Education *Beyond* Education

TEACHING

❧CONTEMPORARY❧

SCHOLARS

Joe L. Kincheloe & Shirley R. Steinberg
General Editors

Vol. 5

PETER LANG
New York • Washington, D.C./Baltimore • Bern
Frankfurt am Main • Berlin • Brussels • Vienna • Oxford

JOHN BALDACCHINO

Education *Beyond* Education

Self and the Imaginary in Maxine Greene's Philosophy

PETER LANG
New York • Washington, D.C./Baltimore • Bern
Frankfurt am Main • Berlin • Brussels • Vienna • Oxford

Library of Congress Cataloging-in-Publication Data

Baldacchino, John.
Education beyond education: self and the imaginary in Maxine Greene's philosophy /
John Baldacchino.
p. cm. — (Teaching contemporary scholars; vol. 5)
Includes bibliographical references and index.
1. Greene, Maxine. 2. Education—Philosophy. 3. Self. I. Title.
LB875.G8353A3   370.1–dc22   2008044668
ISBN 978-1-4331-0355-1 (hardcover)
ISBN 978-1-4331-0356-8 (paperback)
ISSN 1533-4082

Bibliographic information published by **Die Deutsche Bibliothek**.
Die Deutsche Bibliothek lists this publication in the "Deutsche
Nationalbibliografie"; detailed bibliographic data is available
on the Internet at http://dnb.ddb.de/.

The paper in this book meets the guidelines for permanence and durability
of the Committee on Production Guidelines for Book Longevity
of the Council of Library Resources.

© 2009 Peter Lang Publishing, Inc., New York
29 Broadway, 18th floor, New York, NY 10006
www.peterlang.com

Printed in the United States of America

For Maxine

passionate teacher, generous colleague and loving friend

Contents

Acknowledgments

This book would have been impossible without the generosity and assistance from a number of friends, colleagues and students. However, before I mention and thank them, I would like to mention a very special person, without whose support this book would have never been written. This special person is Professor Maxine Greene.

I am honored to call Maxine a colleague and a friend but most of all a great mentor. I have known Maxine only since 2004 when I came to New York City to take my current academic position. As I relocated with my family to this great city, and as we learnt to live, enjoy and survive the stimulating and daunting environs of Teachers College Columbia University, we found in Maxine a great source of hope and encouragement. Not unlike the many colleagues and students before me who have basked in her wisdom and inspiration, I remain constantly enthused by her work and faith in human possibility and the imagination. From the day that I met and heard her speak, I resolved to engage with her work in depth by embarking on this book project. I hope that in recognition of her great work, this book goes toward thanking Maxine for her selfless personal kindness, academic generosity and faith in the educational and philosophical possibilities of women and men.

There are other colleagues and friends I would like to thank. First I would like to thank Thomas James, Provost and Dean of Teachers College Columbia University for his attentive support and for the generous grant that his Office gave me to facilitate this project. Special thanks go to John Broughton, whose friendship and mentorship were instrumental in making this project succeed. My various discussions of Greene's work with John helped me shape up the approach that I took in this book. John's wit, sense of humor and insight remain a source of great inspiration. I would also like to thank Judith Burton and Graeme Sullivan, Program Director and former Department Chair, respectively, for their collegial support through their mentorship and advice, and in helping me organize my time and various other commitments. Thanks also go to my colleagues in art and art education Renee Darvin and Olga Hubard, and my colleagues in philosophy of education David Hansen and Megan Laverty, whose friendship and understanding I greatly cherish.

Without my graduate assistants Christina Soriano, Harrigan Bowman and Tiffany Lee, it would have been impossible for me to have at hand most, if not all, of the Teachers College Gottesman Libraries' Maxine Greene Archive. Christina, Harrigan and Tiffany have taken a lot of their time printing, copying, as well as cataloguing and filing material for me.

Special thanks go to Peter Lang Publishing, their editors and staff, particularly Chris Myers, Joe Kincheloe, Shirley Steinberg, Sophie Appel, Valerie Best and Phyllis Korper for their generous support.

I also remain grateful to all my students, who, in one way or another, continue to give me feedback and encourage me to persist in my academic work.

Last but certainly never least, I want to thank my wife Laura and my daughter Claudia. Living with an obsessed academic is not an easy life, and I thank them for putting up with me. Without their constant support, patience, friendship and love, this book would have never happened.

John Baldacchino
Teachers College Columbia University
New York City
August 2008

Indefinite Readings

The time may have come again for the painting of murals.
—Maxine Greene, "Between Past and Future" (NDa, p. 13)

This book develops a theme *in dialogue* with Maxine Greene's philosophy. The theme is that of the self and the imaginary as dynamic categories of learning. Greene's work provides a unique approach and a way out of the *impasse* in which philosophy finds itself to be less and less potent in its struggle against the professionalized standardization of education. Greene's work and life is a solid testimony to the continuous and dedicated struggle against the reduction of teachers into civil servants within a bureaucratic machine that constantly fails to emancipate the poor and the invisible. Undoubtedly Greene's work enjoys huge support from within and beyond the teaching community because many find in it a hope beyond this *impasse*. Yet, even when as an educator I rejoice in this championing, I also think that notwithstanding this substantial following, the comprehensive foundations of Greene's philosophy are still partially read and often made timid by a visible lack of radical earnest within education. Her unique attention to literature and the arts is somehow missed, while the radical import of her approach to education is either fixed in a formulaic reading, or made benign by a liberal *and* Liberal rendition, of which Greene remains a foremost critic. This does not happen because teachers and others cannot engage with philosophy, the arts or literature, but because the vantage points of education are often constrained by the reified knowledge that consigned the study of education to a domain of measure that bears no regard for the sciences, the arts or humanities.

This book is intended to rectify this instrumental and positivist assault on the educational vantage point. As a dialogue with Greene's work, this book invites the necessary releases of both meaning and the imagination in order to recognize, start, continue or resume the struggle for those possible freedoms without which there is neither knowledge nor being. Here one must not expect a systematized reading that assumes to be a 'correct' reading of Greene's work. Far from it! Neither am I suggesting in any way that Greene's work must be read biographically. Here I have made the conscious decision not to make any allusion to Greene's life. Apart from not being a biographer, I feel that biographical analyses of philosophical works could be potentially misleading, and especially in Greene's case, a biographical analysis would reify the spirit with which she works, and furthermore will fix it in formulaic assumptions. If there is a 'correct' reading of Greene's work, it insists on remaining indefinite and inconclusive—just as Greene would assert the power of incompleteness in philosophy, the arts and education.

With this qualification in mind, I propose Greene's work as a way of revealing and reinforcing the inherent plurality of subjects and discourses, especially those that bring together Continental and American traditions, particularly in philosophy and aesthetics-education. Here I want to draw readers' attention to the manner by which Greene's work empowers us as *learners of the possible* by dint of the imaginary, where the imagination provides a horizon over which the self and an "expanded community" would claim back our right to learning through what she rightly presents as the "dialectic of freedom." This is why, far from a philosophical biography of Maxine Greene, this book is written as an engagement with key arguments through which Greene offers a strikingly original way that empowers us to *see* and re-*position* education beyond what is customarily limited to education. Hence the running title, *Education beyond Education*.

At the same time this dialogue with Greene's work follows suit in further conversing with a number of notable authors and philosophers, such as Virginia Woolf, Toni Morrison, Albert Camus, Jean-Paul Sartre, Hannah Arendt, Maurice Merleau-Ponty, Alfred Schutz, William James, John Dewey, Richard Rorty and many others. By adding another layer of authorship in this dialogical genealogy, and by following the method set by Greene's example to her readers, I would invite readers to understand and engage with Greene's work dialogically and make their own choices in terms of what they, as teachers, artists, philosophers, students, activists most care about. In this way we sustain an interpretative dialogue with Greene, as she teaches us all that a reading is never complete but remains *indefinite* and open to further readings.

The field identified with what could be called 'Maxine Greene studies' continues to expand in various publications that take her work as its major inspiration. At present this is solidly done through two avenues: (a) her own prolific and ever-growing body of writings, and (b) edited books that bring together a number of essays written by an array of academics, educators and those working in the arts. There are at least two major edited books of essays on Greene's work: *A Light in Dark Times*, edited by Bill Ayers and Janet Miller (1998) and *The Passionate Mind of Maxine Greene*, edited by William Pinar (1998). A quick book-search on the Internet or Library Catalogues will also reveal the wide-ranging interest that Greene's work arouses across the arts, aspects of ethics in education, and arts- and aesthetics-education.

What this book does differently is that while it recognizes the great importance of these commentaries on Greene's work, it wants to widen the discussion while focusing on her philosophy of the self and the imaginary. By this I mean that while Greene's work is firmly based within the passion for education and learning, it is also a work of philosophy that takes education outside the parameters within which it has been traditionally exercised in Anglophone schools of education. While educators and aesthetic educators must always claim Maxine Greene as their champion, this could also result in an oversight of her strong standing in other realms such as aesthetics, ethics, literary and visual theory, political philosophy and, indeed, philosophy of education. Thus my decision was that while mindful of the extended discussion of Greene's educational theory, in this book I concentrate on aesthetics, political philosophy and critical theory, while reframing the attention to education from the very sources of the philosophy and literature that Greene discusses.

Greene's diverse and original approach to philosophy, the arts and literature robustly supersedes the so-called Anglo-American–Continental distinction within scholarship. Like Stanley Cavell, Greene claims back the versatile and diverse character of an intellectual tradition that comes straight from Emerson, James, Pierce and Dewey, a tradition that, though distinctly American, extends over and beyond the Atlantic and rightly claims its own Continental sources. Mindful of this intellectual tradition, this book seeks to remind its readers that Greene's work also reaches beyond education and toward the wider realms of aesthetics, culture and politics. Greene has been dedicated to precisely doing this, by physically and intellectually working within fields that are often resisted by the disciplinary restrictions that reduced education into a branch of professional studies. In this respect, one could also argue that this book takes full account of educational studies, but at the same time adopts the view of the artist, the literary and cultural theorist, the political scientist, and more so the view of the philosopher whose interest in education forms part of a wider engagement with the world.

By way of introducing the general tenor of this book, I visit some of the issues that emerge from seeing *with* Greene where, as argued in the opening chapter, a number of philosophical and literary traditions shape her discussion of community, the self and the aesthetic imagination. To see with Greene is to discuss those contexts that Greene the philosopher draws from. For example, while Greene's idea of the community is backed by her engagement with Hannah Arendt's work, this is then returned to a larger picture where Arendt's political philosophy is read against the challenges of the crisis of representation as discussed by Gillian Rose. This reframing is intended to further understand Greene's reading of Arendt, which runs in parallel and often converges with Greene's contemporaries. Overall, this chapter sets the tone for the book, where continuous layers are read over and against each other resulting in an open sort of reading and an attention to meanings that remain in continuous development. This chapter ends at a crucial point, with a passage from Virginia Woolf's *Mrs. Dalloway*, intended as cue to the following chapter that deals with Greene's dialogical reading of the self, particularly in how Existentialism informs notions of the *situated* self that Greene makes core to her educational philosophy.

In 1967, Greene decided to compile a book of philosophical excerpts from the greats of existentialism and phenomenology. The book titled *Existential Encounters for Teachers*, which somehow prefaced her other great work *The Teacher as Stranger*, has an audience of teachers in mind, brought together around the specific issues of existence, and more so the idea of the self in its encounter with the dread of life. This dread becomes that point of departure where hope is constructed out of a profound understanding of the moment of being. This chapter's title, "If we are to be," implies a conditional case for *being* as one's self affirmation-and-negation with respect to how one views the world and how we are to be in it—a situation to which Greene invites us all. This invitation to engage with existentialism and phenomenology is indicative of Greene's commitment to the mediated meanings of learning, a mediation that is not forced by edicts or dogma, absolutes or totalities, but by the realization that life's contingency is a continuous reminder that the world is in continuous *remaking*. Here she also singles out the American dimension urgently inviting all teachers by citing Albert Camus' call for "a whole civilization to be remade," then adding that we all must "remake by means of education" (EET, p. 18).

As education is not just about schools but originates from how we regard life in general and our individual lives in particular, the third chapter discusses what it means *to observe* and *to be observed*. Here the life and work of Virginia Woolf provides us with an approach, almost a 'method', where *argument* is transformed into *observation* and vice versa, where the observer argues her case by drawing our attention and invites us to see *with* her, and where *seeing* in turn becomes a claim for *argument*. In this chapter, the notion of argument is not set to prove anything. Even less is it a question of opposing someone else's argument, or proving it wrong. Greene's dialogic forms are in themselves pedagogical. Like Woolf she invites us to see *with* her. Like Woolf she wants us to enjoy and even delectate in a pedagogical jousting drawn into the *agôn*, into the polemical arena of learning-as-dispute. As Greene keeps reminding us, to learn is to be situated, and to be situated is to argue one's case for one's own situation. A day in the life of an observer is a day in the *situatedness* of learning. Like Woolf, Greene learns with the *literati*. She is herself a *literata*. She mixes with them and invites us as her guest. We go to Mrs. Dalloway's (*a.k.a.* Woolf's) *soirees* and become socialites. We also take the role of the artist-observer, like Lily Briscoe in *To the Lighthouse*, as we engage with the beauty and the ambiguous nature of everyday living. We thus engage in the life of the *every-human*: a humanity of free and intelligent beings.

Yet to observe without sustaining meaning is to yield to the risk of a meaningless life where one's situatedness goes lost or becomes relative. Chapter four takes on the very notion of meaning and how a polity cannot sustain itself if meaning is dismissed by the excuse of unmediated particularities. Here we start to take a closer look at the radical call within Greene's work. This is prefaced by a discussion of Arendt's attention to the dynamic between *active* and *contemplative* life, between theory and practice and the vantage points that we have in *doing what we do*. The dynamic exchange between theory and practice takes us into meaning as a choice of freedom, and of freedom as a condition that does not simply come from a *desideratum* for a societal, egalitarian or even a delectable cause, but from how meaning is *released* by the self as it is made wide-awake to possibility. In Greene's work, meaning and freedom are closely related to praxis, as these come to inhabit new spaces of action and representation. Greene claims these spaces for *us* (learners, teachers, citizens) and in doing so she positions *herself* politically with the oppressed and the marginalized. In this way, her idea of generosity retains a radical stand that presents several challenges that are ethical as much as ontological. If education is an equal right to *know*, then the cause of generosity is driven by a right to *be*. To be generous does not simply imply supporting charitable causes, but a firm undertaking of empathy as a political pedagogy.

This is where freedom comes under discussion in the fifth chapter, and rather than assume freedom as a done deal or a natural ideal, freedom becomes a matter of possibility. Greene's analysis of liberty poses a fundamental question on generic notions of what it means to be free. This is also where the whole question of liberalism as inherited from the Enlightenment, and as carried by the Jeffersonian ideals of the young American republic, comes under discussion. In her seminal book *The Dialectic of Freedom* Greene clearly guides her readers, who are also asked to pay attention to the real contexts of freedom. With freedom presented as ethical and historical, we are invited to look at the private and public dimensions of freedom. Here the notion of the private self becomes crucial in the understanding of responsibility, particularly in a complexion by which the work of women and men is brought to our attention in terms of how we reach from private into public realms. However, there remains an issue with the heritage of liberty, which John Dewey has struggled with presenting in his work, especially in his *Freedom and Culture* and *Democracy and Education*. Here we re-read Greene's reading of Dewey against other discussions of the notion of liberty, particularly Quentin Skinner's critique of liberalism in his *Liberty Before Liberalism*. The assumption of a private radical and a public pragmatist assumed by Rorty is challenged on the same grounds with which Skinner critiques Isaiah Berlin's theory of freedom. As this discussion evolves, this chapter takes a view that Greene's work moves beyond pragmatism and in many ways avoids the pragmatist predicament by reading the notion of freedom back into history in a somewhat different way from that of Dewey.

It is often argued that the cornerstone of Dewey's philosophies of art and of education is the primacy of experience. This is no less pronounced in Greene's claims for the experiential core of the imagination. However, in chapter six, experience is challenged in terms of the limits of its conceptual possibility. Instead, experience is read against the notions of *anticipation* and *futuring*, which Greene supports through her philosophical dialogues with the work of Alfred Schutz, Jean-Paul Sartre and Camus. In chapter six, the Deweyan lineage in Greene's aesthetics of the imagination is discussed in some depth, proposing a critical approach to its aspects and also analyzing whether the critique of experience as a central node in the pragmatic Canon could or should be further qualified—and if so, indicating as to where and how Greene's philosophy would play a part. Just as Greene questions Dewey's approach to history when she distances him from Camus in chapter two, in this chapter we find Dewey read in parallel to Sartre in Greene's discussion of freedom and art. Here the possible leaps out of the ordinary and the experiential comes from the power of aesthetic imagination, which, however, closely assumes an autonomy that it partakes from art. This chapter also discusses the Hegelian nexus that sustains a common ground with Dewey and the Italian liberal philosopher Benedetto Croce. Central to this reading is the dialectical character that both Croce and Dewey sustain in their aesthetic philosophies; a dialectic that Greene takes further into art and with Sartre and Camus reassembles into non-identitarian contexts where paradox is recognized as central to art; as an aesthetic category that neither Dewey nor Croce would entirely recognize.

This is where it is proposed that Greene's work sustains risk as a core aesthetic category. Chapter seven, titled "Risking the aesthetic," takes Greene's work into the aesthetic education of women and men, which is distanced from Schiller's attempt to reintegrate the good with the truth via the beautiful. But Green has no interest in constructing makeshift bridges between the true, the good and the beautiful. If aesthetics-education were meant as an ethical or a metaphysical tool—even for the purposes of philosophical forms of 'reconciliation'—then learning and the arts would be trapped into an *instrumental* structure. Greene's notion of aesthetic education is based on risk—a risk that would even stake the relative safety of catharsis. As she pushes the aesthetic into riskier realms, where the imagination is 'let loose', the idea of risk itself becomes a catalyst of aesthetic autonomy. Far from being an instrument, the aesthetic avenue upholds autonomy while making it imperative for all of us to consciously engage with the realities by which we have to face the world.

It is here that the penultimate chapter, "Pedagogical imaginaries," proposes that the idea of 'imagination' is re-read from the wider horizon of 'the imaginary'. Here it is argued that Greene's notion of the imagination is a matter of being and not an instrument of *learning-what-one-must-know*. The imagination turns knowledge into *being*, and it opens wide the possibilities that one gains from experience as a horizon of *anticipation*. To know is to imagine, as one extends knowledge into the field of generating possibilities by ways of anticipation *qua* experience. Greene's philosophy of imagination is neither benign nor does it 'flow' into a magical world of certainty. Rather, the imagination is an act of presencing where we all engage with the diverse subjectivities that construct the world as it is and as it might be aesthetically and teleologically projected. Within the parameters of a philosophical imaginary, one can also extend the grounds on which the juncture between experience and the imagination converges on the arts and how through the arts we recognize ourselves as plural subjects. In this chapter, reference is made to the notion of the female and male subjects referencing the notion of presencing in Woolf's *Orlando*, which is in turn read through the work of Luce Irigaray.

This opens the possibility of seeing Greene's philosophy beyond fixed boundaries. Whether these boundaries are manipulated by any means, the praxes sustained by Greene's ethical discourse radically questions any pre-assumed *order*, especially when it comes to the existence of men and women as a history of discrimination. This chapter extends previous discussions of how the question of otherness in terms of class, sex, gender and race plays a role in Greene's work. It is argued that in the same way Greene's work offers a different and original take on the question of social and racial discrimination, its attention to the question of difference is a radical perspective that is in turn articulated within a much more significant political and philosophical horizon.

By way of concluding this book, I propose that for education to go beyond itself, it cannot favor one paradigm of education over another as in the conservative-liberal-progressive split, but it must result from what Greene prioritizes as the teacher being a stranger who holds a passion for incompleteness. In this respect the last chapter revisits three possible 'places' from where to view education: the *polis*, the *agôn* and the *khôra*. Broadly representing the *political*, the *polemical* and the *indefinable*, these 'places' assume a horizon over which education is proposed to recognize and assume its own *groundlessness*. In a way, this last chapter is an inauguration of further discussion—which is what the main spirit of Greene's work is all about, and to which one hopes this book does some justice.

As one engages with Greene's work, one cannot but feel a great deal of anxiety in that the freedom it exudes could well be taken liberty of. In the entirety of this work I paid great attention and respect to make sure that when my voice comes in, it is distinguished from Greene's. Far from trying to make my point by invoking Greene, I have always felt that Greene urges us to take on a dialogue with her and with the myriad interlocutors that characterize her work. Yet what remains fundamental in her work is the urge to take the leap, to move beyond and to take on what is unfamiliar yet new and full of possibility. This recalls Friedrich Nietzsche's essay "Schopenhauer and Education" where he states: "There is one single path in this world on which no one but you can travel. Where does it lead? Do not ask, just take it. Who was it who made the statement: 'A man never rises higher than when he does not know where his path may lead him'?" (1995, p. 174). One almost feels tempted to answer Nietzsche's question with a very loud cry: "Maxine Greene!"

CHAPTER ONE

To See with Greene

[T]he artist might well say, as Joseph Conrad once did: "I want to make you see." His intention to enable the reader to "see" may be embodied (almost visibly) in the work he made. To see what? Certainly not the absolute, the really real. Not the Leviathan; nor the heavens; nor the pit. To see, rather, the resemblances, conjunctions, illuminations revealed by metaphor; to see human beings, created human creatures, separated out from the flow of everydayness, given a particularity, a presentness within the domination of art; to see the shapes and details of the perceived world as evoked by the protean work of language; but, most of all, to see inside the self, the consciousness.

—Maxine Greene, "Literature and Human Understanding" (1968b, p. 15)

While most of us despair over an intellectual culture that abdicates from its political responsibility, Maxine Greene teaches us otherwise. Far from losing hope, Greene is a philosopher committed to change. Greene regards philosophy as that intellectual capacity by which we uphold human dignity and claim back truth. Her claim to truth is not a profession of the 'clear and distinct' realms within which Descartes rediscovers human reason.

"Cogito ergo sum" he asserted, and the words have rung through the centuries. Released from the mists of prejudgement and sensation, he [Descartes] was convinced that he was able to conceive "clear and distinct" ideas corresponding to those in the mind of God. The body, for him, was thought of in sensory and organic terms. Will and consciousness both were associated with the disembodied mind. Decontextualized and detached, that mind rejected the partial and the perspectival. (Greene 1994a, p. 428)

Like Dewey, Greene values experience in its entirety. She is not a positivist who poses mere fact as reason's slide-rule. She does not claim experience as a process of parts that make a perfect whole. Experience is only part of the story, and the story is not finite. Experience is also something other than the facts by which empiricists proclaim knowledge. As Wittgenstein (1979) insists, "philosophical problems are not solved by experience, for what we talk about in philosophy are not facts but things for which facts are useful. Philosophical trouble arises through seeing a system of rules and seeing that things do not fit it" (§1, p. 3).

Wittgenstein's clarification is necessary to philosophy and to anything else that lay beyond our philosophical needs. He likens philosophical problems to "advancing and retreating from a tree stump and seeing different things. We go nearer, remember the rules, and feel satisfied, then retreat and feel dissatisfied" (Wittgenstein 1979, p. 3). Greene places experiences in a slightly different frame, but not in contradiction to Wittgenstein. For her, "to 'do' philosophy in the domains of the artistic-aesthetic is to think about one's thinking with regard to the ways in which engagements with the arts contribute to ongoing pursuits of meaning, efforts to make sense of the world. It is to reflect upon perceived realities as well as those that have been conceptualized, and to ponder the phases of remembered experiences with the arts" (Greene 1991, p. 123). Here she qualifies the act of *doing* philosophy by the domains of "the artistic-aesthetic," which is where the "things for which facts are useful" (to use Wittgenstein's term) would thereby include that which Descartes' 'clear and distinct' conclusions would reject as 'partial and perspectival'.

"... so that we all become different"

The 'partial and perspectival' is what makes philosophy worth pursuing. To do philosophy is to discover things that make facts useful, and more so things that make life hopeful. Greene's is a philosophy of hope. Assuming hope as a philosophical position implies taking the risk of the imagination. Thus we are invited to see the world *with* Greene. William Ayers beautifully accounts for this when he describes his own experience of *doing* philosophy with Maxine Greene:

> "Where is the nearest school?" Maxine Greene asked. "And how do state regulations affect that school? Does the curriculum include both physics and chemistry? Such questions, obviously, are variously answerable—like questions in the social sciences and even natural sciences. But they are not the queer questions Berlin had in mind. Contrast them, then, with these: How are we to understand freedom? How are we to understand fairness, and how can it be reconciled with individual rights? How can we justify a commitment to critical reflection, aesthetic awareness, open-ended growth, or intellectual understanding to a public preoccupied with the need to focus on skills and proficiencies alone? Or more specifically, is it fair that my child be bussed to another neighborhood to school? Is it possible for the child of fundamentalists, say, to study Darwinian evolution in school and still accede to the creationist position? These are the types of questions that arouse the philosopher." (1998, pp. 4–5)

A philosophy that invests human reason in risk and hope requires a leap of faith beyond a world of cruelty, discrimination and senseless competition. So while one turns numb by the shivering fact that embedded forms of discrimination insistently besiege the very foundations of society, Greene's answer is unambiguous: "Passions, then, engagements, and imagining. I want to find a way of speaking of community, an expanding community, that will take shape when diverse people, speaking as *who* and not *what* they are, come together in speech and action, as Arendt puts it, to constitute something in common among themselves" (1992, p. 250).

I read Greene's notion of community as the only possible horizon on which we could play with ways of *re*-imagining and *re*-conceiving difference as an act of being. Difference in its ontological sense (of *being*) supersedes the limits of diversity as an epistemological statement (as an accounting exercise of knowing). One never finds this distinction front loaded, as it were, in declarative ways by Greene. However, any argument for a community of *who* rather than *what* you are predicates the need for a further distinction: between *gnoseology* and *epistemology*. The Greek distinction between *gnosis* and *episteme* differentiates knowledge as *consciousness*, as knowledge *in itself*, and knowledge as a *science*, as a *form* of knowledge. Gnoseology implies knowledge *in se*, as consciousness, which in discussions about education carries a deeper meaning than that of forms of knowledge—thereby implying subject matter, method or forms of inquiry. Although this distinction is often blurred and seemingly the word epistemology is more commonly used, one must bear in mind that gnoseology has a distinct approach to knowledge that would resist the transformation of knowledge into structures of power (Foucault 1991). Equally a gnoseological approach to knowledge is an effective way of surpassing the curricular stalemate where knowledge is reduced to an epistemological hierarchy. Although Greene does not make direct reference to gnoseology, her approach to knowledge as it becomes coterminous with being situated directly corresponds to *gnosis*.

One's being situated within communities of difference is premised by choice and "breaking loose from anchorage."

> [Maurice Merleau-Ponty and Virginia Woolf] move me to reach into my own story, into the ambivalence of my own choosing to act in such a way that I break loose from anchorage and that I stir others to break loose along with me, *so that we all become different, that we all engage in a dialectic to reach beyond where we are.* (RI, p. 110, my emphasis)

In this recognition of community, difference is made possible by dint of its apparent opposite: a human *sameness*, where we are all the same because we are all different. By being different we become social beings. As beings of the same, we are beings of otherness. But there is a caveat: sameness has to recognize the parameters of an otherness that is not simply assumed by some liberal decree that forgets the uniqueness of the one as articulated by the discrete power of the multiple. One way of reading Greene's expanding community is to discard the easy recipes of immediate dualism between difference and sameness, and dispose of the epistemic mechanisms of immediacy.

A rejection of immediacy is ethically premised and therefore politically expressed. Although one could make political assumptions devoid of ethical responsibility, this is always precluded by Greene's position. Even in her ethical investment of political mediation, her notion of 'community' never becomes a sentimental formula of 'doing goodness'. Laying claim to the notion of 'community' is to ask for acts of *political* mediation. So if we go with Greene's premise of an expanding community, this is primarily an expanding *polity*—that is, a political relation between groups, sub-groups and individuals. Any form of mediation is political, and Greene's is the mediation of an incongruent and asymmetrical multiplicity, albeit ethically construed as a means of breaking off from those historical anchorages that have precluded the community. To simply call for the unity of one human race, one human society and one call for freedom is to fall short of the political action that these forms of unity would ideally portend. Like Hannah Arendt, Greene calls for more: "if there is some abstract totality, some generalized certainty, or even some concept like 'humanity', it exists on the horizon, forever on the horizon, to be sought *en route*, on the way. To be on the move in this fashion requires a degree of thoughtfulness" (1990, p. 69). Citing Arendt's *The Life of the Mind: Thinking*, Greene explains that this approach to the idea of 'humanity' "requires that we be awake to the 'claim on our thinking attention' made by events and facts as they impinge on us" (ibid.).

Greene's consistent ascription of her political philosophy to Arendt's warrants close attention. It is all too tempting to derive similarity from their shared Jewish ancestry. This would fall foul of Greene's and Arendt's opposition to totalizing assumptions. A supposition of theoretical commonality based on gender is equally deficient. In fact when it comes to the latter, Greene is attentive to what she calls the "multiple requirements" and "multiple realities" by which one could identify what is distinctive in women. So while arguing that "there are innumerable cultural differences, class and ethnic differences, factors that go beyond gender when it comes to understanding 'women's ways of knowing'" (Greene 1994a, p. 451) multiple realities and multiple requirements also demand that inquiry can never be "like the air (...)

expected to be 'pure'" (ibid.). Dismissing gendered monoliths and monolithic genders alike, Greene presents us with the distinctiveness by which women "are as hospitable as they tend to be to openness and indeterminacy when it comes to research and to inquiry. Incompleteness, as we now realize, is a significant concern when it comes to what are thought of as 'new' epistemologies" (ibid.). This is not far removed from what Gillian Rose said about Arendt, Rosa Luxemburg and Rahel Varnhagen:

> They reveal how posited universality of 'rights of man' and 'rights of society' deposits customary statuses within the violence of civil society. Yet this tension of middle-womanship is sustained in all three authorships: they neither opt to abandon political universality, even though it is demonstrably spurious; nor to resolve its inconsistency and antinomy in any ethical immediacy of love: 'community', 'nation', 'race', 'religion' or 'gender'. Remaining *within the agon of authorship* they cultivate aporetic universalism, restless affirmation and undermining of political form and political action, which never loses sight of the continuing mutual corruption of the state and civil society—whether the state is separated from or united with gender, religion, politics. (1992, p. 155, my emphasis)

Like Arendt, Luxemburg and Varnhagen, Greene has no time for seamless worlds or the fiction of appropriate irenic suppositions: "We can no longer talk in terms of seamless totalities under rubrics like 'free world', 'free market', 'equality' or even 'democracy'." This is because "publics, after all, take shape in responses to unmet needs and broken promises; and human beings are prone to take action in response to the sense of injustice or to the imagination's capacity to look at things as if they could be otherwise (1992, p. 258).

An expanding polity makes the *case* for a cause. This *case* gives human reality to individual *existence*, where the human is ascertained as a horizon of disjointed histories and traditions that could be seen to entertain a common right to the *same* and the *equal*. But there is a further caveat: *equality* and *democracy* cannot be simple words used as miraculous tokens. As in Rose's comments on how inconsistency and antinomies cannot be resolved by an "ethical immediacy of love" that is so often made falsely benign by the spurious notions of 'community', 'nation', 'race', 'religion' or 'gender', Greene is equally dismissive of the immediacy of "seamless totalities under rubrics." If there is a common right, or a way of living through the inconsistencies and antinomies that make communities what they are, then in Greene we find a route via *existence*—this time not as a term in a rubric, but as a claim that is made right from within what Rose terms as "the agon of authorship."

In Ancient Greece, the *agôn* represented a space where disputes were settled. *Agôn* as 'the ground of assembly' also recalls the word *ágo*, which in its Greek original denotes the 'act of leading'. From this it isn't difficult to infer

that *pedagogía* (pedagogy) is not limited to the *paedeia* (the child and her education) but extends to the *agôn* (the space of dispute and leadership). Just as the
polity can never become a totalized harmonious ground, in Greene's *agôn* of
authorship one finds a *pedagogical* assumption that extends beyond fixed rubrics of learning. Far from simply learning or knowing, pedagogy acts by the
political prerogative that the *agôn* presents.

Greene's *agôn* of authorship is a space where literature moves away from
the text to "radiate through consciousness": "We know now that we are not
asked to seek buried meanings in Toni Morrison's *Beloved* or in Virginia
Woolf's *To the Lighthouse* or in Albert Camus' *The Plague*" (Greene 1994a, p.
456). We are reminded that Morrison, Woolf and Camus are as real as *we* are.
Their texts engage with a world in which we *all* live. In this world, meanings
may be bent and hidden; they may come across as convoluted and paradoxical;
but they are neither buried nor immaterial. Meanings are made by and for us.
At the same time Greene poses a responsibility by which we are made aware
that this experience is not simply ours as isolated individuals. As I in turn read
Greene reading Camus, Woolf and Morrison, I realize that though one can
read in isolation, one may not necessarily become literate. "Yes, becoming literate is also a matter of transcending the given, of entering a field of possibles.
We are moved to do that, however, only when we become aware of rifts, gaps
in what we think of as reality" (RI, p. 111).

Greene exercises her prerogative from within her *agôn* of authorship as a
way of urging us to exercise our own right to agree or remain freely in dispute,
as different members of a polity in continuous expansion: "We are challenged
to bring each text alive in our experience, to allow it to radiate through consciousness and open up new perspectives on the lived world" (1994, p. 456).
In this way the assumption of an engagement with texts as forms of consciousness is inverted. The cards turn on us as readers, and this time we are
led from the front by a reader among other readers: Greene herself. On such a
pedagogical terrain, the art of teaching is neither that of immediate facilitation
nor a means to simplistic reform. Greene's pedagogical stance is radical. She
cites Marcuse's *The Aesthetic Dimension* (1977) and how when he "speaks of the
qualities of art that allow it to indict established reality and evoke images of
liberation, he may be suggesting, as I am here, the relevance of art in overcoming the inability to see others" (RI, p. 136). This position transcends any simplistic assumption of diversity. It reclaims an aesthetic position that allows us
to make possible what pragmatically seems restricted. Beyond our inability to
see others, we become conscious of inhabiting the spaces of dispute and learn-

ing, a space that communities could assume for themselves as expanding polities of difference.

Uniquely Incomplete, Yet Hopeful

To assume that one could freely share one's political space with others is not a foregone conclusion, nor even a case of wishful thinking. As a philosophical concept, *sharing* is a difficult concept. What does one share? On what basis and by what ethical prerogative should one legitimize an economy of sharing within a community that is characterized by difference? It is even harder to extend this argument in terms of the pedagogical spaces of dispute and learning, where we are expected to be our own teachers and our own arbiters. This does not simply impinge on our life as citizens and individuals who abide by the agreed laws of a political space. It also has a huge bearing on us as *selves* —that is, as political, artistic, pedagogical, social ... selves—and therefore as beings with existence, as existent beings.

In all of her work, Greene's position is *uniquely* existentialist. I say *uniquely* and not *necessarily*, *commonly* or *typically* existentialist for a reason. Her existentialist argument is neither fatalist nor cynical, but *real*. This reality is acquired by a forfeit where the existent self gives up the certainty presumed by the discursive rubrics of the *real* for the uniquely existent 'facts' by which fixity is defied. This is where we "become aware of rifts, gaps in what we think of as reality" (RI, p. 111). In the uniquely existentialist, one does not find a univocal voice that assumes an existence for the *sake* of existence. Neither is the *unique* a proto-religious concept where everyone is declared unique 'in the eyes of God'. On the contrary, to supplement Greene's existentialism with the *unique* is to assume existence by dint of a larger state of affairs where it is just possible that political, artistic, philosophical and pedagogical fatalism will be avoided.

Greene knows and wants us to know that after Auschwitz we could still write poetry, or at least turn incompleteness into an aesthetic possibility. Adorno famously argued that "perennial suffering has as much right to expression as a tortured man has to scream; hence it may have been wrong to say that after Auschwitz you could no longer write poems." But he qualified this, adding that "it is not wrong to raise the less cultural question whether after Auschwitz you can go on living" (Adorno 1990, pp. 362-63). Adorno did not pair the *writing-of-poetry* with the *going-on-living* in some kind of symmetry. Yet to argue for poetry and living in a shared horizon of incompleteness would invariably pose another question: whether poetry could survive the incomplete in the same breath as asking whether life is worth anything beyond the experience of genocide.

Though not alluding to Auschwitz, Adorno's work or the possibility of writing poetry in a life that appears incomplete, Greene approaches the notion of the incomplete by recognizing its intrinsic power. This is especially tangible when she takes Beckett's *Krapp's Last Tape* as a play that "can never reach a conclusion for the actor: there are always new intonations, new facial expressions, new modes of shuffling or staggering or pacing, as more and more meanings unfold" (VBG, p. 155). At first one could assume that this is just a way of reading Beckett's choice of dramatic form where an apparent use of incompleteness suggests a larger picture in terms of pairing poetic decisions with life's many options. However, Greene is far from suggesting symmetry between poetics and life. Instead she argues for the *power of incompleteness* as a means to exist. This does not mean that she adds a teleological or pedagogical resolution to the poetics of incompleteness. Rather, she widens what she identifies as "the power of incompleteness" to the realm of upholding it as it is: incomplete. This is what a good existentialist will do with the notion of an unresolved life.

> If any of you were in a work-shop concentrating on the Beckett piece, you remain aware that, no matter how often, how deeply you tried to plunge, you could never entirely realize the potential in that strange duet of tape and old man's voice: the cut of memory, the instants of poetry, the almost inexpressible desolation. And yet it was through the trying and the reaching that you felt yourself enter into the enactment, pour in your energy, bring it to life in your own experience. And, having brought it to life, many of you discovered dimensions of your own lived life, past and present, that you had never known. (VBG, p. 155)

So while never adding an end or ascribing a means by which the incompleteness in Beckett would in any way be completed for us, Greene urges her students to willfully experience the incomplete realms of Beckett's play. There, she tells them "you discovered dimensions of your own lived life, past and present, that you had never known." One might suggest that maybe in discovering the never-known dimensions of life, in Beckett one will also discover what Adorno calls his "frightful answer to art":

> Beckett's oeuvre gives the frightful answer to art that, by its starting point, by its distance from any praxis, art in the face of mortal threat becomes ideology through the harmlessness of its mere form, regardless of its content. This explains the influx of the comic into empathic works. It has a social aspect. In that their effectively blindfolded movement originates exclusively in themselves, their movement becomes a walking in place and declares itself as such, just as the unrelenting seriousness of the work de-

clares itself as frivolous, as play. Art can only be reconciled with its existence by exposing its own semblance, its internal emptiness. (Adorno 1999, p. 250)

Complementing Greene with Adorno risks false attribution. Greene's references to Adorno are mostly *en passant*, though this does not diminish her
recognition of his work, especially when she explains how the *Dialectic of Enlightenment* (Adorno, Horkheimer 1979) "made us grasp the ways in which the
Enlightenment rationalized the early extremes of capitalism and may have
generated the forces that made Auschwitz and Hiroshima technically (and
morally) conceivable" (Greene RI, p. 193). *Prima facie* this may appear to be a
cursory interest in Adorno's position from Greene's part. Yet in their different
readings of Beckett there is mutual resonance, and perhaps more than a coin-
cidental parallelism. Greene's reading of Beckett helps us read Adorno's own
Beckettian analysis. Reading Adorno after Greene, as it were, tends to clarify
how his notion that art "has a social aspect" while it "can only be reconciled
with its existence by exposing its own semblance, its internal emptiness"
(Adorno 1999, p. 250) brings home the dialectical tensions that characterize
Greene's attention to the aesthetic imagination.

In the fifth chapter of *Landscapes of Learning*, a chapter aptly titled "The
Agon of 'Basics'," Greene wonders whether many members of the public and
many young people know "what to make of their being in the world. Because
it afflicts them as if it were objectively meaningless, they deny the need for
thinking and look for technique instead" (LL, p. 79). The context for this remark is a society that is driven by 'measure' and by dissatisfaction with educational and productive outputs. "If the newspapers say that Johnny and Susie
are not being taught to read, if it is assumed that reading has something to do
(...) with 'making it', with success, they cannot but turn their anger and frus-
tration against the schools" (LL, p. 76). Unlike Greene, essentialist education-
ists who cannot see beyond the notion of 'units of analyses' would suggest a
quick solution. As education is seen as an elusive category that could somehow
become simplified in one set of issues, the essentialist would lay claim on
those 'basics' that would accordingly provide a blueprint for success. The
grand narrative of simplistic 'basics' is given in lieu of a critical approach to
questions of learning.

Greene's answer is that "the simplifications attached to the call for basics
cannot be simple." "For some of us," she says, "the world of risks and pursuits
is far more appealing than the world of arrivals and assurances" (LL, p. 85).
Against the essentialist's view, Greene poses what is not far removed from a
unique sense of existence, that which Sartre (1982) alludes to in his vision of
existence in *Nausea* where "never up until these last few days had I suspected

the meaning of 'existence'." Sounding Antoine Roquentin's inner voice, Sartre (1982) recounts the existential moment:

> It took my breath away. Never, until these last few days, had I suspected what it meant
> to 'exist'. I was like the others, like those who walk along the sea-shore in their spring
> clothes. I used to say like them: 'The sea *is* green; that white speck up there *is* a sea-
> gull', but I didn't feel that it existed, that the seagull was an 'existing seagull'; usually
> existence hides itself. It is there, around us, in us, it is *us*, you can't say a couple of
> words without speaking of it, but finally you can't touch it. (p. 182)

Greene speaks of a 'wide-awakeness' that offers "no guarantee about what [it] can achieve" (LL, p. 84). She hopes for an expanding dialogue, a wish to see "an intensified concern for the qualitative dimension of life." She further qualifies wide-awakeness, which Alfred Schutz originally defines as "a plane of consciousness of highest tension" (LL, p. 163; Schutz 1970, p. 69). Greene adds that Schutz "is also pointing out that human beings define themselves by means of their projects and that wide-awakeness contributes to the creation of the self" (LL, p. 163). Not unlike Sartre, Greene looks at forms of human representation, at the arts, in the hope that one's encounters with them will "offer opportunities for persons to become present to themselves" (LL, p. 84). How does one present one to oneself? Far from solipsism, the claim to present one to oneself is a claim for the unique individual who assumes responsibility for what he or she must stand for in relation to others. This is what I mean when ascribing to Greene's existentialism a dimension of *the unique*. A uniquely existent being does not portend the solipsistic myth of the exclusive being who rejects the world and everyone in it. Arendt reminds us that "living beings, men and animals, are not just in the world, they are *of the world*, and this precisely because they are subjects and objects—perceiving and being perceived—at the same time" (1978, vol. 1, p. 20).

The unique thus carries a proviso for living individuals to be *of-the-world*. The unique is relational in that it is subject and object, presenting others and being presented by others. By implication the uniquely existent is a *modus vivendi*, a way of life that assumes the risk to say with Camus (2000): "I leave Sisyphus at the foot of the mountain! One always finds one's burden again. But Sisyphus teaches the higher fidelity that negates the gods and raises rocks. He, too, concludes that all is well. (...) One must imagine Sisyphus happy" (p. 111). To take on one's burden is neither humiliating nor denigrating, but humanizing. This is what gives Sisyphus a unique existence. Far from accepting the sentence of solipsism, Camus' Sisyphus claims back the world and turns his captivity into a "higher fidelity that negates the gods and raises rocks." Sisyphus's call is not distanced from what Camus calls the artist's difficult calling: "*The Myth of Sisyphus* poses mortal problems, it sums itself up for me as a lucid invitation to live and to create, in the very midst of the desert" (p. 7).

One always tries to understand the question of existence by engaging with one's own 'factual' existence, often through that of others. Greene's unguaranteed *wide-awakeness* reveals the reality of the risk of the self, a risk that permeates the entirety of her work in the form of a commitment to what the self can achieve in its relatedness to others by which we realize the possible via the imagination. The imagination is possible because individuals presume other individuals. This also means that the self, as that which imagines, can also relate with life's contingent nature, when there is no guarantee as to what will happen from now to then. Not knowing what is going to happen in the next moment is the kind of *wide-awakeness* with which Camus assesses the world's meaning: "I don't know whether this world has a meaning that transcends it. But I know that I do not know that meaning and that it is impossible for me just now to know it. What can a meaning outside my condition mean to me? *I can understand only in human terms*" (2000, p. 51, my emphasis).

This is why Greene takes the question of existence seriously and seeks no shortcuts away from what could turn out to be inconvenient and unsavory to those who assume, by common sense, that contingency must be either overcome by constructed metaphysical myths or simply ignored. When Camus says that we can understand only in human terms, he is neither constructing a new metaphysic nor ignoring contingency. Rather, like Sisyphus, he takes stock of truth as a human reality and not simply as a human set of assumed facts or mere occurrences. If I can understand only in human terms, then it is possible to know more than just 'facts'. To understand in human terms is to take responsibility of what one cannot understand beyond the parameters of the world we live in. To understand in human terms is to be wide-awake and fully aware of a world that includes everything: stuff to be proud of as well as stuff to be ashamed of. Given this is all we've got, there is no choice but to take ownership of a world that we reveal to each other, as each other's others. Sartre (1956) suggests that the engagement of the self with the other could spiral down to situations where (as in systems of education) one is even made to be ashamed of oneself for many reasons: "the Other has not only revealed to me what I was; he has established me in a new type of being which can support new qualifications" (p. 222).

Any economy (or indeed curriculum) of the self is duty-bound by dint of being a political economy of selves. This economy does not simply allow the individual to take on herself without the *other*, and therefore without the *others* that make up her polity. The polity is diverse and disparate. It is not fixed because if that were fixed, equality would simply become an "agon of 'basics'," a veil that estranges communities from their disparate polities. When fixed, neither the politics of sameness nor that of otherness could make any existential—let alone *educational*—sense. Neither the other nor the same are fixed or simply run in parallel. The congealment of the other into a fixed existential relationship is anathema to Greene: "The subject, as many existential phenomenologists have believed, is always in process, creating herself or himself by means of a project within a social context that prohibits both fixity and autonomy" (1994a, p. 450).

In Greene's definition of community, the existential dynamic of the self also presents us with an expanding polity that is distanced from philanthropic essentialism. Communities must interrupt and break through monolithic 'forms' such as race or culture, sexuality and gender. These 'forms' should never be lined up or patterned out in symmetrical shapes or relations. Greene makes us aware of a horizon that is never flat, but runs *in*, *out* and *across* a multiple relationship between 'other' and 'same' in the plural—as an affair of 'otherness-es' and 'sameness-es'. For Greene the political project is to bring this possible plurality into constant being. This is where she extends the notion of an expanding economy of difference to those "perspectives never tapped, observations never heeded, understandings ignored" (1994a, p. 451). This invites us to participate in no less than a *passionate* cause that confronts all the assaults on human decency. Greene would be the last of all humanists even if all humanists were to either give up or be swallowed by this inclement and obscure earth.

The Algebra of Fragile Dreams

Many would rightly regard Greene as an inspiring philosopher who promotes and teaches the wise lessons of humanistic liberalism in the form of a doctrine of freedom and democracy. In this doctrine, it is assumed that the imagination reigns supreme in a life well examined by the means that experience—more so, *aesthetic experience*—lends us in the form of a released power of the imagination deposited within the deep segments of the visual and performing arts, music and literature.

Yet Greene's shining optimism is never an attempt to conceal the melancholic character of the human condition. In her work there is anger—an anger that is justified by the need to oppose what is unjust. Indeed an anger that is never privatized in self-indulgent grief. Being a philosopher she cannot reduce anger and protest to media-friendly sound bites or soapbox activism. Her radical stand is neither mediatized nor immediate. Rather it is mediated by an incessant love of scholarship that often takes the form of a passionate plea for the recognition of forms of agency by which freedom is already present *dynámei*, potentially, as a form of conviction.

Greene is rightly described as passionate in her many lectures and in the artistry of her philosophical writing. This passion is palpably evident in the way she embraces scholarship. She has never been inhibited by the false rules of 'staying within' or 'being faithful' to a fixed notion of education-as-a-discipline tied to political essentialism or empirical practicism. Her approach to scholarship, within and outwith *education-as-a-discipline*, remains an open work throughout. There is always a sense of wonder, a spontaneity by which she approaches art and literature with the enthusiasm of a young artist who has just embarked on changing the entire world by means of the vivid, the challenging, the shocking and the lively. Greene's open spirit recalls another young artist, Joyce's Stephen Daedalus, who solves the strictures of history, literature and philosophy by removing all hindrances through the precision of algebra:

> Sitting at his side Stephen solved out the problem. He proves by algebra that Shakespeare's ghost is Hamlet's grandfather. Sargent peered askance through his slanted glasses. Hockeysticks rattled in the lumberroom: the hollow knock of a ball and calls from the field.
>
> Across the page the symbols moved in grave morrice, in the mummery of their letters, wearing quaint caps of squares and cubes. Give hands, traverse, bow to partner: so: imps of fancy of the Moors. Gone too from the world, Averroes and Moses Maimonides, dark men in mien and movement, flashing in their mocking mirrors the obscure soul of the world, a darkness shining in brightness which brightness could not comprehend. (Joyce 1992a, pp. 29–30)

Greene's work refuses to be reduced to an Educationist's textbook, or a researcher's handbook. She gives no formulas. Her work often comes as that most-desired antidote to all purist assumptions of what philosophy must or should be. Like Joyce she extracts darkness from brightness and shines it in the corners of our imagination—an imagination that knows no walls, boundaries or strict definition. Nor is she a literary critic or an art theorist who abides by supposed rules, methods or discipline. In her scholarship, Maxine Greene emerges as the Woman of Letters *par excellence* who continues to reach out beyond the boundaries of disciplinary limitations and who enthusiastically invites everyone to share and engage with a wider horizon of knowledge, discourse, dialogue and learning. However, as a Woman of Letters, Greene also reclaims and opens wide—this time for and to the oppressed—the grounds on which an Emerson or a Thoreau would have walked in the relative (and maybe solitary) peace of their own genius:

> The question of whether freedom can be achieved apart from institutions and social arrangements will continue to preoccupy us, as it has preoccupied reformers and educators over the years. Even now we cannot but ask ourselves whether Emerson could have made himself understood by Lucy Larcom or the other mill girls at the Lowell mills. Could he have made himself heard by the "sheet-white girls," by the men on the docks, by the steamboat captains, by the Jay Goulds and the Commodore Vanderbilts and the Gatsbys of the new world? (DOF, p. 36)

Far from a criticism of Emerson, this falls in line with Greene's preoccupation with the 'fragility of their dreams' as she raises similar questions with regards to Thoreau, even when in both his and Emerson's work we find the strongest of cases made for the possible and for human agency:

> The metaphor, the sense of possibility remain potent, if we can free them from the sedimentations of cliché. Thoreau's appeal was to the consciousness of personal agency, so often obliterated by thoughtlessness or by accommodation to a system or submergence in the crowd. Without the consciousness of agency, no human being is likely to take the initiative needed for the achievement of freedom. For Thoreau, however, his writing and his abolitionism exhausted his urge to action. Both *Walden* and *On Civil Disobedience* still function as potential pedagogies in the sense that they aim at raising the consciousness of those willing to pay heed. Perhaps we can view Thoreau in the company of utopian socialists like Robert Owen, Frances Wright and Robert Dale Owen as harbingers of an alternative tradition in this country, for all the tension between their points of view, the fragility of their dreams. (ibid.)

Here we are presented with the fragility of the intellectual's dreams of freedom, moot tenets of the liberal's blissful certainty over freedom and intelligence. Yet Greene is quick to remind us—albeit indirectly—of the tensions that this misguided bliss contains: a tension between the willful generosity of spirit, by which liberals claim an argument for personal freedom, and the vulnerability of the liberal's willful acts of social commitment, which more often than not are flawed with a disproportionate anxiety over 'individual freedom'. This is not far removed from the dilemma of Robert Owen's political benevolence and radical earnestness, which is quickly shattered by what Marx and Engels (1988) identify as the utopian socialist's "inverse relation to historical development":

> In proportion as the modern class struggle develops and takes definite shape, this fantastic standing apart from the contest, these fantastic attacks on it, lose all practical value and all theoretical justifications. Therefore, although the originators of these systems were, in many respects, revolutionary, their disciples have, in every case,

formed mere reactionary sects. They hold fast by the original views of their masters, in opposition to the progressive historical development of the proletariat. (p. 241)

The social dilemma of contemporary liberals is no less perplexing, particularly when even the Left itself, emerging from its critique of liberalism, has failed to solve the problems that it rightly identified in the fragile dreams of the utopian socialists and their radical enthusiasm (Inglis 1982). In many ways one wonders how many willful social liberals are aware of the weakness that Greene recognizes in Thoreau's and Emerson's fragile dreams. Unless this weakness is identified in tandem with the claim to possibility and human agency without being aware of the fragility of the intellectual's dreams, one would be missing the point of Greene's stand as a Woman of Letters.

Although many are right in 'seeing' Greene's work as an emblem of the power and polity of the freed imagination, it is easy to fail to really 'see with' her the limitations that normally foil the same imagination. This is because in the liberal tradition many still fail to recognize that praxis is not simply a form of social critique. Yet in terms of political action, it is obvious that praxis cannot simply begin with individual freedom. Rather, praxis must begin with a political understanding that is shared with the mill girls at the Lowell mills, the "sheet-white girls," the men on the docks, the steamboat captains (...) and so on. In the failure to assess the fragility of the philosophical dream, hasty social and liberal democrats have cut themselves off from the lineage by which Greene (1994) declares unequivocally that "realizing that no metanarrative can offer guarantees, educators may come together in local spaces and struggle to create humane communities, playful communities, at once beautiful and just" (p. 459).

Greene's work sits firmly within what Wollstonecraft bequeathed in *A Vindication of the Rights of Woman*. Wollstonecraft (1987) warns against "pretty superlatives, dropping glibly from the tongue" as these would "vitiate the taste, and create a kind of sickly delicacy that turns away from simple unadorned truth." This also recalls Gillian Rose, another contemporary Woman of Letters, who just before she lost her battle with cancer in 1995 argues that "politics does not happen when you act on behalf of your own damaged good, but when you act, *without guarantees*, for the good of all—this is to take *the risk* of the *universal* interest. Politics in this sense requires representation, the critique of representation, and the critique of the critique of representation" (1997, p. 62).

To take 'the risk of the universal interest' might be mistaken for a benign vision of freedom *qua* a liberal endeavor. Yet in Rose's assumption of political freedom any argument for risk in the universal requires recognition of the tension that exists between the particularities by which we see the world and the risking of these particulars to a universal that is never identified. Rose insists (against the prevailing postmodernist's rejection of the possibility of representation) that representation in its critical case has to be made palpable enough to afford us the risk. Otherwise the risk is no risk at all. In Rose one finds a line of argument that is not dissimilar to Greene's call for a "struggle to create humane communities, playful communities, at once beautiful and just" even when we are told that there are no more metanarratives to find refuge in.

So when Greene's will to representation (as well as its critique and the critique of its critique) appears in her call for the released imagination, one cannot fall back on defaulted utopias. We have already seen how Greene considers herself as one of those for whom "the world of risks and pursuits is far more appealing than the world of arrivals and assurances." In this respect our reading of her aesthetic pedagogy must be rooted in other than a simple lineage between aesthetics and education, even when *prima facie*, this is what everyone seeks out.

This is where we take Greene's invitation and risk all, as Woolf does in her art:

> Was he not like Keats? She asked; and reflected how she might give him a taste of *Antony and Cleopatra* and the rest; lent him books; wrote him scraps of letters; and lit in him such a fire as burns only once in a life-time, without heat, flickering a red gold flame infinitely ethereal and insubstantial over Miss Pole; *Antony and Cleopatra*; and the Waterloo Road. He thought her beautiful, believed her impeccably wise; dreamed of her, wrote poems to her, which, ignoring the subject, she corrected in red ink; he saw her, one summer evening, walking in a green dress in a square. "It has flowered," the gardener might have said, had he opened the door; had he come in, that is to say, any night about this time, and found him writing; found him tearing up his writing; found him finishing a masterpiece at three o'clock in the morning and running out to pace the streets, and visiting churches, and fasting one day, drinking another, devouring Shakespeare, Darwin, *The History of Civilisation*, and Bernard Shaw. (Woolf 1994a, p. 93)

CHAPTER TWO

If We Are to Be

I remember dread [*miedo*] as a permanent metallic taste in the mouth.
—Isabel Allende, *My Invented Country* (2003, p. 180)

The human being must experience difficulty and unease if he is to be.
—Maxine Greene, *Existential Encounters for Teachers* (EET, p. 32)

Isabel Allende's dread, her anxious fear, left her with nothing but a metallic taste when on September 11, 1973, a military coup led by Augusto Pinochet bombed Chile's presidential palace *La Moneda* and crushed the democratically elected government that was inspired, conceived and led by President Salvador Allende, her father's cousin. Twenty-eight years later, the same dread came over her when, now a citizen of the United States, she witnessed with the rest of the world the horror of September 11, 2001. Both tragedies happened on a clear bright Tuesday at more or less the same time of day.

The coincidence was too uncanny to bear. For Isabel Allende this augmented the sense of dread a hundredfold. Chile's September 11 remains largely forgotten by many who either by denial, ignorance or simply indifference still know next to nothing about who was involved and by whose backing the military junta decided to crush the democratic will of the Chilean people. Indeed Allende's democratically elected revolutionary government—the first of its kind in the world—may have lost its initial utopian fervor. Historians remain at odds on whether his *Unidad Popular* lost the support of its base. As we have seen in the wake of Augusto Pinochet's arrest in 1998, Chileans remain split over Allende's legacy. Yet whatever the argument, no one had the right to crush Chilean democracy. Just as nothing would justify the massacre and oppression of the Chilean people by the say so of a bunch of fascist generals prompted and supported by the interests of Empire.

For Isabel Allende, as for those who were exiled, or whose relatives were tortured, oppressed, murdered and forgotten in Pinochet's Chile, September

11 remains an indescribable moment of existential dread. A point zero. An absolute nothingness. A human history in fragments.

> I realize today that I am one person in the multicolored population of North America, just as before I was a Chilean. I no longer feel that I am an alien in the United States. When I watched the collapse of the towers, I had a sense of having lived a nearly identical nightmare. By a blood-chilling coincidence—historic karma—the commandeered airplanes struck their U.S. targets on Tuesday, September 11, exactly the same time in the morning—of the 1973 coup in Chile, a terrorist act orchestrated by the CIA against a democracy. The images of burning buildings, smoke, flames, and panic are similar in both settings. That distant Tuesday in 1973 my life was split in two; nothing was ever the same: I lost a country. That fateful Tuesday in 2001 was also a decisive moment; nothing will ever again be the same, and I gained a country. (Allende 2003, p. xii)

Allende's words capture what Kierkegaard calls "persistent striving" as that "ethical life view of the existing subject." Maxine Greene articulates this ethical view as the origin of 'learning' and 'being', where "in order to learn, in order to be, [the individual] must struggle against blankness and inertia, and commit himself to his 'fundamental project,' which is the achievement of his full human reality" (EET, p. 19).

The learning to which Greene alludes is not something that one gets from someone or from a situation. Learning is not a game of passing the epistemological parcel from the knower to the unknowing. Nor is it a form of power exerted by those who claim to know over those who are deemed to be 'in need' of teaching. To understand the world from within the dread of the existent is to take 'to learn' into the constituency of 'to be', that of Being in- and for- itself, as Sartre puts it in *Being and Nothingness*. The qualification of being is essential in any discussion of learning, especially when learning pertains to one's understanding of how *being situated* also means that one becomes aware of one's existence, an existence that is unpredictable as much as it is unconsciously *owned* and consciously *dreaded*.

As to who owns (by subsequently fearing) one's existence becomes a major political—and by implication, a cultural-pedagogical—question. In Allende's sense of existential ownership-as-dread, September 11 becomes a fear of belonging but at the same time a return to one's own(ed) country. As a space where one presumes to belong, one's country is lost one day and gained the other. Maybe, as Constantine Cavafy reminds us, the sense of belonging—which is the city that we all carry within us—will remain the same when it persistently seeks itself elsewhere: "You will find no other place, no other shores. This city will possess you" (2007, p. 73).

"... somewhat later than Dewey's"

Reflecting on existence, we often find ourselves in the predicament of contradiction and paradox. One's existence comes into focus while being *with* others, but also while feeling *without* others. Often there is a sense of existence without being. This feels like an entrapment, a perpetual state of being *in-between*. In this sense, one feels trapped in an existence that lacks the very life one aspires to live. This is not simply an anxiety over the loss of the certainty of an absolute or totality. This feeling comes from a realization that existence may not be an end in itself, and yet it is all we have. Dread from what could be feared as a termination of one's taste and zest for life becomes a discovery of one's existence per se—of existence *as such*, in and for itself—in terms of what becomes a peculiar form of reassurance where what is the norm is uncertain, but also where we realize that uncertainty can never be the norm. Life as we know it may not be what we wish it to be. But then what is certain is that whether realized or not, one's life *exists indeed*, and it is because one *exists* that he or she could hope and imagine the self in all its possibilities.

Reviewing Sartre's *Nausea*, Albert Camus explains that "in the best ordered of lives, a moment always comes when the background collapses. Why this and that, this woman, this job and this appetite for a future? To put it in a nutshell, why this fever for life in these legs that are going to rot?" (1967, p. 146). Camus does not stop with the rot. To take life's contingency into account is not a cue to desperation. Absurdity in itself is not the consummation of hope, but a step to somewhere else, a beginning. For Camus "the realization that life is absurd cannot be an end in itself but only a beginning. It is a truth which nearly all great minds have taken as their starting point. It is not this discovery which is interesting, but the consequences and the rules for actions which can be drawn from it" (1967, p. 147).

In her book *Teacher as Stranger* Greene reads Camus within the context of the life and work of teachers. As individuals coming to terms with existence, teachers do not live in a vacuum. The School is not an isolated unit that has nothing to do with reality. One becomes a teacher within the stark realities that face everyone. Yet, it is also true that facing the challenges of her profession the teacher has to take personal decisions that risk compartmentalizing her life. Powerless in a system that expects them to obey orders, measure up to irrational expectations and to act "like clerks, subjects of a remote authority that issues orders, supervises, and asks little more than conformity to custom," teachers often "accede" to this form of compartmentalization (TAS, p. 5). The

very nature of teaching—indeed the very *act of being* a teacher—continuously
faces an existential dilemma:

> There are, clearly, manifold ways of adjusting—and manifold ways of refusing. Too
> many of them involve denials, evasions of confrontation. In self-protection, a teacher
> develops techniques for avoiding full consciousness; he postpones "real life" until the
> hours after school. After all, when one becomes self-conscious, one is present as a per-
> son in any situation; the mechanisms of denial and detachment do not work. One is
> compelled to put oneself and one's commitments on the line. New possibilities may
> be terrifying in the vistas they disclose. *It is not easy to take one's authentic stance, to
> choose oneself as personally responsible.* It is never easy to act upon what one—for good,
> defensible reasons—truly believes. (TAS, p. 5, my emphasis)

Beyond what Greene decries as the futile slogans and all too easy shortcuts
by which educational policy makers continuously misrepresent learning, there
remains her strong belief that it is possible for teachers to take an authentic
stance in their life and profession. This authenticity does not emerge from following the hollow assumptions made by the educational policy maker. Nor
does it assume that education is the systematization of learning. Rather, the
stance is philosophical, and more specifically that of *doing* philosophy. This is
because philosophy is not a "distinctive structure of knowledge" but "a way of
approaching (or looking at or taking a stance with respect to) the knowledge
gained by the natural and human sciences, the awareness made possible by the
arts, and the personal insights into existence each human being accumulates as
he lives" (TAS, pp. 6–7). In this way the teacher is not simply a unit within a
system, a clerk who obeys, or a knower who 'gives' knowledge to those who
'need' it. Rather the teacher takes on his "vantage point as actor (...) from the
vantage point of his newest experience and his most recent fears" (ibid., p. 7).

The exchange between experience and fear characterizes the philosophical
event as it emerges from dread and its existentialist sense for the absurd. Citing the "vantage points" of experience and fear as the origin of the teacher's
philosophical deed, Greene invites us to consider education as a philosophical, more specifically, existentialist event: "To do philosophy, as Jean-Paul Sartre says, is to develop a fundamental project, *to go beyond the situations one
confronts and refuse reality as given in the name of a reality to be produced*" (TAS, p.
7, my emphasis). How does one refuse this *given* reality? What urges us to dis-
tinguish between *reality*, a *given* reality, and a reality *to be produced*?

In one of her early essays, aptly titled "Existentialism and Education,"
Greene argues: "the point is that man, living man, is *doing* experiencing, not
having or reflecting experiences. If existence signified 'standing out', emerging,
then living man is a man always becoming, endeavoring to choose himself in
his situation, to transcend himself, to come to be" (NDb, p. 7). Greene's exis-

tentialist position is neither gratuitous nor rhetorical. Neither is it limited to the teacher's predicament or the failure of a system driven by educational bureaucrats. In her engagement with the teacher's vantage point of newest experiences and recent fears, she positions the notion of the self within the scope of philosophy where activity originates in the act of refusal that politically enacts a distancing from realities that are given instead of (if not simply *forced* on) other realities.

> I think we must begin with the notion of existence as emergence, self transcendence, and assume that the existentialist concern in the classroom can only be with the fulfillment of the individual in his full reality, of the person in his world. For all his concern for inwardness and his preoccupation with personal isolation, the existentialist recognizes that the living person must be understood in the context of his situation at a particular place and time. (...) The 20th century teacher must be cognizant of the universal aspects of man's predicament: his longings for support and recognition; his anticipations for transiency, loss and death; and he must also take into account the fragmentation, multiplicity, and flux within societies today. (NDb, p. 8)

In doing philosophy, one's fundamental project is a refusal of a manufactured reality that dwells on unheeded fears and unexamined experiences. Greene reminds us that the existentialist "is less interested in gathering evidence than in what the individual does with the evidence; he is concerned not so much with scientific or rational solutions, but with solutions deriving from the emotional, aesthetic and moral dimensions of the self" (NDb, p. 7). While teachers engage with others, they become others. Likewise teachers become strangers who look at the world from a different angle, wondering what's the next step, what should be done? Teachers often feel like Meursault in *L'Étranger*, who Camus describes as "not a reject, but a poor naked man, in love with a sun which leaves no shadows" (1986, p. 118). Being in love with "a sun which leaves no shadows" is not a hopeless situation, but rather, as in the case of the absurd, a realization of one's situatedness, a condition by which one takes ownership of one's truth. Camus is reassuring: "This truth is as yet a negative one, a truth born of living and feeling, but without which no triumph over the self or over the world will ever be possible" (ibid.)

One cannot assume the truth as a case (or indeed a cause) without situation. In this respect, the notion of the absurd is no less historical than the situation with which we all, teachers and learners, citizens of the same polis, members of society, would have to assume our positions when doing philosophy. Yet the business of doing philosophy—and with it, the questions of 'method' and 'knowledge'—become matters that are not limited to one's grappling with the notion of the truth of fact in science and or that of meaning in the arts. This is limited not only to teachers and learners, but also to humanity whose wider context is the thrust of learning and teaching.

In many ways the relationship between teachers, humanity and the need to do philosophy presents us with a cyclic dilemma, what philosophers call a *tautology*. Doing philosophy cannot be reduced to method and knowledge. The matter of method and knowledge is not restricted to the so-called professional philosopher but is a concern for everyone, including teachers and non-teachers. However, because knowledge and understanding are not restricted to philosophical or scientific methods, they become a major concern for philosophers and scientists. This is the tautology that directly affects the teacher. The teacher, as it were, remains at the center of this tightrope between the method of understanding presented by science as a series of facts and problems to be solved and the situated realities that, philosophers would insist, need to be liberated from the facts and problems that the social and natural scientists present to us as 'resolvable'. While philosophers and scientists might retreat in their quibbles, teachers cannot afford to do so because they deal with learners—that is, everyone—and by consequence with themselves, who are the most conscious of learners.

Thus although Camus reassures us about the absurdity of the situatedness by which we become conscious of our subjective truths as all that we have to begin with, we are also made aware of the certainty by which natural and social science claims to 'deliver' us from what it sees as the subjective uncertainties that afflict the world. One must bear in mind that these uncertainties are not indecisive situations such as war or disease, but the same phenomena with which humans have imagined and still strive to create a world with a modicum of beauty, goodness and truth. After citing Camus, Greene captures this predicament succinctly: "Poetry nor mathematics: neither can fully explain. Nor can either assuage the desire for a world that is reasonable in ordinary human terms" (TAS, p. 107).

Greene turns to Dewey, whose philosophy, *prima facie*, seems to accommodate both poetry and mathematics: "[Dewey] meant that a reflective man maintains a certain continuity in his habits of thinking and acting. In this context, a philosophical disposition enables such a man to continue probing, learning, seeking connections and meanings. In fact the disposition to find out best equips the human being to bear vicissitudes and pain" (TAS, p. 108). Initially seeing a certain similarity of positioning between Dewey and Camus—that is, how in their different ways they valorize the indeterminacies of life—Greene goes on to explore this in terms of the historical character of the unease that arises between the certainty of science's objective truths and the subjective meanings of the self:

For Dewey it might stem from some dislocation in social life, a moral dilemma, or an unanswered question in one of the sciences. Camus was speaking out of a sense of predicament that might well be alien to Dewey because it was not really susceptible to conceptualization or definition. The predicament was irremediable because of the human being's habitation in a universe that refused to be reduced to terms of thought. (TAS, p. 108)

So far it seems that Dewey and Camus are only at odds with how and where they position philosophy. One might even go as far as saying that they do not agree over what philosophy should do. However, they seem to be approaching the dilemma in a way that remains open and ultimately converges, where from an existential point of view one cannot presume causality as a fixed determination and concern of human thinking and being, and where from a pragmatic point of view causality does not follow a uniform pattern and therefore does not obstruct the accommodation of diverse and unexpected situations. In other words, both Camus and Dewey seem to accept the idea of contingency.

However, the apparent commonality and possible convergence between Dewey and Camus over indeterminacy and contingency disappears when it comes to sheer history. Though their life span might have overlapped (Dewey died in 1952, aged 93, Camus died in 1960, much younger, at 47), their attention to history turned out to be radically different. By consequence their philosophies might converge in some ways, but would quickly part company. This does not occur in terms of their philosophical sensitivity, but more so in terms of the acuteness with which history intervened in what Dewey and Camus stood for and responded to. As a philosopher who is equally sensitive to the truth of history, Greene cannot fail to observe this difference:

The dilemma has to do with man's feeling of homelessness at a moment in history (somewhat later than Dewey's) when science, by dint of mathematical description, had indeed achieved an abstract totality although a kind of totality unassimilable by ordinary men. Hence, the predicament, as Camus saw it, cannot be equated with the Deweyan problem; it cannot be solved reflectively. Nevertheless, confronting his predicament, the individual *can* choose to adopt certain attitudes, which may well be dispositions to rationality. (TAS, pp. 108-9)

Far from choosing between Dewey and Camus, pragmatism or existentialism, Greene re-positions the question of how we do philosophy within the historical realities that urge us to choose our "dispositions to rationality." It is all too easy to simply dismiss this choice as a casualty of events and claim that philosophy transcends historical occurrence. In electing an argument that allows us to do what we do within the indeterminacies of life and without losing our disposition to rationality, Greene could have made an elaborate argument for pragmatism and like Richard Rorty she would claim Dewey as the paragon of such disposition (Mouffe 1996). In not choosing to do so, she never rejects Dewey inasmuch as she chooses history over an all too tempting engagement with rationality. Clearly her disposition is first historical and then, by the same consequence, existential. Yet this is not a privileging of a philosophical assumption of history over existence or reason, but rather a responsible recognition of what *our history* has come up with—"somewhat later than Dewey's."

As history recalls ominous names such as Hiroshima and Auschwitz, we cannot simply ignore the fact that doing philosophy somehow shifts and becomes different from Dewey's way. In short, it is a question of what *doing philosophy* can afford us, and in turn, what we can afford in *our* ways of doing philosophy—a distinction that Dewey would probably corroborate. To that effect we now add other names to our history: two tragedies of September the 11th—both Chile's *and* New York's. If September 11, 1973, seemed 'affordable' to the many who chose to forget, after September 11, 2001, one cannot keep forgetting that men, women and their political systems are well capable of terror and mass murder. And just as the recent genocides in the Balkans, Rwanda and now Darfur remind us that Auschwitz remains part of the human condition, we come to realize with Greene that "there are other dangers as well, perhaps not as great as this [she refers to anti-Semitism] but potentially almost as damaging. One of them derives from irresponsibility, when the individual does not seize the initiative in and the responsibility for his own coming to be" (EET, p. 55).

Disruptive Choices

"At the end of this voyage to the frontiers of anxiety," Camus tells us, "Sartre does seem to authorize one hope: that of the creator who achieves deliverance through writing" (1967, p. 147). In 1967, Greene took Sartre's 'authorization' in her stride. She goes on to edit and publish a volume of existentialist texts, ranging from Tolstoy to Sartre, Kierkegaard to Heidegger, Rilke to Buber, Marcel to Jaspers, which takes "six weeks or so" to write (Greene 1998, p. 11). She names the book *Existential Encounters for Teachers*, where evidently her intended audience is expressly that of teachers, and more intently the American teacher whom she invites, citing Camus' call for "a whole civilisation to be remade," and adding that we all must "remake by means of education" (EET, p. 18). Even forty years later, this book presents us with Greene's vision as one of genuine belief in the power of philosophy, the arts and literature. It also reinforces the image of a teacher and philosopher who never hesitates to confront, challenge and fight officialdom and bureaucracy in Education. No holds barred, Greene exhorts teachers to talk of passion, subjectivity and becoming (EET, p. 17). To this very day, such speak is still frowned upon by many in Education, which as a discipline is fraught with positivist fallacies, short-termism and standardization. Greene's deep encounters with existentialism and phenomenology form the foundation of all her work. Her renowned passion for education is qualified by her passion for the fundamental project, the achievement of full human reality:

> Doing, acting, choosing—these are the watchwords of existential thinking and existential education. *The world remains open; the world remains strange; and history is possibility.* The teacher, then, may conceive himself to be a metaphysician, an ironist, an artist; but, first and last, he must conceive himself as a living man. (EET, p. 152, my emphasis)

A life unexplained is strange. Its screaming silence is terrifying. The dilemma of meaning remains unbearable, while truth retreats from fact. Yet life attracts further lives. The empty street becomes full. We speak of it together. We argue about it. We re-enact it on stage, on television, in the cinema. We depict it to each other. We write poems and make music from it, where dissonance becomes assonance and *vice versa*.

Re-citing Greene's words—"The world remains open; the world remains strange; and history is possibility"—one recalls Edward Hopper's paintings of lone figures sitting in apartment rooms in works such as *Eleven AM* (1926) and *Hotel Room* (1931). These works recall the mood in Odysseus Elytis's poem "Sunday 19" from his *Journal of an Unseen April*, where a Sunday's calm evokes "the likelihood of death" as a "droning still" permeates a room of removed sentiments (Elytis 1998, p. 65).

Where does one begin with Hopper's depiction of women, most of whom rest in a state of undress on a bed bathed in the light coming from a window overlooking what feels like a morose cityscape? Why do these solitary figures have to be women and not men? Why is it that when Hopper depicts solitary men they are mostly sitting outside and fully clad, as in that other canonical work, *Sunday* (1926)? To what extent does Hopper's work reflect life? Or is he more intent on constructing a reality that disrupts the certainty by which the majority of his audience views his work? Are Hopper's existentialist narratives (if one could call them 'existentialist') a painted version of a common thread in all the arts of Modernism?

To Greene's mind, Hopper's work recalls the sense of estrangement that surrounds us, but of which we are not always conscious:

There are strangers all about us now, presumably autonomous people moving in the shopping malls, up the elevators in glass and metal buildings, through antiseptic corridors, in large and muffled rooms. There are masses of strangers on the main streets; but the cities are marked in many places by the emptiness and silences seen in Edward Hopper's paintings. Suburbs and small towns are deserted in the daylight; at night, the walls close people in; and, everywhere, television screens glimmer and speechless onlookers gaze. (DOF, p. 19)

Is Hopper's a painted version of a moody void, one of those moments that Vladimir, in Samuel Beckett's *Waiting for Godot*, gloomily declares to be "too much for one man," but then upon reflection he changes his mind and cheerfully suggests: "On the other hand what's the good of losing heart now, that's what I say. We should have thought of it a million years ago, in the nineties" (Beckett 1979, p. 10)? It is not even clear whether Vladimir really has a change of heart, or whether he cannot even make up his mind. He also says that he is yet to try everything. To many extents, any judgment that he might make about his own predicament is held in reserve, distracted by questions over the utility of his own queries. There is nothing exactly conclusive in what he says because there is nothing to conclude. Better put, once the dialogue on life is concluded there is no need for, or way of, going further. So the resolution of a situation's meaning cannot be precipitated. What appears to be a sense of hopelessness is in effect an optimistic way of keeping life going. Like Beckett's Vladimir, Sartre's Antoine Roquentin holds his judgment, and in doing so he remains hopeful: "Perhaps some day, thinking about this very moment, about this dismal moment at which I am waiting, round-shouldered, for it to be time to get on the train, perhaps I might feel my heart beat faster and say to myself: 'It was on that day, at that moment that it all started'" (Sartre 1982, pp. 252–23).

Yet Hopper's characters inhabit paintings, not plays or novels. Even if Beckett's plays and Sartre's novels appear to remain unresolved (hence read as full of hope, albeit *prima facie* bizarre and perverted), Hopper's paintings offer a different kind of promise. This promise is found in what Georges Lukács (1971) calls art's *speciality*, as a membership of a 'special' world that emerges from the specificity of the aesthetic. The aesthetic specificity of the work—as a painting, in Hopper's case—opens the possibility to *argue* art beyond its point of origin. Without taking account of art's aesthetic specificity, one loses track of art's speciality and considers art as a mere instrument where Beckett's work becomes nonsense and Sartre's notion of absurdity remains ... simply absurd! Because of art's speciality we realize that Hopper's painting is not a medium that intervenes between art and existence, but a human construct that *becomes* and therefore *partakes* of the human self in a meaningful and autonomous way.

This is where one needs to clarify the relationship between art and existence, especially when following Greene's stand on aesthetics-education. The fact that one elects to engage with existence through an aesthetic experience occasioned by a painting could contribute to an inflationary attribution of situational contexts to works of art. This inflation is not uncommon in art. T.J. Clark (1999) identifies it as "the excess of reality," for which artists such as Caravaggio and Chardin tried to make amends by using a series of transitions from light to dark, focused to generalized and so on (pp. 44–45). This excess of reality could be caused by the degree to which the artist adds a detailed presence of visual referents in the work for the purpose of narrative or composition. Another excess (to which Clark makes no direct reference) is caused by over-interpretation. In some cases, art appears to be suffering from an overage of a myriad attributions that mean something only to those who use them as referents of interpretation. This excess of possible meanings contributes to an intentional fallacy that ties art to assumed origins (Wimsatt & Beardsley 1954). This fallacy is compounded by its direct opposite: where some assume that the arts must be 'experienced' just as one experiences life in its various modalities. One could say that in the latter case another excess happens— where reality is inflated by the manufacture of wrongly attributed experiences. Whether one's experience of art should be attributed to one's daily experience (often on the whim of observation) or whether it must be always assumed that an original intention is key to art's meaning is a question that has a bearing on art's relationship to the immediacy of the *here and now* and its subsequent questioning.

When Greene speaks of the individual's existential experience, she argues that for learning to take place, everyday life must be disrupted. Here we are not speaking of learning as an apprehension of knowledge, but learning as an existential project. So what is meant by *disruption* implies that knowledge is not apprehended but becomes part of what it means to be.

> There is, in consequence, something irreducibly problematic about the situation in which true learning takes place. The everyday, the ordinary are in some sense disrupted; the questioning student must break with the ready-made, with conventional wisdom; he must choose himself as a conscious being—choose himself to know. (EET, p. 127)

Just as in its disruption with the ordinary, a painting gains a sense of being—even when it appears to depict the quotidian (as in Hopper)—the speciality that brings about an aesthetic experience cannot be anything but a disruption with one's daily encounters. I dare suggest that 'learning to know' must be predicated by the notion of 'learning to be'—*always* and not simply in moments of aesthetic rupture. In other words, one might argue that to attribute aesthetics to learning would mean overloading the notion of existence with the preoccupations of art, and by consequence, mediate existence with life through the disruption—rather than the mirroring or imitation—of the ordinary.

As I argue later in this book, any claim for a widening of one's understanding—of life, art or anything else—can be placed only on experience when it is understood as a process of *anticipation*, rather than a mechanical method that *replicates* the experienced events. Although I cannot attribute this distinction directly to Greene, her work does imply that to open one's imagination through one's experience of the arts is never a mechanical repetition of the immediate. Greene may or may not agree with the notion of experience as anticipation, but surely her idea of the primacy of the disruption of the everyday suggests that experience cannot be taken for granted as some instantaneous form of learning. A mechanical assumption of experience could only *replicate*—artistically, pedagogically, conceptually—the limits of what is assumed to 'happen' in terms of 'what one experiences'. On the contrary, the widening of experience to the concept of *anticipation* denotes women's and men's ability to transcend the limits of what they experience. Thus while Greene never says that experience anticipates anything a priori, her idea of *the disruption of the ordinary* supposes that experience is not a unitary notion, but stands for a multiplicity of possibilities—which is where one could safely say that as *possibility* one's ability to break with everyday experience is predicated on the need to release one's imagination. Arendt clearly confirms this state of affairs when she says that "all thought arises out of experience, but no experience yields any meaning or even coherence without undergoing the operations of imagining and thinking" (1978, vol. 1, p. 87).

Greene's notion of the disruption of everyday life prefaces Kierkegaard where he explains why his soul always turns to the Old Testament and to Shakespeare: "I feel that those who speak there are at least human beings: they hate, they love, they murder their enemies, and curse their descendants throughout all generations, they sin" (EET, p. 130). This is indicative of the need to learn to engage via contexts that disrupt life in its immediacy. After all, a painting of a solitary figure in a room is not equivalent to the actual experience of a lonely person in a room. Thus we could speak of Hopper's painting as disrupting *our* conscious engagement with life by means of what *someone else* makes *us* conscious of. This *someone else* is not simply Hopper the artist or his original intention. Rather it is an otherness that comes as a negotiation between the individual viewers of the work, and how the work in its distance from actual life makes one aware of the dread that triggers an interest in life. But this does not mean that art's meaning is left to the whims of one's experience. Rather, the anticipation with which one approaches the work is often disrupted by what appears, as in Hopper's case, as a deceptively 'easily understood' painting. It soon becomes clear that even in the misleadingly mimetic character of Hopper's figurative work, the viewer's initial certainty could not be saved from the abyss that will ultimately engulf his or her aesthetic experience. As in Narcissus's attraction to the lure of mimesis, the risk remains fatal. And to learn this fatality is to encounter one's existence. Valéry famously captures this luring risk in his poem *Narcisse parle* (*Narcissus Speaks*) saying how "the deceitful moon raises its mirror" until the hidden messages of the waters are quenched (Valéry 1963, p. 43).

The Free as Reflective

Introducing her translation of Sartre's *Being and Nothingness*, Hazel Barnes explains that "throughout the book Sartre has been stressing the fact that in imagination the object is posited either as absent, as non-existent, as existing elsewhere, or as neutralized (i.e. not posited as existing). Now in order to effect such a positing, consciousness must exercise its peculiar power of nihilation (*néantisation*). If an object is to be posited as absent or not existing, then there must be involved the ability to constitute an emptiness or nothingness with respect to it" (Barnes 1956, p. xiii).

One cannot imagine anything that is immediately in front of him. To imagine a horse one cannot be looking at a physical horse or its image. In other words, what we posit in consciousness, we must negate in our imagination, and inversely, to imagine something is to negate its presence. What the imaginary assumes, our consciousness must first eliminate from immediate experience. As the emptied space of *néantisation* makes it possible for the self to imagine beyond the limits of immediate consciousness and experience, the condition of nothingness becomes an occasion for the possibility of a larger imaginary context where the promise of life becomes infinite. In this way, nihilation is not a destruction of reality, but an opportunity to imagine other than what is immediate.

The centrality of the imagination in Greene's philosophical project emerges from this dialectical positioning of the immediate senselessness of nihilation and the actualization of human possibility. Greene adds to this dialectic a location where the assumptions of learning as a concern for being are situated within everyone's reach, where the possible and the real converge in the self's *facticity* and where facticity serves as the dialectical fulcrum for the pedagogy of the imagination. Greene argues that even as the child "projects himself forward, he carries with him an awareness of brute existence—of 'senselessness'—which all the arrangements of social life are devised to obscure" (EET, p. 87). Policy makers and curricular engineers are the first to argue that the School is there to eradicate all traces of "senselessness" and "awareness of brute existence" in the child. Yet Greene argues the very opposite. It is this senselessness and awareness of brute fact that would actualize the self's imagination: "there is in the perception of meaninglessness (or of 'facticity') a potential opportunity to impose meaning, if only by contemplating or ordering the past, or by telling 'stories' about existing in the present" (EET, p. 87).

To identify Greene's philosophical origin in Existentialism is not to make a point of exegesis that ties all her subsequent work into a false sense of 'coherence' without any possibility of evolution. Rather, as we have previously argued, Greene's choice is rooted in her valorization of historical truth. Already in *Existential Encounters for Teachers* one finds a rather protestant reading of Existentialism where there isn't a univocal reading, and where there is no one Canon. In this way, she characterizes existentialism as a cue to exploration, rather than as a set of conclusions: "the existentialist would consider education to be an exploration of value, above all else; and, at some point, he would have to consider the difficulty of dealing with human choices without working through some common reflective method of handling them" (NDb, p. 8). Greene makes no apologies for making no attempts "to identify what are, in philosophic contexts, significant differences between rigorous phenomenologists like Martin Heidegger and 'literary' existentialists like Jean-Paul Sartre" (EET, p. 5). A discussion of Greene's existentialist origins is an occasion to provide oneself (as a reader of her work) with a point of introduction into a much wider horizon. This also prepares one for one's engagement with her work in conversational mode.

We have already established that Greene's work is an occasion for dialogue, where an *agôn*—as a space for learning—is claimed. To claim a space for learning, and by consequence a learning space, is both political *and* philosophical. It is to pose the great questions of the self within the greater possibilities of the imagination. This is done not for sheer delectation but by one's commitment to freedom, where we come to realize the responsibilities that the horizons of emancipation continue to promise us by means of the dialectical nature of human potentiality. As in all potential situations, there is always the risk of failure, or even fatality. We know from history that freedom can be fatal, but it is worth dying for. The same goes for the risk of the imagination as it becomes charged with a desire to engage with its aesthetic possibilities. We all have been warned of the risk, as Schiller reminds us in his Ninth Aesthetic Letter where he says that the artist, being the child of his or her time, must not be "at the same time its ward or, worse still, its minion!" (1967, §IX, p. 55). Schiller augurs that the child is taken away by a beneficent deity for the child to grow into a mature individual and then to return to one's century: "let him return, a stranger, to his own century; not, however, to gladden it by his appearance, but rather, terrible like Agamemnon's son, to cleanse and to purify it" (p. 57).

The risk of the self that is lured to existence's mimesis recalls Narcissus's risk. Like Narcissus we seek into the depths of aesthetic reflection and there we see nothing but ourselves. However, to make this risk worth its while, one must be made aware that the sweetness of reflection (as *mimesis*, as imitation-and-representation) also hides the daemonic desirability of an end (as *thanatos*, as death) to be feared. (One cannot forget that self-reflection in the abyss of mimesis was fatal to Narcissus.) Yet it is by the power of this fear that we can hope in learning to handle the delectation of mimesis and its deadly essence. And while Greene would not put it this way, there is something of this need for fear when she states that although the individual must not choose irrationalism, one would "neither feel his freedom nor the risks of reflectiveness if he satisfies himself with general statements and syllogistic arguments, if he stops asking existential questions at the 'boundaries' of his life" (EET, p. 68).

So while retaining Narcissus's risk, how would one save Narcissus from himself? Could the lure of a deadly mimesis (which is not that different from Greene's notion of the "risk of reflectiveness") fulfill what Schiller augurs to the returning artist when he urges him or her to be like Orestes, the avenging son of Agamemnon? Is the abyss of reflection possible without its risks? Should Orestes be pacified by historical amnesia? Should the murder of Agamemnon by Orestes' mother Clytemnestra and her lover Aegisthus be forgotten? As there is nothing to do with the inevitability of Narcissus's death and Orestes' defense, and while the risk and the inevitable remain possible, we are also reminded that neither mimesis nor possibility belong to a benign rite of felicitous Adventism.

The vindication of Agamemnon and the memory of Narcissus form part of the truth that actualizes human potential. This is because even when the self opts for *néantisation* for the sake of the imagination, the same self can do so because it is corporeal, and furthermore because it is *lived* and therefore *em-bodied*. If being begets nothingness in order to imagine a fuller actualization of the potentiality that lies beyond the limits of the *here and now*, it can only do so because the self is what Merleau-Ponty (1989) calls *"le corps vécu"*—a body that brings together reality as a lived event; thus a lived body, or as Roger Poole (1972) put it, an *embodied subject*.

Poole's take on embodied subjectivity illustrates the fundamental relation-ship between the predicament and risks of representation as it emerges from the self (here likened to Narcissus's curiosity with his own image) and the vin-dication of the polity, which Schiller (using the figure of Orestes) urges the art-ist to take in his or her return to one's century as an alien figure. While the figurative narratives of Narcissus and Orestes might be confusing, they remain potent narratives of a necessary disruption with which knowledge is chal-lenged. In his *Towards Deep Subjectivity*—which roughly coincides with the time when Greene published her *Teacher as Stranger*, following her writings on Exis-tentialism—Poole takes the example of the Spring Revolution in Czechoslova-kia, a revolution that was ended by the brutal Soviet invasion of August 20, 1968. Though crushed, the Czechoslovak rising came to symbolize the robust disruption of the objectified totality of Soviet ideology. As the tanks leveled themselves with individuals, Leonid Brezhnev's intransigence was met by a col-lective positioning of subjectivities:

> As embodied subjectivities, the protest marchers and sitters-in of the 1960s have mounted a series of moral questions in visual form. By denying the validity of what is the case, and implicitly suggesting the desirability of what is not the case, a series of indirect communications have in fact been filtered from *one section of rationality to the other*. (Poole 1972, p. 21, my emphasis)

As "one section of rationality" filters into another, one can see how the "disposition towards rationality" that Greene claims in her discussion of Ca-mus and Dewey (TAS, pp. 109) is not simply *pertinent* to history, but is an *act* of history. The embodied subjectivities that took their moral question to the streets in Prague were not irrational, but on the contrary they amounted to a most tangible disposition toward rationality. It was also mounted, as Poole puts it, "in visual form" and in doing so it found an effective way of dirempt-ing what is from what is not the case. This diremption was enacted as a form of indirect communication, where deep subjectivity and the body in visual form—as sign—become one. Poole takes (and later expands) the notion of indi-rect communication from Kierkegaard, as a form of communication that "must be distinguished from its expression" (Poole 1993, pp. 158ff). In the case of the Spring Revolution, the embodied subjectivities of the protesters find expression in the figure of Alexander Dubcek, whose indirect communication gradually becomes present to the Czechoslovakians: "Suddenly he corresponds to a deep subjective need in his fellow-countrymen, and in an act of sudden insight they *identify* in him" (Poole 1972, p. 26).

The ultimate existential moment of the historic diremption by which reason filtered from the side of ferrous objectivity to that of embodied subjectivity has become memorized by Jan Palach's ultimate sacrifice. In the wake of the Soviet invasion, Palach made the ultimate sacrifice, setting fire to himself in protest. Poole argues that in taking his life Palach's communication holds no answer:

> There is no answer to the communication of Jan Palach. The statement is final and absolute (...) his act establishes a whole network of validities for the body as sign. The body is established as the final, and perhaps only, dense secure moral value in our world. Nothing else is shared as surely as it ... (pp. 26-27)

As the ultimate risk of reflectiveness becomes an act where reflected and reflection are consumed into one event, the choice remains stark. Given that the body is all we have, our rational dispositions must take account of the space that our bodies create and inhabit. In this respect, the context of learning, like everything else, remains relational and thereby critical; active and thus responsive; reflective and so observable. If for Palach his self-consummation meant the ultimate sign of protest against the brutal objectification of the self, his sacrifice consumed all that the body could 'learn'.

As our bodies learn from Palach's final statement, we only hope that in our modest statements we achieve the power of a collective answer—if only to be able to resist what constantly threatens our embodied subjectivity. Here, Greene suggests a way to understand live dilemmas like those we are confronted by, such as Palach's final statement. Ultimately freedom is a question of choice, what Greene calls "boundary" choices, which embody the possibility of anticipation, "the anticipation of the unpredictable, even with death."

> Education, suggests the existentialist, may make people aware of what the yearning means by helping them name and feel the edge of it. Perhaps only a confrontation of such longing can make existentialist freedom possible, the freedom to choose oneself, to engage one self with others, to commit oneself to values, to ideals that will make men in some sense "irreplaceable". (NDb, p. 8)

CHAPTER THREE

Lives Observed

And this, Lily thought, taking the green paint on her brush, this making up scenes about them, is what we call 'knowing' people, 'thinking' of them, 'being fond' of them! Not a word of it was true; she had made it up; but it was what she knew them by all the same. She went on tunneling her way into her picture, into the past.
—Virginia Woolf, *To the Lighthouse* (1995, p. 187)

Lily Briscoe, unmarried woman painter, sees the sea-surrounded Hebrides world quite differently than does the analytical Professor Ramsay. Both viewpoints are at odds with those of the various children, the aged poet, or the lighthouse keeper. When the characters are seen to view things differently, this phenomenon may make readers conscious of the inadequacy of some of the patterns or interpretations they themselves have produced along the way. They may become self-reflective.
—Maxine Greene, *Releasing the Imagination* (RI, p. 97)

Virginia Woolf writes on how she "came to think of life as something of extreme reality" (1985, p. 137). Three deaths in her family provide a context to this extremity, three deaths which left her in one of her deep bouts of depression. Roger Poole contextualizes Woolf's 'extreme reality' as "given to the world in the novels." "In a sense," he explains, "the novels are about just this: what is 'reality'? And the origin of the sense 'extreme reality' is in the abrupt and violent deaths of [her close relatives in] 1895-1906, which temporarily shook her balance" (1995, p. 107).

In Woolf's art, extreme reality emerges within the norm. It appears in a day in the life of her characters, like Mrs. Dalloway whose life seems to be characterized by a constant and dedicated engagement with the world—hers as well as others'. Reality is also embodied in Woolf's rendition of Mrs. Ramsay's character, her beauty, her strength and her tender care towards her family. Yet as life's extreme reality turns norm into exception, the author who writes is also, at face value, the author who observes others *beyond* quotidian normality. In Woolf's case, these *others* may appear as characters in a story line, but surely they become more recognizable—as *they become us*—while we, as the readers, engage with the common grounds by which we try to define human 'life' and therefore each other. More than an audience that reads someone else's stories, that engages with the artworks that someone has made, or that views the film that someone has directed, as Woolf's audience we *live* all the instances that her art comes to represent.

Through the Looking-Glass of "Depicted Consciousness"

As works of art and literature invite us to engage with the mind of an author who willingly opens herself to all who want to understand and engage with life as such, we become self-reflective protagonists. As protagonists we are constantly presented to ourselves and to each other, over and over again. In others we immediately recognize ourselves as if we are looking at curious mirrors that, instead of reflecting what's in front of them, somehow suggest a personal, historical and imaginary lineage that helps us recall who we might be and what we might look like. However, these mirrors never imitate what's in front of them. Rather, they *connote* and *suggest*, thus leaving us with an open interpretation as we look for new passages in case we get trapped in the mirror:

> How would you like to live in Looking-glass House, Kitty? I wonder if they'd give you milk in there? Perhaps Looking-glass milk isn't good to drink—But oh, Kitty! Now we come to the passage. You can just see a little *peep* of the passage in Looking-glass House, if you leave the door of our drawing-room wide open: and it's very like our passage as far as you can see, only you know it may be quite different on beyond. (Carroll 1996, p. 10)

What *we might look like* in this curiously selective form of reflection is what makes the individuals and communities whom the author, artist, playwright, poet or filmmaker imagine and converse with. What *we might be* stands a good chance of becoming similar to what the author seeks to emulate when she also enters into 'character mode' and follows us through the looking-glass. Even though this is never the case—because invariably disjunctive moments of the 'inexperienceable' will emerge as gaps between us, art and the artist—Greene reassuringly argues that such gaps are surmountable (1994b, p. 212). Commenting on moments in Woolf's *To the Lighthouse*, she remains optimistic over the readers' ability to build *their own* experience into literary experience as a way of rewriting a "life text": "the scene of the work being read, after all, is *depicted consciousness*; because it is reader consciousness that has been provoked to invent the illusioned world" (ibid., my emphasis).

By dint of our 'reader consciousness' we become observers of our lives as well as of others. The observer of one's life also wants to be observed, even when a hidden observation remains unknown. In Greene's words, "the reader is allowed a free fictive use of perceptual experiences; since no one can contain or prescribe them with any specificity" (ibid.). One could add—and this might not be Greene's position—that the reader's "free fictive use of perceptual experiences" could explain how a juxtaposition of realities (the reader's and the author's) might work.

Elsewhere Greene argues that in the mutual relationship between author and reader, the latter becomes "conscious of the inadequacy of some of the patterns or interpretations they themselves have produced along the way" (RI, p. 97). One could infer from this that such misinterpretations do not pertain to some 'true' meaning that lies encrypted among the metaphors, characters and story lines of art or literature.

When one talks of the hermeneutic nature of works of art and literature, one does not imply codified meanings that are 'meant to be discovered' by literary or artistic detectives. The penchant for secrets is not a matter for literature and art, even when literature and art continuously entertain audiences with the subject of conspiracy—good examples being Umberto Eco's novels and more so the mystery classics, like Arthur Conan Doyle and Agatha Christie's great works. In Conan Doyle, Christie and Eco, the hermeneutic nature of the work does not emerge from the question "Who did it?" but primarily relates to how one understands and ultimately *learns* to move within and negotiate the human relationship between selves, their stories, and history. One must never forget that the primary aim of hermeneutic science is pedagogical; more specifically the enfolding of a *magisterium*—a body of learning—from where humanity learns *with* the logos as the words by which we ultimately articulate, recognize and partake of the world's immanence. In this immanence—in this interiority—the Scholastics perceived a divine design. Somewhat differently, some modern philosophers recognize immanence in how our existence pertains to *being-there*, or as Greene would put it after Merleau-Ponty, how women and men become conscious of *being situated*.

What is hermeneutical about mysteries is not the perpetrator of the crime in a detective story, but the need to construct a structure of questioning that, in Hercule Poirot's immortal words, would exercise those little gray cells, and ultimately teach us something solid about the weaknesses of the human condition through the strength of logical reasoning: "'This affair must all be unravelled from within.' He tapped his forehead. 'These little grey cells. It is "up to them"—as you say over here'" (Christie 1984, p. 151).

This is especially the case when the work is evidently constructed on the observation of a life whose interlocutors are *subjects-of* as well *subject-to* the stories that they construct. This also has a lot to do with the historical attributes of hermeneutics where the text in its historicity also relates to history as a life-form, as lived by women and men in their everyday lives.

This state of affairs is pretty much clarified by Jacques Rancière, who argues that "it is not a matter of claiming that 'History' is only made up of stories that we tell ourselves, but simply that the 'logic of stories' and the ability to act as historical agents go together. Politics and art, like forms of knowledge, construct 'fictions', between what is seen and what is said, between what is done and what can be done" (2006, p. 39). Though at first glance it appears as mysterious, even the unpredictable nature of human history foils any conspiratorial temptation to refashion art as a hermetically sealed meta-story. In history's indeterminate ways, but also in the ways we become, willingly or not, *historical* beings, what we come to tell of 'history' as a story cannot be hierarchized into a faked order of aesthetic meanings. Instead, how we narrate is an expression of the consciousness by which the arts provoke us "to invent the illusioned world" (Greene 1994b, p. 211). This world is not estranged in any way from our being situated in specific time frames or spaces. To the contrary, it helps us understand and appreciate the sense of one's now.

> The point is to live our lives because they are ours. Or to shape our narratives in ways that do not duplicate other narratives. At least we can work to render them the kinds of stories that open out to possibility. This does not depend upon representation; it depends upon creation and invention, preferably among others who are also in quest, who recognize us for what we are striving to be and who win our recognition for what they are not yet. (Greene 1994b, p. 218)

Landscapes of the Many

As the role of the subject exchanges and moves within and outside the reality that is *given* by the work of art, the notion of meaning remains open and fluent. It is because of this fluency of subjects and meanings, Greene suggests, the readers "may become self-reflective" (RI, p. 97).

To assert the self without falling into solipsism is the main challenge of a reflection on life, a reflection directed to the self where one's sense of one's *now* is not an unmediated form of reflection or learning, but an awareness of reality as being both *pragmatic* and *immanent*. In other words, reality is a world that is practiced through experience, but which also beholds an inner meaning to whatever we come across in everyday life. This notion of a pragmatic-yet-immanent world attracts particular attention to how ventures like educational philosophy could be done from what Greene calls "the vantage point of the person involved." Even when the world seems split between its practical and immanent sides, Greene remains hopeful: "There is the chance of increasing clarity: the ability to say what one means and can defend, to provide good reasons for what one believes. There is the chance of intensified commitment to values. There is the chance of combating the sense of meaninglessness and nihilism which afflicts so many—indeed, of transforming the world" (TAS, p. 37).

To recover one's sense of one's now is not to look at the self from an external vantage point that pretends to objectify and invest its assumed evidence into matters of fact. However, one's engagement with life cannot be a glorified form of navel gazing. It would certainly make no sense at all to assert the self only to transform it into an *object*. However, it would be dubious to value existence and the body from the position of the solipsist. Even when they seem to reach the obscure depths of subjectivity, neither Beckett's Vladimir nor Sartre's Roquentin abdicates from *observing* a reality 'out there', even when, in Beckett, this reality often seems to be stranger than the oddest takes on the norm, and in Sartre, reality becomes so uncanny that it is easily mistaken for a form of alienation.

Greene sees a way out of this dualism when she talks about the *vantage point* that teachers have at their disposition. Here Greene specifically cites Arendt's *The Human Condition*: "the vantage point of our newest experience and our most recent fears is nothing more than to think what we are doing" (TAS, p. 6; Arendt 1998). In Arendt's mind, to think of nothing more than what we are doing "deals only with the most elementary articulations of the human condition, with those activities that traditionally, as well as according to current opinion, are within the range of every human being" (1998, p. 5). More than a question of reason in the sense of ratiocination, the vantage point of *what we do* is firmly positioned within the political, and just as Arendt cannot be read without taking the political into account, nor would Greene make any sense if her stand would be simply assumed as some form of liberal enthusiasm. A liberal position, in this sense, would merely suggest political opinion. But like Arendt, Greene is a radical, not a liberal.

The nature of a vantage point, as understood through Arendt, is plural, and plurality is not limited to mere *position*, but portends a radical assumption. In *The Human Condition*, Arendt singles out three human activities that are fundamental: labor, work and action. While labor is seen as corresponding to the biological process, and work as that which "provides an 'artificial' world of things," action is "the only activity that goes on directly between men without the intermediary of things or matter." More important, this activity "corresponds to the human condition of plurality, to the fact that men, not Man, live on earth and inhabit the world." Arendt goes even further: "while all aspects of the human condition are somehow related to politics, this plurality is specifically the condition—not only the *conditio sine qua non*, but the *conditio per quam*—of all political life" (1998, p. 7). Greene's reference to and use of Arendt's idea of a vantage point is radical in this sense. It follows that any vantage point will be useless if there was only an acknowledgment of multiple positions. Plurality is not simply an existence of multiples, but a political condition that cannot be ignored. To argue for a plural vantage point is to say that there is a political condition by dint of humans being *many*. Humanity is, ultimately, *il maggior numero*, as Gramsci (1975a, p. 27) put it. It is *the largest number possible*, where qualitatively speaking, in terms of sheer diversity, being human has to do with sheer quantity. Arendt cannot be bolder: "Plurality is the condition of human action because we are all the same, that is, human, in such a way that nobody is ever the same as anyone else who ever lived, lives, or will live" (1998, p. 8).

Trying to sum vantage points in terms of singularity or universality would be futile. To pose a choice between the singular and the universal, contingency or necessity, would add nothing to teachers, or anyone else who claims a vantage point. The teacher, Greene argues, "is not required to choose himself as a predominantly rational man *or* a sensuous man; an objectivist *or* a subjectivist; an activist *or* a quietist. In a multifarious culture, no single schema or category can be sufficient for organizing the flux of reality" (TAS, p. 9). However, this would not imply a relativist choice. Not to choose between objectivism and subjectivism, activism or quietism does not mean that one simply implies the other. Greene's italicization of the word 'or' is not there for emphasis, but to highlight the equivocal nature of *choice*. Having to choose between objectivism and subjectivism would lead to a partial, one-dimensional engagement with the world.

Herbert Marcuse describes one-dimensionality as a thought and behavior "in which ideas, aspirations, and objectives that, by their content, transcend the established universe of discourse and action are either repelled or reduced to terms of this universe. They are redefined by the rationality of the given system and of its quantitative extension" (Marcuse 1986, p. 12). In a similar vein to Marcuse's critique of "a false consciousness which is immune against its falsehood" (ibid.), Greene argues that

> we do not philosophize to answer factual questions, establish guidelines for our be-
> havior, or enhance our aesthetic awareness. We philosophize when, for some reason,
> we are aroused to wonder about how events and experiences are interpreted and

should be interpreted. We philosophize when we can no longer tolerate splits and fragmentations in our pictures of the world, when we desire some kind of wholeness and integration, *some coherence which is our own*. (TAS, pp. 10–11, my emphasis)

It is because of the need to re-appropriate a "coherence which is our own" that the consciousness by which one would philosophize *the* world—rather than *about* the world—ultimately has to radically oppose the immunity of the one-dimensionality. In other words, philosophizing must not be frightened of the distinctions between reality and existence. A coherence of our own does not mean a leveling down into unanimity. Rather, it is the opposite. To seek coherence in the context of Greene's philosophy is not to revalue and reclaim contradiction. As Greene continuously argues, the dialectic is what characterizes philosophizing. Contradiction remains of essence to coherence. Philosophizing is the re-appropriation of wonder and with it, the appropriation of philosophy as "a process of arguing" (Laclau 1993, p. 341). It is in this context that one could then understand how a "coherence which is our own" is radically opposed to the notion of a one-dimensional *whole*, even when this is often presented to us as holistic and liberal. As one "can no longer tolerate splits and fragmentations in our pictures of the world" and as "we desire some kind of wholeness and integration" (TAS, p. 111), we invariably claim our right to the now as that point where the self could wander beyond contrived dualisms and fragmentations but without being trapped by one-dimensionality.

In effect, one-dimensionality has manipulated the desire to understand the world by suppressing the human aspiration to higher forms of culture, to higher forms of understanding, to higher forms of coherence where the dialectic was once the ground for this higher understanding. Marcuse explains how "today's novel feature is the flattening out of the antagonism between culture and social reality" (1986, p. 57). What Greene calls our philosophical desire to reach a "coherence which is our own" is precluded by a "liquidation of *two-dimensional* culture" that does not happen "through the denial and rejection of the 'cultural values', but through their wholesale incorporation into the established order, through their reproduction and display on a massive scale" (Marcuse 1986, p. 57). Greene comments that "when we consider how effectively modern society has absorbed the most startling products of the *avant garde*, and even the revolutionary imagination, it is easy to understand Marcuse's view" (LL, pp. 23–24).

Marcuse also remarks how "in the realm of culture, the new totalitarianism manifests itself precisely in a harmonizing pluralism, where the most contradictory works and truths peacefully coexist in indifference" (1986, p. 61). The result is a cultural amnesia where learning is obstructed because possibility is suppressed by the fact that in the immediacy of life, distinctions are replaced by a form of instant gratification that avoids the very notion of alienation between the actual and the possible. On the other hand, Marcuse tells us, "prior to the advent of this cultural reconciliation, literature and art are essentially alienation, sustaining and protecting the contradiction—the unhappy consciousness of the divided world, the defeated possibilities, the hopes unfulfilled, and the promises betrayed" (ibid.). Though few would agree that eliminating pain is equivalent to curing a disease, the one-dimensional form of cultural reconciliation that Marcuse talks about has done exactly this. It has convinced many that the consciousness of pain must be eliminated so that a semblance of peace and social harmony becomes reality. And where would the hegemony of one-dimensionality strike if not within those realms of culture and learning where the symptoms of inequality and oppression are most sensitized? What one-dimensional society does is desensitize the pain, and attempt to eradicate the truths of contradiction and the dialectic from our reasoning. As Greene puts it,

> in the writings that questioned bourgeois society in years past, there was a 'conscious transcendence of the alienated existence,' as Marcuse says. In fact the incompatibility between the images of life to be found in that prose and poetry and the normal 'order of business' may be evidence of their truth. Readers, over the years, have been able to perceive that truth when they have opened themselves to these works. In so doing, they have taken new standpoints on their normal life situations; they have gone beyond their own taken-for-grantedness. Marcuse also points out, however, that modern society has so much absorptive and assimilative power that the critical elements in this kind of literature have been obscured. (LL, p. 23)

With this analysis as a potent backdrop of hegemonic assimilation, Greene proposes that education must find a way to break through. Ultimately, the breakthrough must be a way of recollecting what Marcuse sees as art's prior ability to sustain and protect the contradiction. Greene is hopeful "that an adequate pedagogy might still enable modern learners to break with this assimilative power and reconstitute certain works of art as *occasions for transcendence, self-knowledge, and critique*" (LL, p. 24, my emphasis). Citing Sartre, who argues that the writer must animate and penetrate the world with his freedom, Greene makes a very powerful argument for pedagogy: "The pedagogical task is to make the 'worlds' in literature available. The works to be opened up might come from any tradition, but there appears to be a special value in the literature that belongs to the Western adversary tradition, largely because of what afflicts us today" (LL, p. 24).

To better understand what Greene means by the "Western adversary tradition," one must resort back to Marcuse, who explains how this has worked in art forms where contradiction is sustained and protected so that art's criti-cality continues to help us rebut assimilative hegemonies.

> The tension between the actual and the possible is transfigured into an insoluble con-flict, in which reconciliation is by grace of the oeuvre as *form*: beauty as the "promesse de bonheur." In the form of the oeuvre, the actual circumstances are placed in an-other dimension where the given reality shows itself as that which it is. Thus it tells the truth about itself; its language ceases to be that of deception, ignorance, and sub-mission. Fiction calls the facts by their name and their reign collapses; fiction subverts everyday experience and shows it to be mutilated and false. But *art has this magic power only as the power of negation*. It can speak its own language *only as long as the images are alive which refuse and refute the established order*. (Marcuse 1986, pp. 61–62, my empha-ses)

Greene's proposed pedagogy reclaims art's "power of negation," by which an awareness of the contradictory nature of reality is regained through the criticality by which art approaches the world. In the second chapter of her *Landscapes of Learning*, Greene discusses an approach to a number of writers of the Western adversary tradition, which has "a special capacity to arouse us to wide-awakeness in our own time and that this kind of arousal is a necessity if there is to be transcendence" (LL, p. 37). While stating this Greene also re-marks that, like everyone, teachers also partake of the one-dimensionality that continues to assimilate learning into a positivism and scientism (LL, pp. 25–26). "Teachers (artlessly, wearily) become accomplices in mystification. They have neither the time, nor the energy, nor inclination to urge their students to critical reflection: they, themselves, have suppressed the questions and avoided backward looks" (LL, p. 38). Here, Greene knows she is not playing safe at all. She knows that she is "arguing against conventional wisdom" by proposing "aesthetic encounters that are bound to disturb, if they do not simply con-fuse."

> I am asking that attention be paid to a literature that seems, on the face of it, irrele-vant to teacher education, a literature whose critical elements have been effectively absorbed. The reason, again, is that literature may have an emancipatory function for people whose selves have become attenuated, who have forgotten the function of the "I." I do not see how individuals who know nothing about "the power of darkness," who account for themselves by talking about "chance, circumstances, and the times," can awaken the young to question and to learn. Learning involves a futuring, a going beyond. Teachers who feel themselves are submerged, who feel in some sense "fin-ished," like the desks before them or the chalkboards behind, can hardly move stu-dents to critical questioning or to learning how to learn. (LL, pp. 38–39)

Yet Greene remains optimistic: "It ought to be possible to bring teachers in touch with their own landscapes" (LL, ibid.). And who better reminds us of the function of the "I" and "the power of darkness" by bringing us back in touch with our landscapes than one of the most notable literary artists of the Western adversary tradition: Virginia Woolf.

"The glove's twisted finger"

There is a great passage in Woolf's *To the Lighthouse* where in her many dialogues—often appearing as mental monologues—Lily Briscoe is confronted with a sense of the now that emerges from a dialectic between a memory of the subject and the embodiment of both:

> (...) gathering a desperate courage she would urge her own exemption from the universal law; plead for it; she liked to be alone; she liked to be herself; she was not made for that; and so have to meet a serious stare from eyes of unparalleled depth, and confront Mrs. Ramsay's simple certainty (and she was childlike now) that her dear Lily, her little Brisk, was a fool. Then, she remembered, she had laid her head on Mrs. Ramsay's lap and laughed and laughed and laughed, laughed almost hysterically at the thought of Mrs. Ramsay presiding with immutable calm over destinies which she completely failed to understand. There she sat, simple, serious. *She had recovered her sense of her now—this was the glove's twisted finger.* But into what sanctuary had one penetrated? Lily Briscoe had looked up at last, and there was Mrs. Ramsay, unwitting entirely what had caused her laughter, still presiding, but now with every trace of willfulness abolished, and in its stead, something clear as the space which the clouds at last uncover—the little space of sky which sleeps beside the moon. (Woolf 1995, pp. 57–58, my emphasis)

As one 'follows' Lily's thoughts, it becomes clear that what appears to be a subjective escape from others is in fact the opposite. The subject embodies the surrounding environment and absorbs a sense by which other lives come to define the sense of now in its multiplicity. In this case, what brings the mind 'back' to the now is the awareness of one's body as it recalls another's: "Then, she remembered, she had laid her head on Mrs. Ramsay's lap." Lily's reaction manifests itself in a rapture of laughter, the meaning of which Mrs. Ramsay could not discern. At that moment both Lily and Mrs. Ramsay seem to be locked in mutual mystery, as they look at each other while failing to understand each other's reaction. "Was it wisdom? Was it knowledge? Was it, once more, the deceptiveness of beauty, so that all one's perceptions, half way to truth, were tangled in a golden mesh? Or did she lock up within her some secret which certainly Lily Briscoe believed people must have for the world to go on at all?" (ibid., p. 58).

One's sense of one's now becomes an act of continuous exchange. While Lily recovers this sense by suddenly coming back to her corporeal reality (realizing that her head was rested on Mrs. Ramsay's lap), the affection that was clearly established between her and her mentor causes her to lose her sense of the real once more, only to recoup it by engaging with the serenity on Mrs. Ramsay's face, a serenity that resembled a "little space of sky which sleeps beside the moon."

Yet Lily's serene (albeit uncertain) feeling jars with her clear judgment of another member of the family—Professor Ramsay—whose ability to 'talk nonsense' about Locke, Hume, Berkeley and the French Revolution ultimately convinces her that "teaching and preaching is beyond human power" where "if you are exalted you must somehow be a cropper" (ibid., p. 52). This contrast between Lily's affection to Mrs. Ramsay and her disdain for Professor Ramsay's intellectual arrogance presents Woolf's own take on the matter of reality and the extents to which one's sense of the now gains complexity. Clearly, for Woolf the sense of the now is not signified by the clarity emerging from the empirical world of a Locke or a Hume, but rather, as something resembling a "glove's twisted finger." Poole's discussion of Virginia Woolf's irritation with G.E. Moore's attitude toward what he saw as the precision of language further clarifies this position:

> It was of the essence of Virginia's genius that what she had to say, to show, was not capable of being further verbally reduced from the expression she had already given it. If anything, her mind led her to describe inclusively, and to expand upon certain aspects of what was described, rather than to exclude more and more from the description. The description and the intelligibility had to belong together. It might take fifteen pages to describe a mark on the wall. The Moorean attitude had no patience with such descriptions. Its question was, so to speak, 'Is it a stain or is it a nail?' Virginia was trying to draw attention, however, not to what the mark in fact empirically *was*, so much as to the process of human vision which allows such enormous and radical imprecisions. (Poole 1995, p. 67)

Greene reminds her readers that "it takes at least what the poet William Blake once described as a fourfold vision—derived from feeling, sensation, and intuition as well as mind—to encompass one's experience adequately and humanly" (TAS, p. 9). This is what Virginia Woolf does in her work, and this is why her approach to the details of the world is echoed in Greene's own philosophical claims on the world "when, for some reason, we are aroused to wonder about how events and experiences are interpreted and should be interpreted" (TAS, p. 10).

In Woolf's work one finds an approach, almost a 'method', where *argument* is transformed into *observation*. Argument is a continuous dialogue, a process of future possibility and a widening attribution that gives rise to an unrestrained imaginary. Woolf's is an expansive way of reasoning that is diametrically opposed to essentialist analyses and arid formulae. In Moorean speak, a mark on the wall remains a mark—whether it is a stain or a nail. On the other hand, the Woolfian imaginary transcends the mark and lifts it above its accidental condition. Whereas Moore's logic sees no value in what a mark could possibly become, thus dismissing it as an accident, Woolf transforms a mark into a sign. As a sign, the mark tells a story of human relationships in continuous expansion. What was then a mere mark is now a defining moment, the latter end of an expansive act that "allows such enormous and radical imprecisions" (Poole 1995, p. 67). More so, for Woolf, the mark on the wall becomes an occasion for a conversation that is *observed* and *observing*, where the observer argues her case by drawing our attention and invites us to see the world *with* her.

As previously argued, to *see with* is distinct from an invitation to see *through* someone's eyes or thoughts (chapter one, this volume). An observation that is *observing* also entails a polite distance that portends an ethical dimension to the act of seeing with one another. Seeing with someone else still requires one's own eyes and one's own vision. In addition, *seeing with* is an occasion for an expansive *argument*. As they expand, arguments and conversations are open to imprecision, accident and guesswork. Argument is not set to prove anything. Nor is it there to find essentials that proscribe any further conversations. Even less is it a question of crushing those who argue differently from one's own. In common parlance, argument might suggest a combative mood. Yet to argue one's case necessitates dialogue with one's world in a way that does not necessarily limit itself to the spoken or factual world. In seeing with others one becomes dialogical by dint of one's argument being observant of, and thereby *learning*, the other's position, by seeing the other's perspective in a way that one has never seen before.

> If learning is, in one dimension, to reconstruct experience, it may be said that the reader has "learned," even though what he has learned cannot be stated discursively, cannot be translated into fact nor assimilated in some fund of knowledge. He has been enabled to *see* what he may have never have seen in quite that fashion. (Greene 1968b, p. 16)

The way we are invited by Greene to look at the world around us recalls how Woolf lifts the veil off the deceptive gentility of the English bourgeoisie, particularly in *Mrs. Dalloway*. But rather than decry and condemn the affluent and the genteel, the lifted veil reveals not only a complex world of anxiety and fear, but also a degree of love toward the other. Mrs. Dalloway is not a snob, and any hasty judgment suggesting a would-be elitism would be simply shortsighted. Mrs. Dalloway seems to exude the innocence of the generous socialite whose philanthropy is not a matter of duty, but a question of innate generosity—a human need. Thankfully, the class war rhetoric of a benign proletariat confronted by an evil bourgeoisie has long been consigned to the dustbin of pseudo-ideology. So one could dare argue that the socialite Mrs. Dalloway is not short of being a socialist who believes in the good of society by way of her being attentive to the world in its dynamic plurality. As she observes, Mrs. Dalloway remains both politically and humanly observant of the ethical dynamic implied in a sense of the now, a sense that she shares with the world around her:

> She would not say of any one in the world now that they were this or were that. She felt very young; at the same time unspeakably aged. She sliced like a knife through everything; at the same time was outside, looking on. She had a perpetual sense, as she watched the taxi cabs, of being out, out, far out to sea and alone; she always had the feeling that it was very dangerous to live even one day. Not that she thought herself clever, or much out of the ordinary. (…) She knew nothing; no language, no history; she scarcely read a book now, except memoirs in bed; and yet to her it was absolutely absorbing; all this; the cabs passing; and she would not say of Peter, she would not say of herself, I am this, I am that. (Woolf 1994a, pp. 12–13)

Greene's dialogic forms are in themselves pedagogical. Like Woolf (*and* Mrs. Dalloway) she invites us to see *with* her. Greene wants us to enjoy (even delectate in) a pedagogical jousting drawn into the *agôn* of reasoning. In Dalloway's/Woolf's reasoning there is neither bombast nor naivety, but "a perpetual sense" formed by means of common observation: "She knew nothing; no language, no history; she scarcely read a book now, except memoirs in bed; and yet to her it was absolutely absorbing; all this" (Woolf 1994a, p. 12). Greene's close and continuous attention to Woolf's work is not fortuitous. Woolf presents a different yet familiar take on the power of observation, and Greene takes serious note of it. Woolf's is a philosophy that comes by the default of being in the world and making of the world one's life project, even when we have no choice but to make do with it, and on which we have a single bet to place. Woolf observes by arguing and argues by observation. There is nothing else one can do with the world but take it on by observation—which is just as ominous. This is what Lily Briscoe, Mrs. Ramsay and Mrs. Dalloway do. In this sole simple choice of method, an entire world emerges as Woolf engages us, her readers, with her ways of reasoning out why someone is doing *this* while others do *that*, and this when "she would not say of herself, I am this, I am that" (Woolf 1994a, p. 13).

Likewise Lily Briscoe looks around her world, and realizes that "Her world was changing: they were still" (Woolf 1995, p. 121). By 'they' she meant the trees, but it was not just the trees and maybe everyone else was still. "The event had given her a sense of movement. All must be in order. She must get that right and that right, she thought, insensibly, approving of the dignity of the trees' stillness, and now again of the superb upward rise (like the beak of a ship up a wave) of the elm branches as the wind raised them." The artistic *persona*, embodied in the character of Lily Briscoe is pivotal to Woolf's *To the Lighthouse*. Away from the literary critic's precise and attentive framing of whom might she represent in Woolf's life, Lily Briscoe brings out a persona that is very relevant to our attention to the self, understood, as it were, through the eyes of someone whose life is expressed in form and color. Briscoe would never become a famous artist, nor would she seem to be happier had she become one. Yet she is far from being a dilettante. Lily's art is intent on self-assertion. As a visual artist, Lily Briscoe becomes a vehicle for Woolfe's own views about the artist. The artist as a young and then a middle-aged woman in the person of Briscoe never becomes ancillary to the bigger picture.

> Taking out a penknife, Mr Bankes tapped the canvas with the bone handle. What did she wish to indicate by the triangular purple shape, 'just there?', he asked.
>
> It was Mrs Ramsay reading to James, she said. She knew his objection—that on one could tell it for a human shape. But she has made no attempt at likeness, she said. For what reason had she introduced them then? He asked. Why indeed?—except that if there, in that corner, it was bright, here, in this, she felt the need of darkness. Simple, obvious, commonplace, as it was, Mr Bankes was interested. Mother and child then—objects of universal veneration, and in this case the mother was famous for her beauty—might be reduced, he pondered, to a purple shadow without irreverence.
>
> But the picture was not of them, she said. Or, not in his sense. There were other senses, too, in which one might reverence them. (Woolf 1995, pp. 59–60)

Lily's persona seems to affirm that there is nothing to prove in being an artist, yet there is far more to be gained from doing art. Although Mrs. Ramsay is the central figure in *To the Lighthouse*, Lily is not on the periphery. She is a powerful interlocutor. Also fascinating for those who, like Lily, do art is the precision of words by which Woolf describes the dialogue that goes on between the painter, her subject and her medium. Woolf's description of the act of painting bears the hallmark of an attentive and careful rendition of the direct relationship between the materiality of the paint and canvas and how this materiality is integral to the artist's sense of her self, as she engages with the *now* that her pictures aim to construct, rather than simply imitate, capture or represent.

> With a curious physical sensation, as if she were urged forward and at the same time must hold herself back, she made her first quick decisive stroke. The brush descended. It flickered brown over the white canvas; it left a running mark. A second

time she did it—a third time. (...) Here she was again, she thought, stepping back to look at it, drawn out of gossip, out of living, out of community with people into the presence of this formidable ancient enemy of hers—this other thing, this truth, this reality, which suddenly laid hands on her, emerged stark at the back of appearances and commanded her attention. (Woolf 1995, p. 172)

When one reflects on *To the Lighthouse* from the artist's point of view, another protagonist takes center-stage—but this time it is not human, but a painting. Lily keeps returning to her painting of Mrs. Ramsay and James. The painting keeps bringing out that other thing; "this truth, this reality, which suddenly laid hands on her." This is the continuous return of a reality that emerges "stark at the back of appearances" and continues to command her attention. Far from perspective and composition, what frustrates the artist is the question that Bankes posed: why isn't there any attempt at likeness? The question seems to hone in on the very question of meaning. Perhaps, the issue of meaning begins with the issue of existence, as Greene would remind us that "the only meanings, the only 'points' there are, are those men create for themselves" (1965, p. 127).

CHAPTER FOUR

Meaning's Cause

Our question, What makes us think?, does not ask for either causes or purposes. Taking for granted man's need to think, it proceeds from the assumption that the thinking activity belongs among those *energeiai* which, like flute-playing, have their ends within themselves and leave no tangible outside end product in the world we inhabit.
—Hannah Arendt, *The Life of the Mind* (1978, p. 129)

My particular interest is in the ongoing life of meaning. I want to treat it in the continuity of its development from the time it comes into being before we even begin to speak to the first discoveries of sense and meaning in sensible experience. I want to describe how it advances through the assimilation of a speaking power and the growing ability to mediate between intentions and words. I want to draw attention to the growing capacity to express thought, and by means of such expression, to become more and more aware of what is real.
—Maxine Greene, "Language, Literature and the Release of Meaning" (1979, p. 124)

To make of learning a societal, egalitarian and meaningful cause is more than just indulging in the rhetoric of progressive education. This is because the idea of progress in and of itself means nothing without an inherent dialectic. What Greene terms the *dialectic of freedom* could be misleading if read from an assumption of inevitable *progress* guaranteed by the miraculous *praxes* of critical pedagogy. These terms have a specific meaning in Greene's work. More than entries in the rhetoric of social justice or educational equity, in Greene's terminology, words such as 'praxis' and 'freedom' inhabit a diversity of *spaces* that articulate values ranging from ethical responsibility, choice, conscious situatedness, to the cause of human generosity. Notwithstanding the loss of meaning—the loss of *ground*—with which Greene struggles all the time in terms of her desire for a value-laden world, she still holds faith onto learning as the act by which we have a stake in the wide horizon of human possibility. This is more the case when many times it appears that the "articulation of experience and communication about the world" is dominated by "the convention of 'meaninglessness'" (Greene 1968a, p. 54).

As we are all situated somewhere or another, when it comes to education we have no choice but to engage with the relational nature of learning. "A dialectical relation marks every human situation. (...) Each such relation presupposes a mediation and a tension (...) the tension cannot be overcome by a triumph of subjectivity or objectivity; the dialectic cannot be fully resolved" (RI, p. 52). To take a humane stance is to take note of a dialectical approach to life's relational nature: "If we teachers are to develop a humane and liberating pedagogy, we must feel ourselves to be engaged in a dialectical relation" (RI, p. 52). The relational ground on which Greene presents this dialectic is clarified within the context of praxis and how she defines it. While her work takes continuous account of the tradition of what, after Gramsci, one could loosely term as the *philosophy of praxis* (1975a), Greene further extends its definition. Reading Greene, one encounters a wider sense of *praxis*:

> (...) *praxis* involves critical reflection—and action upon—a situation to some degree shared by persons with common interests and common needs. Of equal moment is the fact that *praxis* involves a transformation of that situation to the end of overcoming oppressiveness and domination. There must be collective self-reflection; there must be an interpretation of present and emergent needs; there must be a type of realization. (LL, p. 100)

In Greene, praxis adds ever-changing caveats to the idea of political transformation where education as *conscientization* (*conscientização*) (Freire 1996) is returned to the tensions revealed within the "dialectical relation [that] marks every human situation" (RI, p. 52). Praxis is a pedagogical opening to the imaginary by which we speak through the truthful horizon of the arts and the speculative grounds of the sciences. Our engagement with the arts, the sciences, and human knowledge *as a whole* presupposes more than political action.

Greene urges no less than a radical intervention in the idea of education in general and aesthetic pedagogy in particular. Radical interventions exert the imagination as our most potent force: the force of the possible. This is where the imagination becomes a praxis that education must cultivate. After Greene, one could safely say that the imagination precedes and anticipates any form of knowledge. Without the imagination, knowledge is not just stale and reduced to mere information, but virtually impossible. The imagination is never limited to the affective domain or the 'education of the senses'. The imagination is that human ability with which women and men cope with the unresolved tensions that characterize the relational dialectic where life finds meaning.

For praxis, Greene advocates *situatedness* as it reveals the realities of everyday life. Beyond its pragmatic-reflective relation with experience, the *desire* for the recognition of situatedness in education characterizes Greene's work by its open embrace of the antinomies and paradoxes that embody our imagination. In her *Dialectic of Freedom* she states,

> It is with a similar concern for the human vocation and for situatedness that I speak of the "dialectic of freedom" in the chapters of this book. I am eager to reaffirm the significance of desire along with the significance of thought and understanding; I want to break through, whenever possible, the persisting either/ors. There is, after all, a dialectical relation marking every human situation: the relation between subject and object, individual and environment, self and society, outsider and community, living consciousness and phenomenal world. This relation exists between two different, apparently opposite poles; but it presupposes a mediation between them. (DOF, p. 8)

The mediation between the opposite poles that characterize life also presupposes a fundamental approach that is central to Greene's work. To discuss Greene's definitions of freedom, praxis and the imagination would mean nothing if one fails to recognize how she empowers the educational cause with generosity. Greene's notion of generosity prompts a call for justice, as this presents us teachers, learners and citizens of the educational polity with an ethical, and more so ontological, challenge. If education constitutes a polity whose members have an equal right to *know*, then the cause of generosity is driven by the right to *be*. To be generous does not entail philanthropy or charitable deeds. As Freire reminds us, "true generosity consists precisely in fighting to destroy the causes which nourish false charity. False charity constrains the fearful and subdued, the 'rejects of life' to extend their trembling hands. True generosity lies in striving so that these hands—whether of individuals or entire peoples—need to be extended less and less in supplication, so that more and more they become human hands which work and, working, transform the world" (Freire 1996, pp. 21–22). Generosity is a firm undertaking of empathy as a political pedagogy. In other words, generosity is the call to be *radical*.

The *Skholé*'s Radical Call

Hannah Arendt's argument that in being the same we are all different is a lesson in radical thinking. It goes straight to the root of the human condition (Arendt 1998). Arendt's lesson poses action as *the* human condition. Active life (*vita activa*) gives specific meaning to how we engage with the now. This means that the traditional renunciation of the now in favor of contemplative life (*vita contemplativa*) makes no sense anymore, just as the now can never be divorced from how we think about—how we *contemplate*—sheer existence as we go on doing what we normally do. As observation could be said to be *theorized*, theory can no more exclude the here and now. Rather, we theorize for the sake of us all, for what we do, what we have done and what we hope to be doing. Just as Virginia Woolf extends the accident of a mark on the wall to the realms of human possibility, Arendt's work returns theory to the fold of the observing many, however erratic and inchoate these observations might be.

In describing Aristotle's distinction between the ideal of contemplation (*theôria*) and action (*praxis*), Arendt sets the scene for a relationship that ultimately deconstructs the very origin of this distinction:

> Aristotle's very articulation of the different ways of life, in whose order the life of pleasure plays a minor role, is clearly guided by the ideal of contemplation (*theôria*). To the ancient freedom from the necessities of life and from compulsion by others, the philosophers added freedom and surcease from political activity (*skholê*), so that the later Christian claim to be free from entanglement in worldly affairs, from all the business of this world, was preceded by and originated in the philosophic *apolitia* of late antiquity. What had been demanded only by the few was now considered to be a right of all. (1998, pp. 14–15)

Arendt tells us that inasmuch as this hierarchy is reversed in Marx and Nietzsche, the problem with this ordering has to do with how the active life potentially remains generic and undefined.

> (...) the enormous weight of contemplation in the traditional hierarchy has blurred the distinctions and articulations within the *vita activa* itself and that, appearances notwithstanding, this condition has not been changed essentially by the modern break with tradition and the eventual reversal of this hierarchical order in Marx and Nietzsche. It lies in the very nature of the famous "turning upside down" of philosophic systems or currently accepted values, that is, in the nature of the operation itself, that the conceptual framework is left more or less intact. (1998, p. 17)

If we take Arendt's concern into the realms of the relationship between learning and the situated contexts of the here and now, it is easy to see how the relationship between active and contemplative life corresponds to the relational dialectic of theory and practice in education. It is in this framework that Greene locates her philosophical engagement with education, as she approaches theory and practice from a context that is found within the mores of the active life—in short, within *praxis*. Greene refuses to take praxis as the excluded remainder or the unwanted appendage of *theôria*. The active life cannot exclude theory because "there is, after all, a dialectical relation marking every human situation" that "exists between two different, apparently opposite poles; but it presupposes a mediation between them" (DOF, p. 8).

It is not difficult to see how the realm of *skholê* enters the realm of the school. The link made between the modern meaning of *school* and the ancient notion of *skholê* is not made out of etymological indulgence, but expresses the desire to make of learning a form of life (a *bios*) that appears to remain unfettered by the here and now. However, on a closer look, if the assumption of *skholê* in its ancient context of *apolitia* remains unchanged, it would handicap the whole project of learning, because it limits the notion of *theôria* by the traditional definition of an active life as something that is excluded by a higher contemplative order of living.

Because *skholê* denotes the "freedom and surcease from political activity" (Arendt 1998, p. 14), it is sometimes assumed that education must be a leisurely activity that abdicates from active life. However, this becomes problematic in the context of modernity. This misconstruction of *skholê* as an uncommitted pursuit may be right in the ancient Greek and later Scholastic contexts of the distinction between *vita activa* and *vita contemplativa*, *praxis* and *theôria*, the political and apolitical. But as this distinction comes to us already challenged by the modernist resolve to reverse and ultimately do away with this false hierarchy between practice and theory, the equation of *skholê* with the apolitical and non-practical becomes anachronistic. This is confirmed by Greene's entire work, where such distinctions are far superseded by the position that learning is situated, where by force of its act of *being*, praxis becomes a form of consciousness that weds activity to contemplation.

In an article she wrote in 1959, titled "Philosophy of Education and the Liberal Arts: A Proposal," Greene fully recognized the role of philosophy of education within the modernist resolve of an active life related to *theôria*:

> History, viewed as a cooperative and creative act extending over centuries, orders inchoate fact (...) Education, in turn, is a process of selecting and structuring certain elements in cultural experience, fixing them in words, and making them available to human minds; and the part played by philosophy of education is not very different from the aesthetic vision in literature or the interpretive mind, itself philosophical, which distinguishes history from mere record. Philosophy of education, however, stands in a special relation to such disciplines as history and literature, since these provide the substance, the source of raw material for the philosopher concerned with schools. The problem remains to transform this relationship into a productive transaction, one of practical importance for the subject-focused teacher-to-be. (1959, p. 52)

As she insists on her fundamental argument that learning pertains to being situated, Greene forecloses any hierarchy or duality, and instead she dons philosophy of education with a transactional role. The role of philosophy of education in this transaction operates in many ways and at various *levels*, where the student "becomes a double agent, potential actor as well as learner, potential doer as well as one who undergoes" (Greene 1959, p. 53). In an essay on social work education, Greene reiterates her definition of philosophy as "an activity characterized by the framing of distinctive questions to be put to experience and to the cumulative knowledge available to the one who asks." These questions "are not answerable by factual statements, not soluble through formal or empirical inquiry." They have to do with "the exposure of hidden preconceptions and assumptions" (1966, p. 22). This throws the education of social workers straight into a relational domain where the facts of active life are underpinned by the questions of human conduct, which, in effect, situate individuals within societies and the world in general. If anything, the apolitical context of the *skholê* can only serve as a *terminus a quo*, a point of departure.

> The social worker, like the teacher, must be equipped to order his field by means of theory and to know what the categories of behavioral science reveal. Both social worker and teacher, however, are persons committed to working with their fellow human beings in the midst of life; and both can benefit from the imaginative engagements which heighten the sense of involvement in the human situation *per se.* (Greene 1966, p. 23)

Here the *skholê* enters the realm of *vita activa*, where the learner reflects on the learning process and discovers how it works by means of her direct involvement with the situations of meanings and 'facts' that, at face value, may not be quantifiable, but whose reality remains as tangible as the empirically measured contexts that we find, make and live in the world. When Greene argues that the philosopher's challenge is to integrate his discipline with the humanities, she sets a scenario where the student "may recall how Oedipus's affirmation of responsibility and Hamlet's acknowledgement of his obligation to set things right in Denmark flared out of their contexts and struck sparks in their mind" (1959, p. 53). Here theory and praxis are not simply blurred. Their distinction becomes irrelevant. It becomes clear that in Greene's work, far from an apolitical school, we find a pedagogical conception subscribed to active life that is inclusive of contemplative practices. In fact, one could derive from Greene a concept of *skholê* that corresponds to a learning space, an *agôn* (cf. chapter one, this volume). As *agôn*, the *skholê*'s learning space makes possible the radical return of the political.

This time, the return of the political takes the form of a plural event by which we realize that we are the same, as many. It is also within this context that we must consider seriously new radical democratic possibilities that would not fall in the usual traps of total rejection of liberal-democratic frameworks, but which would be no less radical in terms of proposing real change in our democratic state of affairs. "There are many ways in which the democratic 'language-game' can be played," says Chantal Mouffe, "[to] bring about new

meanings and fields of application for the idea of democracy to be radical-
ized." For Mouffe the effective way to challenge power relations is not to adopt
an abstract negation, "but in a properly hegemonic way, through a process of
disarticulation of existing practices and creation of new discourses and institutions" (Mouffe 2005, p. 33).

The political return is not simply practical, but must be viewed as also occasioned by *theôria* as it opens the possibilities through which everyday life signifies what could possibly lie beyond existence's immediate whereabouts. This
is why, as we have seen in the previous chapter, Moore's ferrous logic fades in
the presence of Virginia Woolf's attention to detail. This attention is characterized by the *simplicity* that Woolf regales a mark-turned-sign with immediate
access to the *complexity* of the world's immanence. In Henri Bergson's words,
simplicity denotes the way of intuition, by which we can grasp the meaning of
the world in one go, as *durée*, as duration. Duration needs to be taken directly.
"It is no use trying to approach duration: we must install ourselves within it
straight away. This is what the intellect generally refuses to do, accustomed as
it is to think the moving by means of the unmovable" (Bergson 1983, p. 299).
Schutz clarifies Bergson's notion of duration, arguing that it brings forth
something new within a stream of consciousness that is, more often than not,
undifferentiated: "Indeed, when I immerse myself in my stream of consciousness, in my duration, I do not find any clearly differentiated experiences at all.
At one moment an experience waxes, then it wanes. Meanwhile something
new grows out of what was something old and then gives place to something
still newer" (Schutz 1970, p. 61).

Far from being naïve, the simplicity of intuition and the moment of duration form part of the privilege that we have as human beings in wedding the
intuition of an active life with the mediation regaled by rational contemplation. Perhaps more than anything, the concept that embodies these two aspects of life constitute Merleau-Ponty's notion of *le corps vécu* where "I regard
my body, which is my point of view upon the world, as one of the objects of
that world" (Merleau-Ponty 1989, p. 70). One must add that it is also because
of the recognition of such deep subjectivity that the assimilation of a one-
dimensional polity could be resisted and ultimately revoked. While a one-
dimensional totality objectifies everything—thus leaving the body without any
power to view itself as one of its own objects—the body as a lived subject rejects
this assimilation. Conscious of space as a differentiated state of affairs, one
catches it "at its source" and thinks "the relationships which underlie this
word, realizing then that they live only through the medium of a subject who

traces out and sustains them; and pass from spatialized to spatializing space" (p. 244).

The pass from a (passive) *spatialized* to (an active) *spatializing* space indicates a move that we would recognize as existential and more so pedagogical. This pedagogical take of spatializing becomes more tangible, when, as Schutz reminds us, a conscious assumption of time as *durée* is an experience where "something new grows out of what was something old and then gives place to something still newer" (1970, p. 61). Here Schutz's reference to Bergson's notion of "conscious life" and how Schutz relates it to his concept of *wide-awakeness*—which, as already argued, Greene adopts—warrants citation:

> One of the central points of Bergson's philosophy is his theory that our conscious life shows an indefinite number of different planes, ranging from the plane of action on one extreme to the plane of dream at the other. Each of these planes is characterized by a specific tension of consciousness (...). By the term *"wide-awakeness"* we want to denote a plane of consciousness of highest tension originating in an attitude of full attention to life and its requirements. (1970, pp. 68–69)

It seems to me that the act of spatializing space is an act of wide-awakeness where, as Green puts it, "individuals can be provoked to reach beyond themselves in their intersubjective space" (DOF, p. 12). This is the only way to resist the "one-dimensional 'excellence'" and "economic competitiveness" that teachers are asked to deliver. While one-dimensional educational policies become spatialized points of *arrival*—assuming knowledge as an epistemological hierarchy of subjects—Greene suggests a spatializing point to a continuous form of *plural departures*, where "it is through education that preferences may be released, languages learned, intelligences developed, perspectives opened, possibilities disclosed" (ibid.). It becomes evident that we are faced with an education beyond education—a distinction between one concept of a spatialized form of passive learning and a spatializing *wide-awake* praxis of education, which, as a multi-dimensional construct, could effectively strategize political change.

Rioters in the Courtyard

It is by a concern for learning as the rejection of one-dimensional polities that a political argument for schooling gains fuller relevance. Theory and practice form the nexus of Greene's philosophy of education, where *vita contemplativa* and *vita activa* are integrated in the lived experience of learning.

When he [the student] reads a drama like *Oedipus the King*, he ought to be able to conceive it not only in the context of Athenian culture with its belief in a ruling 'lo-gos', in fate and oracles, but also as a function of a specific historic moment different from the moment that produced *Agamemnon* earlier or *Medea* later on. With a culmi-nating act of the imagination, he ought to relate what he reads and learns to himself and to the culture of his own day, with the understanding that whatever appreciation he feels denotes a relevance, an immediacy in the patterns of the ancient work. (Greene 1959, p. 52)

Because situatedness is plural, it requires the theoretical force of the school's *agôn* as the prime facilitator of a pedagogy that restores a multi-dimensional polity as an energized space. This moving between the political and non-political is a radical context where the philosopher of education must, in Greene's words, resemble a gadfly (1959, p. 55). While the philoso-pher-gadfly nags and annoys by constantly taking multiple positions without ever falling into relativism, she shows and confirms that education cannot be fixed in one realm or another, but must be marked by the indelible character of radical recurrence. Rather than closing, the philosopher's recurrence re-opens itself in constant perpetuity. "There is no virtue which is final; all are initial," Emerson famously says in his essay "Circles." "The virtues of society are vices of the saint. The terror of reform is the discovery that we must cast away our virtues, or what we have always esteemed such, into the same pit that has consumed our grosser vices" (Emerson 1941, vol. 1, p. 204).

Reading Greene, one cannot miss the point that from its origins as an apolitical activity, the school as *skholé* bequeaths a dynamic political imaginary that empowers the learner to 'think out of the box', as the tired phrase goes. This resonates with how education must engage everyone in the life of what could be called *the every-human*: a humanity of free and intelligent beings, where, I would suggest, the artistic persona becomes a model for the occasion of *theôria* and a horizon of practical (and therefore *ethical*) choices. With the analogy of the gadfly in mind, Greene beautifully concludes her 1959 essay as follows:

Gadfly the philosopher of education must continue to be, but respecter of persons and special skills he must also remain. He may approach his opponent with hand out-stretched and still not sacrifice integrity; and he may say—in candor and in hopeful-ness—that the conversation can be enriched by his voice and eased by the sense of windows opening out to the world. And perhaps he may repeat, this time without bit-terness or guile, the words of Socrates. "You *will* not easily find another like me." (Greene 1959, p. 55)

After all is said and done, the cause of *the every-human*, the generous cause that enables integrity with outstretched arms, may well have to be enacted by stealth. How Socrates' bitterness and guile give way to the generosity by which one offers oneself to the other, and in that sense how it could utter, without immodesty, "You *will* not easily find another like me" is not short of an impossible challenge. The backdrop to this difficult challenge is not the philosopher's arrogance, as in Socrates, but in the environs of meaninglessness and the anxiety that this portends. Back in the 1960s, Greene makes frequent comparisons between the sense of protest then and the sense of protest in the 1930s. In a paper titled "Teaching the Literature of Protest," Greene argues that the sense of meaninglessness that marks the 1960s protests is markedly different from the sense of a future, embodied in the political optimism with which America's marginalized proletarians—immigrants from all nations, creeds and ethnic origins—have sustained their political struggle in the 1930s (Greene 1967). The protests in the 1960s have a different complexion, not simply in the context of how meaninglessness became a cause in itself in the 1960s (as opposed to the meaningful hopes of the 1930s), but more so in how teachers were confronted by a totally different order of questioning, dilemmas and issues that they could not simply ignore in the 1960s.

Writing for *The English Record*, whose constituency is that of the teachers of English, Greene could be seen as advocating a curriculum that accommodates a widened literature that becomes inclusive, in this particular case, of books written by authors of color: "The challenge posed by what we call Negro literature is a challenge to innocence and ignorance" (1967, p. 5). Yet Greene's question goes beyond literature per se, but dwells on how a literature of protest begets distinction from works of art, and in doing so, it demands special attention from teachers who must, ultimately, pass it on to their students. In radicalizing this choice, Greene repositions learning as a form of engagement that attends to literature and the arts, not simply as a curricular horizon, but as a world that needs to be acted upon, a meaning that needs to be shared, understood and *politically* appropriated.

In this period of unrest and riot in the United States and Europe, Greene contributes numerous essays on the subject of protest, education, the young and, most of all, the prevailing question of meaningless. In a comprehensive essay on meaning and meaningless, titled "The Whale's Whiteness"—a title that evokes Moby Dick and the "intangible malignity" that it comes to represent—Greene argues that "the pervasive view of the world as 'meaningless' was a learned view, a response that became conventional" (1968a, p. 56). The thrust of Greene's essay is not an easy one, particularly because in it Greene shows the dilemma that emerges from a state of affairs where "a mode of excessiveness, along with the move to dichotomy" accounts "for the plunge into totally noncognitive arbitrariness where values are concerned." Greene finds this arbitrariness "unwarranted by the facts of the axiological case—but somehow entailed by the posited 'emptiness' of the world" (1968a, p. 67).

This dilemma is not simply caused by the dichotomous theoretical positions like literary-aesthetic vs. cognitive-scientific, or phenomenological vs. empirical, but a dilemma that becomes a matter of convention, where it is difficult to understand or cope with change, because an appropriate language for expression is not yet found, and where new symbols and new conventions become necessary. But where does one find these languages, these new symbols? Greene looks back to 18th and 19th century literature and argues that "deprived of the *consensus gentium* of previous times, confronted with a condition to which the unitary vision of the eighteenth century seemed utterly irrelevant, writers had to create their own symbols and their own semblances of order." Looking back at how these semblances tried to recreate a chain that tied the political and aesthetic imaginary back to what was considered to be an era severed by the onset of massive economic and political revolutions, Greene suggests that "the long struggle to repair that chain created the conventions which shape so many contemporary visions of the world." Her hope in 1968 was not different from the hopes that we still entertain—albeit with altered backdrops and even more shocking political and ideological turmoil: "I am trying to suggest," Greene says, "that an imaginative 'taking over' of what Merleau-Ponty calls the 'operations' involved may give us a somewhat new perspective. And I am hopeful that such a 'taking over', brief as it must be, may offer clues to new alternatives" (1968a pp. 58–59).

As she moves from 19th to 20th century literature, and posing the existentialist definition of the absurd against that of common parlance, Greene reminds us of the hope that Camus invests in Sisyphus, and seeks to distance Beckett's Estragon and Vladimir from the accusation of irrationalism. Greene also challenges the unreasonable dichotomies by which science is ditched against the arts, where fact is posed against ideals and the imagination. Not unlike Arendt, Greene walks slowly but steadily over a tightrope stretched between a useless bipolarity that was (and remains) imposed between theory and praxis. Thus her denunciation of scientism and irrationalism is unequivocal: "Scientism, like the misuse of language, becomes another breeding ground of 'meaninglessness'" (1968a, p. 69). As in her critique of one-dimensionality, Greene is aware of the intricate patterns by which meaninglessness is woven. While a dualism between scientism and irrationalism is a misconstrued assumption, equally misconstrued is the elimination of contingency and multiplicity on the pretext of a total meaning. Just as her argument for "a coherence which is ours" is qualified by her critique of one-dimensionality, Greene's critique of meaninglessness proscribes any form of assimilation under the notion of 'meaning'. So where does meaning find its place? Where does one locate it in the effort to reclaim symbol and semblance? How could one avoid meaninglessness while at the same time reject assimilation?

> Meanings are available, partial meanings, contingent ones, depending on the subject matter, on each delimited area of life. But it is of the first importance to distinguish between them, to resist the temptation to subsume them under some higher (or lower) all-inclusive Meaning—or, yes, Meaninglessness, to deprive them of contingency, of their dependence on language, convention and rule. (1968a, p. 71)

Looking back at the student occupation of Columbia University in the 1960s, Greene recalls "the persisting consciousness of possibility or the feelings that there were connections to be found between idealistic actions voluntarily undertaken—for peace, for children, for the poor—and what might some day happen in public schools" (NDa, p. 3). Here we do not find a denunciation of meaninglessness, but a hope in the meanings that *became* available, which, albeit partial, suggested that what the students were fighting for was quite simple: to be allowed to think, discuss and hope for possibility. Greene's philosophy cannot be read without this context in mind. Her warning against the "danger of going on mad pursuits like Captain Ahab's" (1968a, p. 66) was not against the students who, like her, demanded that new meanings are found, even when these may be partial. The events of 1968 amounted to a plea for meaning in a world where meaninglessness did not come from drugs or psychedelics, but from those who pushed the young and the disenfranchised to drugs and alienation. The call for meaning that came from the rioters' songs and meetings was a loud call for making sense and for the release of meaning to everyone.

Greene fondly remembers when during the riots student activities spilled from Columbia's main campus into Teachers College's courtyards where students' 'leaders' made speeches about 'participatory democracy' and 'articulate public' that reminded her of Dewey, "as if they were John Dewey re-born." "It is hard to forget the sound of guitars in the corridors, the notices pinned up in great disorder, the impassioned arguments in the corners, the disrupted classes (and, yes, the 'liberation classes'), the shriek (very oddly) of kazoos." Then Greene makes an outstanding remark, which very much highlights the central tenets of her thinking: "Even now it strikes me as one of those *interruptions of the ordinary that can* (if people are lucky and smart enough) *lead to all kinds of revisions and renewals,* unless too many folks are investing everything in keeping things the same" (NDa, pp. 3–4, my emphases).

What if the struggle for meaning must be—always!—an *interruption of the ordinary*? What if the ordinary itself is always in need of occasional interruptions? What if meaning is the moment of interruption? Wouldn't that be enough to claim back meaning for everyone? Wouldn't that interruption be a way of *releasing* meaning?

Meaning "Released"

When Greene argues for the "release of meaning," stating that her "particular interest is in the ongoing life of meaning," that she wants "to draw attention to the growing capacity to express thought, and by means of such expression, to become more and more aware of what is real" (1979, p. 124), she indirectly states how the political returns to education. When students claimed back their right to meaning—their right to *their own* meaning—they also claimed their right to their intentionality toward the world. And as this emerged in the form of *an interruption of the ordinary*, the politics of intentionality became more pronounced and more assumed from within women and men's "ability to mediate between intentions and words" (ibid.).

John Searle defines intentionality as "the general term for all the various forms by which the mind can be directed at, or be about, or of, objects and states of affairs in the world" (1999, p. 85). He explains that the role of the mind is to find a form of relationship by which one mediates one's subject with the world. It is what relates us "in certain ways to the environment, and especially to other people." As a subject, I relate to the world, and the way this relationship happens is symptomatic of how I direct my intentionality toward the world. Searle explains that this subjective state, this intentionality, includes "beliefs and desires, intentions and perceptions, as well as loves and hates, fears and hopes" (1999, p. 85).

It seems to me that the issue of intentionality—also as understood by Schutz, as a foundational form of consciousness that is directed to *something* (1970, pp. 50ff and 318)—pertains to the realms of choice. Our intentionality toward the world is a choice that we make *in* the world, which in the very context of meaning implies the need to be able to assume grounds that may well be indeterminate. The possibility that these grounds are indeterminate is not found in the doubt that we entertain, but more so in the uncertainty and, to some extent, in the willed ignorance of what one should expect. In this case the ignorance is willed, and therefore it is not a form of stupidity, but rather a calculated risk—a risk that could only assert choice. Greene says of Ellison's

Invisible Man that he is "imagining the indeterminate as background to what is understood, to what has been expressed in language. And it is of great importance to note that, for the 'invisible man', the patterning he is talking about—the constructing, the articulating—is intimately connected with the sense of his own identity" (1979, p. 125). Thus what is understood is not only a matter of risk, but also a conscious choice that may well turn out to be problematic. Yet this does not deter us from making a choice, because it is in our right to choose, as without choice there is no intentionality.

Elsewhere Greene says that "the present situation demands recognition that the ability to involve himself and the ability to choose are determinant in a professional's life" (1966, p. 30). This does not simply apply to the teacher as a catalyst for the learner's ability to choose, but more fundamentally it has to do with the issue of choice per se. As such, choice and the risks that it brings with it inhabit the realm that comes closer to meaning. Choice must be understood as integral to the intentionality by which we as willed subjects come forth to the world and *throw* at it what Searle identifies as our beliefs, desires, intentions, perceptions, "as well as loves and hates, fears and hopes" (ibid.). In this way our choices "bring meaning to the world" (Greene 1979, p. 126), and by that meaning we invest our interest in the world. Whether common, private, social or individual, our vested interest in the world is also indicative of what we are, and what we expect from what we do.

Greene underpins the act of bringing meaning to the world with specific *qualities* that characterize her larger philosophical picture. To bring meaning implies, most of all, the recognition of the indeterminate and inchoate. As we have seen, this indeterminacy comes down to the risky nature of the choices by which we gain meaning for ourselves, as we see *us* and *others* partaking *of* and *with* the world. This opens wide the horizons of possibility, which also presumes what Greene, after Dewey, calls "grounding in the qualitative": "Drained of the qualitative, art and morals would be reduced to mere abstractions" (1979, p. 126). And why is the qualitative a concretizing factor? Should not abstraction be assumed as an aspect of art and morals? In this context, what is abstract is alienated, estranged from the grounding that art and morals seek. Art and morals may take an abstract form, but they cannot be abstracted from the qualities that make them valuable to the risky choices that we have to take.

As grounding in the qualitative presumes that possibilities must happen on the pretext of a meaningful intentionality, the question of meaning cannot be taken out of its pedagogical assumption. By a pedagogical assumption one should not simply mean a class-based or schooled context. The pedagogical assumptions that Greene makes have situatedness as their qualitative ground. A schooled society, as that which Illich (1999) decries, is an abstraction of art and morals, as well as knowledge and consciousness. This abstraction turns a qualitative ground into a quantified set of standards, where knowledge is abstracted from consciousness and where description estranges our normative choices and interests in learning. A deschooled pedagogy, whether housed in a school, or assumed on a wider plane, resists this abstracted quantification. On such pedagogical grounds of quality, learning not only becomes an interruption of the ordinary, but also surpasses its initial stages of interruption and *leaps* beyond the impasse of the meaninglessness of standardization and accountability. What Greene defines as learning's "orientation to the always possible" sharpens her notion of "how learning is conceived—*as a futuring, a surpassing of what is or has been*" (1979, p. 128, my emphasis). This central idea of futuring highlights Greene's existentialist credentials in terms of how she defines action: "It is always future, the existentialists say; we live our lives and make our choices and, by so doing, we create (and recreate) our selves" (1979, p. 131).

In this context the arts are not merely there, spatialized by a disinterested taste. If choice is central to meaning and intention, then this cannot be *disinterested*. As Schutz puts it, "there is no such thing for the actor as an isolated interest. Interests have from the outset the character of being interrelated with other interests in a system. It is merely a corollary of this statement that also actions, motives, ends and means, and therefore, projects and purposes are only elements among other elements forming a system" (1970, p. 149). Choices imply a point of departure that is another's point of arrival. Interests are at the heart of choices and this implies a responsibility and a context or system that defines and makes choice possible and possibility a matter of what one chooses. Notice that Schutz refers to *the actor*. This is the ethical actor, he or she who makes a choice and who assumes the stage as being his or hers. Here the actor never waits for a director to tell her what to do—to spatialize her.

The ethical actor is a *spatializing* and therefore *active* agent of futurity. If the existent is only defined in the future—just as art could never be defined by a past (because art is never *past* but is always *present*)—then what is always future is always unknown. The move of choice is therefore bold. Existentialism is not just dread, but is a leap from dread to the absolutely unknown. To learn this leap is to learn, period. Not to learn—to remain stupid—is to resist the ignorance of the future. As if the leap to the future is not radical enough, what we actually mean by learning must pertain to the interested creation of the self by which one takes full responsibility of one's present, even when the present seems to be all but lost. But how is this loss communicated? How does this willed ignorance of a future that is always in a state of *becoming* become *meaning*?

Greene speaks of communication "as a mode of action, a mode of *interested* action" (1979, p. 131). This kind of *interestedness* is grounded in the ethical choices that the action presumes. As every action is *interested*, because it is ethically construed, consciously or unconsciously, the choice of meaning faces an even larger, constant, challenge—the risk of being subsumed in one-dimensionality. One-dimensionality allows neither *choice* nor *interest* other than that which assimilates one's choice into a semblance of 'freedom' that in effect re-routes the subject's intentionality into an objectified domain.

It may well be that this is where the interested choices we make become somewhat *alien*, where choice is estranged from us just as "the worker is related to the *product of his labor* as to an *alien* object" (Marx 1977a, p. 68). In this case, the author and artist seek to interrupt the ordinariness of meaning in order to reveal it for what it is—an art and moral that has been abstracted from itself. Thus, Virginia Woolf makes of writing "the creation of meaning, of order in a too often 'severed' world" (Greene 1979, p. 132). Yet in her work Woolf never cedes to alienation, but continuously recoups—even when she is more Sisyphean than Promethean—what is continuously being estranged.

Art's intervention in the alienation of meaning becomes paramount to the author's assumption of a world that must be seen for what it is. This is where the question of meaning becomes central to what appears to make no sense. In so many ways art appears to enter nonsense, only to turn the tables over what is but a semblance of sense. Thus Joyce exhorts us to meaning:

> Let us now, weather, health, dangers, public orders and other circumstances permitting, of perfectly convenient, if you police after you, policepolice, pardoning mein, ich beam so fresch, bey? Drop this jiggerypockery and talk straight turkey meet to mate, for while the ear, be we mikealls or nicholists, may sometimes be inclined to believe others the eye, whether browned or nolensed, find it devilish hard now and again even to believe itself. *Habes autres et num videbis? Habes oculos ac mannepalpabuat?* Tip! Drawing nearer to take our slant at it (since after all it has met with misfortune while all underground), let us see all there may remain to be seen. (1992b, p. 113)

Art can reclaim meaning as a 'possible world' only if one is ready to transcend a state of affairs where meaning is owned by "a being *other* than myself" (Marx 1977b, p. 75), where though one has eyes and ears, one neither sees nor hears. Thus Joyce's indirect reference to what one does not see or hear ("*Habes autres et num videbis? Habes oculos ac mannepalpabuat?*") leaves us hoping that maybe, just maybe, we might draw "nearer to take our slant at it" and "see all there may remain to be seen" (ibid.). But unless I, in *my* active intentionality, am not prepared to see with *others* what all of us are not able to see by ourselves, the apparent meaninglessness of life remains abstract and dry of any moral.

Meaning can be released only if one is ready to give possibility to the leap of seeing. If one agrees with Greene when she says that although "it may sound paradoxical to say that the lived world can be illuminated and enlarged through engagement with imaginary worlds," then we would be able to realize what she suggests as 'possible worlds': "if we are to deal with literary works as works of art, we must recognize that they create alternative realities—what we have called 'possible worlds'. These are worlds that can only be entered by persons willing to break with the ordinary and the mundane. In some sense they have to risk uncoupling themselves from routine, from what we think of a common-sense reality" (1979, p. 133). It is only thus that we would be able to see with others, but more so, recognize the cause of meaning within the realm of radical politics—that is, the politics of *possibility*.

CHAPTER FIVE

Possible Freedoms

Because each had discovered years before that they were neither white nor male, and that all freedom and triumph was forbidden to them, they had set about creating something else to be.

—Toni Morrison, *Sula* (1980, p. 52)

Freedom meant one thing to him—home.
But they wouldn't let him go home.

—Alexander Solzhenitsyn, *One Day in the Life of Ivan Denisovich* (1973, p. 140)

Autonomous people are the ones who manage to be actively attentive to the world around and are aware of what they are choosing when they confront situations in which they *can* perceive alternative courses of action.

—Maxine Greene, *Landscapes of Learning* (LL, p. 155)

If freedom is a gift, then humans are perpetual beggars. No one has the power or right to *give* freedom to other human beings. Freedom is in no one's gift. Who authorizes whom to have someone's freedom in one's own gift, if not by a presumptuous 'right' that has been historically taken by force by one individual from another? It seems simplistic to argue that no human being has the right to be free unless all other humans were equally free. Yet, the sad truth is that freedom has come to mean a liberty that is *taken* at the cost of those to whom freedom is forbidden.

Those Who 'Merit' and Those Who 'Fail'

Many are too ready to claim, in the name of what they falsely assume as *their* libertarian territory, that freedom is closely linked to upward mobility and the myth of merit. The Common Weal from which the hopeful notion of liberty has originally emerged, for too long, has been continuously plundered in the name of a liberal democracy whose modern shibboleths of accountability, responsibility, competition and individualism are uttered at the gates of power. What is even more tragic is that in the name of freedom modern self-proclaimed 'libertarians' are all too eager to agree with Margaret Thatcher's infamous dictum: "There is no such thing as society!" (1987).

Those who argue that the priorities of democracy could be summed up in responsibility, individualism and merit while ignoring equality and social justice consider the ending of the social as the hallmark of a modern state that supposedly invalidates any argument for fair distribution, emancipation and social justice. Even after twenty-two years since Mrs. Thatcher's famous words, the logic that one's freedom is gained by one's own betterment remains prevalent, and continues to be reinforced by an array of political alliances and currents. This typifies the logic of populism where, Laclau (2005) tells us, diverse and opposed demands are tied together in a chain of equivalences that coalesce disparate interest groups that even run across diverse socio-economic spheres and convictions. These unholy alliances find it all too easy to rally around a leader who finds someone to blame for all the ills of the nation. Populist reason substitutes the complex challenges of social responsibility with a simplistic argument: a perverted notion of merit pitted against the straw men of 'entitlement' and 'lazy scrounging'. Thatcherite populism was founded on the widespread conviction that those who merit attention are those who 'look after themselves':

> I think we have gone through a period when too many children and people have been given to understand "I have a problem, it is the Government's job to cope with it!" (...) and so they are casting their problems on society and who is society? There is no such thing! There are individual men and women and there are families and no government can do anything except through people and people look to themselves first. It is our duty to look after ourselves and then also to help look after our neighbour and life is a reciprocal business and people have got the entitlements too much in mind without the obligations, because there is no such thing as an entitlement unless someone has first met an obligation. (Thatcher 1987)

Mrs. Thatcher substitutes society with a romanticized notion of a "living tapestry of men and women and people and the *beauty* of that tapestry and the quality of our lives will depend upon how much each of us is prepared to *take responsibility for ourselves* and each of us prepared *to turn round and help by our own efforts those who are unfortunate*" (1987, my emphases). Her position cannot be simpler and clearer for those convinced that *they* are the only hard-workers and that *their* 'real' entitlement is based on the fact that *they* should be rewarded for looking after their own interests. Everyone knows that the 'helping the other' part falls on the wayside because meritocracy is not based on collaboration but on competition: testing, standards and statistics are the Canons of a manufactured credibility that expects immediate consent. "Today it is as if (...) values and commitments have been swept aside," says Greene. "The reiteration of words like 'balanced budget' and 'inflation' and 'interest rates' have drowned out the sound of words like 'justice', 'equity', 'human rights'. Too many of us sit stunned, uncomprehending" (NDc, p. 7).

Measure and standards legitimize competitive merit. At the same time, merit becomes a form of exclusion, where those 'who do not make it' have no one to blame but themselves. Mechanisms like standardized testing and imposed accounting, which were once coerced into the system, now gain consent and become 'spontaneous' (Gramsci 1975b). Greene looks at this as the manufactured normality of the commonsense world, which "seems so normal, so unquestionable, that you imagine it looks the way it looks to you to anyone with normal eyesight" (NDc, p. 8). Yet this normality is an objectified world that has avoided plural interpretations by being already interpreted for us: "Like people everywhere, we forget that it is a constructed or a constituted or an interpreted world. It appears to be so natural because our interpretations have been objectified to such an extent that we take them for granted—not as subjective processes, but as representations of what is objectively there" (ibid.). This is how the argument for selective education is objectified by the assumptions of testing and school ranking, which, by no accident, happen to be related to the real estate industry, local taxation, and a myriad other socio-economic spheres that are all too readily greeted as objective facts. Test-based meritocracy becomes a form of means-based competition. Parents are convinced that it works because they live in the hope that their children will be motivated by such a system. They seem to have no alternative. Once they succeed in one way or another, these children will pass on their gained merit onto new generations who also hope to be chosen above other children and other parents. Those who 'fail' go to 'failing schools' that statistically are considered as having failed the 'objective' standards set by the system.

Discussing the benchmarks by which schools in England are considered to be 'successful' or 'failing', Ross McKibbin points out that "'Failing' schools are often good at things not measurable by formal criteria—at enabling students of many different nationalities to live together more or less in peace, for example. The result is that some schools, liked by parents and Ofsted [the *Office of Standards for Education*], are in danger of being closed because they do not meet the narrow criteria set by the government" (2008, p. 9). This corroborates Greene's argument that the sound of words such as 'justice', 'equity', 'human rights' are drowned, this time by the words 'tests', 'standards', 'attainment' and 'targets'. Failure is objectified and what is perceived as a 'failing' school is despised as a symptom of what is perceived as a larger context—that of a 'failing' social class, or even a 'failing' society. Note that failure is seen as an action incurred by the 'failing' person or institution on him or itself. Those who supposedly fail are not *failed* by others, but are *failing* by themselves. No government or authority speaks of 'failed' schools or hospitals. Instead the jargon is that of 'failing' schools and hospitals, even when the truth is that children, parents, and patients are being failed by a larger context of social inequality and injustice to which all have to consent. As failure is identified with a generalized group of people, it becomes a category of the same notion of society that was anathemized by the same Mrs. Thatcher whose populist ideology was duly inherited and exercised by subsequent Tory *and* Labour governments. McKibbin is not talking about schools in the 1980s, but current schools as overseen by the current Labour administration. What is even more tragic is that those who fervently consent to this state of affairs are themselves being hegemonized by this fallacy. Even though they don't know it, those who 'succeed' are as hegemonized as those who 'fail'.

To state that meritocracy is blatantly expedient warrants the qualification of a context where what is expedient for those who exert the most influence has always been simply assumed as 'natural'. This is why Mrs. Thatcher was so convinced of her political stance that she had the audacity of reciting Francis of Assisi's Prayer to inaugurate her premiership: "Lord, make me an instrument of your peace, Where there is hatred, let me sow love; where there is injury, pardon (...) where there is sadness, joy." If being an instrument of peace means a war in the Falklands, open support of Reagan's Latin American policies, resisting any sanctions on South African apartheid, continuous support to General Augusto Pinochet, even when under house arrest for crimes against humanity, then pardon and joy are very unlikely to follow. What is even worse is the fact that those who were encouraged to "look after themselves" in the late 1980s were duped into taking massive mortgages. They bought property at inflated prices only to quickly find themselves in negative equity, out of a job, or facing foreclosure.

The fact that history continues to repeat itself at the end of the first decade of this century has nothing to do with the ways of the world—be it tragedy or farce—but because like Thatcher, many continue to believe that freedom is only in the gift of the few who claim to deserve it. The flip side of the story is that the so-called progressive Left not only ceded to this logic, but dispersed into the wilderness, conceding to that other famous Thatcherite dictum: "there is no alternative" and paving its way for a new form of meritocracy (Mészáros 1996).

"... enabled to choose themselves as free"

Meritocracy's twisted notions of upward mobility give no further qualification as to what causes the poverty that ultimately defaults on society to look after those who, far from feeling entitled, hardly entertain any sense of meaningful living. The truth is that more often than not the poor and marginalized are hardly seen. They remain, as Greene puts it, "invisible," where even schooling corroborates to injustice: "for too many years, they [schools] have allowed minority groups and the very poor to remain 'invisible'. The claims of equal opportunity, like the myths of upward mobility, have obscured terrible inequities in our society, inequities we have hesitated to confront, much less repair" (1975, pp. 12–13).

The populist's attack is always directed at specific groups that are easily clumped together, such as the 'lazy opportunists' who live on the dole, or the minorities who 'do not integrate'. These targeted groups are always blamed for not 'making it' and being a 'burden' on the State: the immigrant who is deemed illegal and only interested in benefits; the minorities who fail to integrate because they don't speak English, or have different habits or an unfamiliar faith; the single parent who is frowned upon as being irresponsible if not downright immoral; the child who plays truant, deemed as the future criminal; the unemployed who, according to some, enjoys a comfortable life living off social security. These individuals are said to typify the notion of a *society* that is all too easily dismissed by the typical populist.

Twenty-two years on from Thatcher's political *fatwa* on the political existence of society, we still have no real answer as to why should the notion of society be linked to the opportunistic few who play the system, especially when everyone knows that those who play the system are not the single mother, truant child, immigrant or the unemployed. Invariably there are always individuals who play the system, but those who have effectively bankrupt the system prominently include corporate managers and officials who fool thousands in thinking they could make it by offering massive loans that could never be paid. It is this kind of enterprise that plays the system—which is not that distanced from the idea of self-betterment first. In the name of *their* liberty and freedom of *enterprise*, some companies do not think twice to hire immigrants and the unemployed and pay them next to nothing. This recalls Dewey's explanation of how *enterprise* "is given the significance of a certain desirable trait of human nature, so that the issue is taken out of the field of observation into that of opinion plus a eulogistic emotion. 'Enterprise' like 'initiative' and like 'industry' can be exerted in behalf of an indefinite number of objects; the words may designate the activities of an Al Capone or a racketeering labor union as well as a socially useful industrial undertaking" (1989, pp. 92–93).

All of this begs the question: How is freedom possible for the invisible many when they are blamed for the ills of society, a society dismissed as a political *excuse* for those deemed to have failed in the meritocratic race of 'the *free*'?

Greene's take on freedom is neither teleological nor positivist. She avoids other logics of populism: including that which the Left often followed impulsively with disastrous effects, resulting in other forms of discrimination and oppression. Greene is well aware that populism—neither that of the Right nor the Left—could never create the conditions for a just society. Referencing Milan Kundera's *The Unbearable Lightness of Being*, where he states that "what makes a leftist a leftist is not this or that theory but his ability to integrate any theory into the kitsch called the Grand March" (1999, p. 257), Greene adds that the true function of kitsch "is to serve as a folding screen set up to curtain off death, or to mystify by putting a smiling face on things. It is not enough, however, to recognize it as an illusion or a lie, if the achievement of freedom is our concern. It might lose its authoritarian power, but we might be left in the 'lightness of being', with our figurative ashes blowing in the wind" (DOF, p. 10).

It is not hard to notice in Greene's work a degree of reluctance and hostility to immediate solutions. The political side of an active life is never going to be simply a matter of political parties, or allegiances to the Left, Right or Center. Her careful analysis reinforces the character of her radical philosophy. What matters for Greene is the *qualitative grounding* that allows us to see distinctions and delineate a diverse horizon of situatedness that omits the temptation of totalizing views, which politically have proven to be deadly on all sides of the spectrum. "Justice," Greene remarks, "cannot become the central value if teachers do not learn to act consciously on principle, if they have no means of determining when the distinctions they make are relevant, whether the distribution of educational benefits is fair" (1973, p. 182). Refusing to take a simplistic cause-effect attitude to social and educational disadvantage, she writes: "Concerned about deprivations and injustices, I recognize that they cannot be overcome by treating people the same, no matter how important equality of result may seem." Citing R.S. Peters's *Ethics and Education* (1967), she qualifies her strategy of qualitative grounding: "Fundamental to the question of fairness is the notion 'that distinctions should be made if there are relevant differences or on the basis of irrelevant differences'. It is my impression that the intention behind school reform (...) was to make distinctions (...)

on the basis of differences in achievement due in large measure to previous neglect, segregation, humiliation, and the ravages of poverty" (Greene 1973, p. 182).

This would clarify why Greene considers the notion of freedom from an angle of indirectness. She poses the notion of an *action for* freedom in what appears to be an 'inverse' way:

> We cannot teach freedom or autonomy directly, anymore than we can teach a com-
> mon decency; but we can do something to enable people to achieve them, something
> not unlike what we do when we teach literature or chemistry. Certain acts must be
> performed, certain tasks accomplished *if individuals are to be enabled to choose themselves
> as free.* They are acts involving the posing of problems and the referring of such prob-
> lems to the context of action. (1975, p. 11, my emphasis)

In the first place, Greene clearly states what freedom is. She reminds us that people "choose themselves as free" and are not made free or given freedom by someone else, whether this *someone else* is a teacher, politician, econo-
mist, artist or priest. Freedom emerges from one being *enabled* to realize that he or she is free. When in Toni Morrison's *Sula*, Nel and Sula realized that "freedom and triumph was forbidden to them" they sought to create "something else to be" (1980, p. 52). I read this as setting out to create a way of real-
izing their ability to choose themselves as free. But freedom does not simply come in the form of cerebral exercises; freedom does not come from a *desideratum*. Nel and Sula's creation of another state of being was as concrete as the dirt and the cruelty that surrounded them. Yet their action was equally creative and their struggle was characterized by an indirectness that worked in re-
verse, so to speak.

When at one point, Nel and Sula are confronted by a gang of young men, Sula challenges them by taking out a paring knife and slashing the tip of her finger, as she states in a quiet voice: "If I can do that to myself, what you sup-
pose I'll do to you?" (Morrison 1980, p. 55). The action here appears to be re-
versed, and takes an indirect strategy. But the reversal is neither ineffective nor rhetorical. It is an action that holds the absolute meaning of an intention—an intention that does not stop at motive, but which is larger than the gesture that signifies it.

When Greene speaks of freedom and autonomy as something that cannot be taught directly, she is not that far from this logic of reversal. As she defines action, she mentions acts that have "to do with the assessment of contexts, reflection on the taken-for-granted, decision on what is worth-while, commit-
ment to what ought to be" (1975, p. 11). This action is mainly to do with the interruption of the quotidian. It is a transgression of what is expected, and

thus holds an element of surprise in that it takes the risk of the unknown—a certainty that is sacrificed because what certainty produces is more suffering and exploitation by the conventions that too quickly assume that the victim is always to blame.

Again, the centrality of Greene's project is that of possibility and choice. As we have seen in the previous chapters, in Greene's philosophy choice is neither disinterested nor neutral. Likewise, possibility does not come from dreamlike worlds, but dreamlike worlds are made possible by how our intentionality toward the existent world ultimately converges with that of others as it assumes a value that cannot be ignored. In the context of learning, a main predication of possibility is what Greene calls an "intentional education" that must take place within the public domain—be it that of schools or other spaces that act, directly or indirectly, as an *agôn* for learning. Greene tells us that it is not schools that change the social order, but what makes "*particularistic relationships* possible." However, possibility remains conditional on the qualitative grounds of the social, where opportunity must be recognized, challenged, developed or deconstructed: "if individuals are permitted to relate to one another in a matrix of acknowledged duties and rights, freedom may well exist *as opportunity*" (Greene 1975, pp. 11–12, my emphasis).

The assumption of freedom as a historical given, or as given by someone in history, is false because it assumes that the 'free' individual is a passive recipient of freedom. To learn to choose to be free is to be enabled to realize the possibility that choice, in its interestedness, has all but one ground—the unpredictable. Greene states that "if we treat freedom as an existent, a given, something possessed and transmitted," then we remain in an illusionary predicament. Instead, "freedom, at any time, can only be a possibility—to be acted upon by autonomous persons who, through their actions, identify themselves as individuals while bringing norms into being in the world" (1975, p. 13).

Liberty's Dilemma

In an essay for *The Humanist* in 1964, Greene writes:

> No humanist can ignore the manifold bigotries, fanaticisms, and complacencies which sometimes destroy life itself and, more often, block the release of life, the achievement of humane aims. But, paradoxically or not, there is something anti-human and restrictive about a single-minded dedication to overthrow what stands in the way—be it an institution, a group, a man, or an idea. (1964, p. 34)

Taken out of the philosophical context within which Greene works, this statement might give the impression of political quietism. Yet, Greene's critique of what she calls *karamasovism*—which she sees as an exacting revenge against the authorities who shaped one's life and upbringing—is that the logic of revenge politics is self-defeating.

> It is relatively easy to take the path of vengeance or rejection, especially when most rational people seem to support one's notion of what is right and wrong. It is far more difficult to take the uncharted path, the way of specific remaking, reinterpretation, reform—on one's own behalf and on behalf of human happiness and decency. Yet this is what is asked of humanists—this and far, far more. (Greene 1964, p. 34)

Beyond the impulse of *karamasovism*, there are the demands of situations that cannot be ignored if politics mean more than immediate reaction. Just as the struggle for education implies a grounded quality, just as choice is interested, so is the logic of political change. "Again, humanists may march, perhaps *should* march and picket sometimes and protest; but here too there is more" (Greene 1964, p. 35). The questions that ensue explain what the interestedness and quality of action could entail: "What is 'equality' to be taken to mean, in the cities, in the city schools? Who is to reconcile the demands being raised when preferential hiring is discussed, when 'compensation' is talked about, when responsibility is assigned? Who is to identify the specific consequences of each proposal, the effects on the individual people involved?" The challenge here is to recognize the complexities where what is at stake is "the release of the person to live" (ibid.). This particular article is short, yet full of bold statements that need unpacking. When she draws attention to the question of schools, Greene argues that "more and more people are recognizing that when 'excellence' in the schools is discussed, the community's 'image of man' is at issue." Then she asks: "In what sense is it democratic to encourage the gifted? What should Jeffersonian selectiveness be taken to mean?" (ibid.).

The Jeffersonian legacy partakes of the dialectical contradictions bequeathed by the Enlightenment. This legacy firmly rested on the struggles against the monarchy in the revolutions of 1648 in England and 1789 in France, both of which gave rise to the notion of liberty, where the power taken by a monarch and the aristocracy in the name of a God that legitimized such power was challenged and quashed for the first time since Roman republican Law. Marx describes these revolutions as not English and French, but as "the victory of a new order society."

> The bourgeoisie was victorious in these revolutions; but the victory of the bourgeoisie was at that time the victory of a new order of society, the victory of bourgeois property, of nationality over provincialism, of competition over the guild, of partition over

primogeniture, of the owner of the land over the domination of the owner by the land, of enlightenment over superstition, of the family over the family name, of industry over heroic laziness, of civil war over medieval privilege. (Marx 1977b, pp. 139–40)

In *Liberty Before Liberalism*, Quentin Skinner traces these newfound notions of liberty in ideals that go back to the neo-roman theories of free states. Referring to Thomas Hobbes's *Leviathan*, where the Multitude—the many—redefines sovereignty, Skinner makes an elaborate and solid argument for this connection, adding that modern liberalism has basically eclipsed and distorted the original notions of liberty as these re-emerged in the 17th century. Skinner draws our attention to "the unambiguous claim that the state is the name of an artificial person 'carried' or represented by those who wield sovereign power, and that their acts of representation are rendered legitimate by the fact that they are authorised by their own subjects."

At the same time, there rose to prominence an associated view of the relationship between the power of the state and the liberty of its subjects. To be free as a member of a civil association, it was urged, is simply to be unimpeded from exercising your capacities in pursuit of your desired ends. One of the prime duties of the state is to prevent you from invading the rights of action of your fellow-citizens, a duty it discharges by imposing the coercive force of law on everyone equally. But where law ends, liberty begins. Provided that you are neither physically nor coercively constrained from acting or forbearing from acting by the requirements of the law, you remain capable of exercising your powers at will and to that degree remain in possession of your civil liberty. (Skinner 1998, pp. 4–5)

The inherent paradox within the project of the Enlightenment is evident in Marx's characterization of these bourgeois revolutions. The bourgeois victory hailed a new era where the relationship of power shifts and creates new social formations, new struggles for power, while at the same time sustaining a law that unifies all by the equal choice of freedom. In *Freedom and Culture*, Dewey identifies a similar dialectic in the two founding documents of the United States, the Declaration of Independence and the Constitution, both of which cite a "striking difference in temper":

That the first should be much the more radical in tone is easily explicable by the fact that it was written by the man [Jefferson] who was the firmest and most explicit of all the leaders of the movement in faith in democracy. Conditions conspired to make him the spokesman at this juncture as changed conditions brought others to the front in the Constitutional Convention while he was absent in France. In one case, it was necessary to rally all the forces in the country in the name of freedom against a foreign foe. In the other case, the most urgent need of men of established position seemed to be protection of established economic interests against onslaughts of a populace using liberty as a cloak for an attack upon order and stability. There was also need of compromise to unite various sections in a single federal government. Even during his own lifetime the author of the Declaration of Independence feared lest monarchical and oligarchical tendencies should undermine republic institutions. (Dewey 1989, pp. 46–47)

Dewey fails to agree with a Marxist interpretation of this state of affairs in terms of an economic base from which one could extrapolate a general law of political movement. He argues that the "original democratic theory was simple in its formulation because the conditions under which it took effect were simple" (1989, p. 47). Dewey saw the American theory of liberty emerging from the immediate desire to have individual and personal freedom, a freedom that did not accept any external sources of coercion. This also carried an antipathy and suspicion of governments with excessive power. "Guarantees against this abuse were then supposed to be enough to establish republican government" (1989, p. 48). This hostility to excessive governance was due to two historical contexts. First there was the memory of British rule over the new colonies against which the very purpose of independence emerged. Then there was another factor, which Dewey cites as another fear in Jefferson, that might explain the apparent contradictions that one identifies in his view on liberty, and also education. This was Jefferson's own experience in France. "What he experienced there," says Dewey, "led him to give unqualified support to the saying that in a country with an oppressive government everyone is either hammer or anvil." Dewey adds that although in the young American republic there was no visible enemy to freedom above the horizon, "Jefferson anticipated with dread the rise of such an enemy in the growth of manufacturing and commerce and the growth of cities of large populations" (1989, p. 48). Following this Deweyan analysis, Greene argues that Jefferson's concept of freedom "was associated with a concept of action. It was neither privatist nor subjective; it could only be maintained out in the open among self-directing (and self-supporting) persons" (DOF, pp. 27–28).

Jefferson had a very specific notion of the *polis* in mind. To him the new American republic was the greatest opportunity that history provided, where free individuals would live without the shackles of Empire and become a new polis, a new community of free individuals. "With the voice and style of the eighteenth century, Jefferson was again demanding selective education and, at once, free schools for all" (PSPV, p. 8). This may seem contradictory and failing in the eyes of the 21st century educator, yet Jefferson's context was just the bare minimum, but at the same time it enjoyed the maximum and optimum time in history where a new free society could found a young Republic that would truly defend the rights of man.

The Enlightenment concept of republicanism justified this proposal for a common and an un-common school. The ideal of a Republic governed it, a Republic ruled by free-born philosopher kings. Jefferson had the arrangements of the previous century in mind, those that depended on a gentlemanly balance of political forces, not parties contesting for power. He had in mind the rational consensus which had seemed to underlay the contests of his day, the agreements on core values which had counteracted "special interest" and overcome "functionalism" with good sense. (PSPV p. 9)

It is true to say that Jefferson did not anticipate the larger contexts that led to an urbanization and development of a massive scale. But it is also true that, as Dewey remarks, he harbored a fear of this growth, which would be the foe on the horizon of liberty. Yet, as Greene emphasizes, "for all the dissonance between his view of a state small enough to become a *polis* and the vast, centralized order soon to emerge (...) he bequeathed to us a remarkable conception of the relation between freedom and the public happiness" (DOF, p. 29). And it is here that the dilemma of the "Jeffersonian selectiveness"—which seems to give rise to meritocracy—must be addressed. The dilemma does not consist of a misconception of the historical context that Jefferson lived in, but in the underlying theory of freedom that he espoused. While the contradiction of his "selective education [which] at once [supported] free schools for all" (PSPV, p. 8) ultimately comes down to the strategic issue of policy as opposed to a politics of *selectivism* as we know it now, the problem that still rings with some truism is that of how one defines freedom: how could one critique notions that privilege merit over equality without tracing this in Jefferson's notion of liberty?

One could approach this question from two positions. One is to understand that the notion of liberty, in its original neo-roman context, and as exercised in revolutionary England and France (and, by implication, in the young American Republic) is essentially alien and contrary to modern liberalism—and thus it becomes difficult for us to really understand what we should be doing with issues like meritocracy and individualism. This is Skinner's position. Another way to go about it—which may not be in contradistinction to the first—is to engage with liberty as a concept that is tied to the notions of *possibility* and *situation*. By this I mean that as one tries to understand the 'simplicity' by which the theory of liberty emerged in the new American Republic—as Dewey contends—one must also reassess this 'simplicity' in the light of what consequently emerged as its inherent foe, which Jefferson, Dewey tells us, anticipated with dread: "the rise of such an enemy in the growth of manufacturing and commerce and the growth of cities of large populations" (1989, p. 48).

Taking the latter position to start with, one notices that after Dewey goes through the definition of liberty as "a virtual identification of freedom with the very state of being an individual" and "the extent of freedom that existed [as] taken to be the measure of the degree in which individuality was realized" (1989, p. 48), he qualifies it in two ways:

> According to one view, it was an expression of pioneer conditions; it was appropriate to those conditions but was thoroughly naïve as a universal truth about the individual and about government. According to the other view, while the idea had some of the qualities of a dream, yet it expresses a principle to be maintained by deliberative effort if mankind is to have a truly human career. Call it dream or call it vision, it has been interwoven in a tradition that has had an immense effect upon American life. (ibid.)

But Dewey does not stop there. He goes on to argue that this tradition has two separate implications: "on the one hand, it leads to effort to perpetuate and strengthen the conditions which brought it to existence. But, on the other hand, a tradition may result in habits that obstruct observation of what is actually going on; a mirage may be created in which republican institutions are seen as if they were in full vigor after they have gone in decline" (ibid.). Writing in 1939, Dewey was also defending a democratic ideal that was directly challenged on two, if not three, fronts: the external fronts of Fascism and Stalinism, and the internal dynamics of a capitalist system that had grown so much that some saw it as being further distanced from its republican origins.

Although I do not find the distinction between liberalism and liberty explicit in either Dewey or Greene, the questions that Dewey raises over the theory of freedom as it originated in the young American republic are not that far off from what Skinner regards as "the subsequent eclipse" of liberty by "the liberal analysis of negative liberty in terms of the absence of coercive impediments"—in other words as a notion of freedom that is defined by its negation of impediment, rather than as an affirmation of freedom as being immanent to free citizenry in free states. "With the rise of the liberal theory to a position of hegemony in contemporary political philosophy, the neo-roman theory has been lost to sight that the liberal analysis has come to be widely regarded as the only coherent way of thinking about the concept involved" (Skinner 1998, pp. 112–13). Citing and critiquing Berlin's *Two Concepts of Liberty*, Skinner argues that

> Berlin's critique depends on the premise that negative liberty is jeopardised only by coercive interference. From this it certainly follows that dependence and lack of self government cannot be construed as lack of liberty. But this only follows because the conclusion has already been inserted into the premise. What I have tried to show, however, is that the premise itself needs to be reconsidered. The assumption that individual liberty is basically a matter of non-interference is precisely what the neoroman theory calls in doubt. (1998, pp. 115–16)

More remarkably, Skinner argues that the flaw in Berlin's notion of negative freedom is not uncommon in that he sees it as symptomatic of an intellectual heritage in which "it is easy to become bewitched into believing that the ways of thinking about them bequeathed to us by the mainstream of our intellectual traditions must be the ways of thinking about them" (p. 116). This tautology seems to be inherent in the fallacy that philosophical neutrality could somehow allow us to discern where the flaws are—which is what the liberal tradition has always assumed, as it sets itself between and against instrumentality on one hand and criticality on the other. To unravel this tautological morass, Skinner suggests that the historian of philosophy could prevent us from falling into this trap. In this respect the historian would need to position himself in this role and thereby claim—rightly, to my mind—that this would "prevent us from becoming too readily bewitched":

> The intellectual historian can help us to appreciate how far the values embodied in our present way of life, and our present ways of thinking about those values, reflects a series of choices made at different times between *different possible worlds*. This awareness can help to liberate us from the grip of any one hegemonical account of those values and how they should be interpreted and understood. Equipped with a *broader sense of possibility*, we can stand back from the intellectual commitments we have inherited and ask ourselves in a new spirit of enquiry what we should think of them. (Skinner 1998, p. 117, my emphases)

As I see it, Skinner's argument is that we have been all too bewitched with our attempts to believe our own philosophical assumptions—assumptions that were made neutral in the first place in order for them to be believable and for us to be convinced by them. In other words, we tend to willfully forget our philosophical and theoretical histories and we seem to prefer to either fall prey to entrenched ones or try to neutralize history itself and then get trapped in even more tautologies. It is in this respect that I would dare propose that Greene suggests other than what Dewey proposes in his analysis of the Jeffersonian dilemma. Although Greene's position cannot be attributed to Skinner's, because there is no evidence that she follows his work or does research in the same area, one could argue that in her assumptions of possibility she distances herself from that of liberalism or even pragmatism, and while not being hostile to either, she assumes a radically different approach to both.

Just as Greene distances Dewey from Camus (chapter two, this volume), so would one assume that she would consider her own position as going more with Camus' than with Dewey's when it comes to the matter of an intervening history. In fact it seems that Greene uses the same methods of historical intervention to distance Dewey from immediate liberal assumptions and *read* him back to his Hegelian roots. This is not surprising at all. Greene's own identifi-

cation with Dewey's legacy makes it necessary for her to move away from liberal pragmatism, while moving closer to progressivism, although her existentialist foundations gain their sharpest effect within critical theory. This is
confirmed by how Greene considers negative freedom as inadequate: "where
the problem, indeed the 'dialectic', of freedom, was concerned, there was a
dramatic shift from both the Jeffersonian and the Emersonian definitions, de-
spite the survival of the spirit of Jeffersonian republicanism and Emersonian
idealism. For one thing, there was a recognition of the insufficiency of negative freedom and of the view that freedom was an endowment" (DOF, p. 42).

So where does this leave Dewey? Greene cites Dewey's essay "Democracy
and Educational Administration," where he argues that "the democratic idea
of freedom is not the right of each individual to do as he pleases, even if it be
qualified by adding 'provided he does not interfere with the same freedom on
the part of others'." Far from a liberal notion of negative freedom, Dewey suggests a freedom of action and experience as whatever "is necessary to produce
freedom of intelligence." Dewey knew, explains Greene, "that freedom of
mind and freedom of action were functions of membership and participation
in some valued community." She goes on to position him with Charles Taylor,
Hannah Arendt and Jurgen Habermas, arguing that like them Dewey partook
of the idea "that the person—that center of choice—develops his/her fullness to
the degree he/she is a member of a live community" (DOF, p. 43).

In so doing, does Greene take on the task of protecting Dewey's legacy
from modern liberalism's eclipsing of the original notion of liberty? In aligning
Dewey's notion of freedom with a live community, does not Greene align his
idea of liberty with a freedom predicated on citizenry where "for an individual
citizen to possess or lose their liberty [it] must be embedded within an account
of what it means for civil association to be free"? (Skinner 1998, p. 23).

One can only assume that this is the case, because the only alternative that
would survive the foes that Jefferson dreaded is what Rorty sees as a liberal
demarcation between the public and private spheres, a maneuver that would
at best allow us to become private radicals, while pragmatically engaging with a
public life that one hardly finds as politically edifying. "When Dewey talked
politics," says Rorty, "as opposed to doing philosophy, he offered advice about
how to avoid getting hung up on traditional ways of doing things, how to re-
describe the situation in terms which might facilitate compromise, and how to
take fairly small, reformist steps" (Mouffe 1996, p. 17). In saying this, Rorty
pits Dewey against Levinas, whose politics Rorty likens to a "pathos of the infinite [that] chimes with radical, revolutionary politics" that he does not see as
relating to constitutional democracies in Britain, France and the United
States. In this respect, Rorty makes a perplexing suggestion where a demarca-

tion between radical politics and pragmatic practices are shared out between the private and the public.

> Politics, as I see it, is a matter of pragmatic, short-term reforms and compromises— compromises which must, in democratic society, be proposed and defended in terms much less esoteric than those in which we overcome the metaphysics of presence [which Rorty attributes to Derrida's *Politics of Friendship*]. Political thought centres on the attempt to formulate some hypotheses about how, and under what conditions, such reforms might be effected. I want to save radicalism and pathos for private moments, and stay reformist and pragmatic when it comes to my dealings with other people. (Rorty, in Mouffe 1996, p. 17)

Granting that Dewey's politics are structurally and strategically distinct from how he does philosophy, it remains doubtful whether Rorty's liberal argument for the private radical and public pragmatist could effectively sustain the notion of liberty by which Dewey—and Greene after him—engages with the Jeffersonian dilemma. What is for sure is that Rorty attempts to solve the problematic with which the erosion of liberty itself challenges the pragmatic argument for liberalism. This is partly framed by the pragmatic assumption of experience as that which, like freedom, pertains to an individuality which has a lot to teach us about the world, but which still leaves us with the question of how and whether we must be able to surpass the immediate pragmatic questions raised by experience in order to be able to create a society that could—not without irony—accommodate a demarcation between the private radical and the public pragmatist. Yet one does wonder whether such demarcation holds any value in face of stark oppression or naked poverty, in face of oppression in liberal or illiberal contexts. One wonders whether such demarcation is the luxury of those who find liberal democracy accommodating enough to hide its illiberal and oppressive moments, its poor and those who are legally disenfranchised. And how would this hold true in contemporary Burma, Saudi Arabia or Zimbabwe? How would this have worked in Pol Pot's Cambodia, Honecker's GDR or Pinochet's Chile?

What seems to happen in this Rortian argument for liberalism is not dissimilar from Berlin's position. A premise that is presented as philosophically neutral gives an ensuing political argument the appearance of conforming to specific philosophical desires that never formed part of the picture in the first place. This approach raises more questions than it claims to answer. Questions such as What lies behind the political anticipation of the Liberal state? An unexamined experience? A call for reasonable practices? Or is this a genuine desire to atone for a liberty that is gone forever without, in effect, offering an alternative to this sense of loss? But how could one atone for lost freedoms? What lies beyond the wasted lives of many an Ivan Denisovich?

Shukov gazed at the ceiling in silence. Now he didn't know either whether he wanted freedom or not. At first he'd longed for it. Every night he'd counted the days of his stretch—how many had passed, how many were coming. And then he'd grown bored with counting. And then it became clear that men of his like wouldn't ever be allowed to return home, that they'd be exiled. And whether his life would be any better there than here—who could tell? (Solzhenitsyn 1973, p. 140)

CHAPTER SIX

Anticipations

Once I took such delight in Montaigne, that I thought I should not need any other book; before that, in Shakespeare; then in Plutarch; then in Plotinus; at one time in Bacon; afterwards in Goethe; even in Bettine; but now I turn the pages of either of them languidly, whilst I still cherish their genius. So with pictures; each will bear an emphasis of attention once, which it cannot retain, though we fain would continue to be pleased in that manner. How strongly I have felt of pictures, that when you have seen one well, you must take your leave of it; you shall never see it again. I have had good lessons from pictures, which I have since seen without emotion or remark. (...) The reason of the pain this discovery causes us (and we make it late in respect to works of art and intellect) is the plaint of tragedy which murmurs from it in regard to persons, to friendship and love.

—Ralph Waldo Emerson, *Experience* (1941, vol. 1, p. 245)

Artists are for disclosing the extraordinary in the ordinary. They are for transfiguring the commonplace, as they embody their perceptions and feelings and understandings in a range of languages, in formed substance of many kinds. They are for affirming the work of imagination—the cognitive capacity that summons up the "as if," the possible, the what is not and yet might be. They are for doing all this in such a way as to enable those who open themselves to what they create to see more, to hear more, to feel more, to attend to more facets of the experienced world.

—Maxine Greene, "Creating, Experiencing, Sense-Making" (1987, p. 14)

To elevate experience to a level that would fair with what has been traditionally accorded to theory in academia must be a laudable cause. But one should bear in mind that intellectual history is all too scarred by fierce debates over theory and practice, particularly when it comes to the whole question of how far one could go with experience as a benchmark of truth. One need only recall the positivist dispute in German sociology in the 1960s, where luminaries such as Popper and Dahrendorf, and Adorno, Habermas and Marcuse came head to head with passion and wit over practice and criticality in the study of sociology (Adorno et al. 1976). Twenty years before this dispute, just after the Second World War, Max Horkheimer writes in his *Eclipse of Reason*:

[T]he so called practical world has no place for truth, and therefore splits it to conform it to its own image: the physical sciences are endowed with so-called objectivity,
but emptied of human content; the humanities preserve the human content, but only
as ideology, at the expense of truth. (2003, p. 75)

In the lectures that he gave on moral philosophy in the early 1960s,
Adorno notes that there is "a greater need of theoretical intervention at the
present time":

Theory that bears no relation to any conceivable practice either degenerates into an
empty, complacent and irrelevant game, or, what is even worse, it becomes a mere
component of culture, in other words, a piece of dead scholarship, a matter of complete indifference to us as living minds and active, living human beings. *This even holds
good for art for, however mediated, however indirect or concealed it may be, such a link must
nevertheless exist.* Conversely (...) a practice that simply frees itself from the shackles of
theory and rejects thought as such on the grounds of its own supposed superiority will
sink to the level of *activity for its own sake.* (Adorno 2000, p. 6, my emphases)

The inflation of practice and the fossilization of theory create a scenario
where research is equivalent to organization, where scholarship comes measured by how much money it attracts and where facts and figures assume the
status of sacred passwords of a presumed truth. With a theoretical world relegated to the uncritical attics of analytic neutrality, practice "remains stuck fast
within the given reality. It leads to the production of people who like organizing things and who imagine that once you have organized something (...) you
have achieved something of importance, without pondering for a moment
whether such activities have any chance at all of effectively impinging on reality" (Adorno 2000, p. 6). Greene's critique of positivism is not dissimilar:

Positivism, or a separating off of fact from value, dominates much of our thinking.
Systems are posited that they are to be regulated, not by what an articulate public may
conceive to be worthwhile, but by calculable results, by tests of efficiency and effectiveness. (DOF, p. 54)

Positivist notions of practice are rife in educational studies and more specifically in what could be identified with 'Educationism' as a formalized and
identitarian discipline that erodes the humanist position that has traditionally
deemed education as a bastion of equity and emancipation. While it has often
been argued that the bastion of humanism in education lies in the liberal and
pragmatist traditions by which education took its place in the echelons of progressive politics and brought theory into the public domain, there has been a
direct correlation between the rise of practicism and the failure of liberalism
and pragmatism in education—not to mention the very problematic position
within which humanist traditions have in turn placed themselves. More so,

the unquestioned adoption of positivism in education—disguised as a scientistic methodology that somehow sustains a liberal morality—remains trapped within the underlying empirical assumptions made by the same progressive theories that, devoid of criticality, find it too easy to subscribe to a positivist paradigm that at the face of it promises a delivery from the fallacies of metaphysics and the superstition of religion, but in reality have fossilized theory and reduced everything to the limited pathos of the empirical. Far from such a delivery, Educationism sustains a totalized ground that is shared between liberals, pragmatists and progressives alike, all singing from the same hymn-sheets of accountable actions and standards that continuously mistake diversity for difference, equity for egalitarianism, standards for quality, lobbying for reform, policy for politics and 'affirmative' platitudes for emancipation.

Rather than achieving the desired academic and scientific legitimacy for which education has for better and worse continuously craved, in the name of *practice* and *experience* Educationism has systematically impoverished the study of education, where schools of education—particularly across the Anglophone world—have witnessed a steady decline of the humanities, especially through the marginalization of philosophy, the arts and related cognate subjects. It is now customary to assume education to be a professionalized field where what matters is a quantified, measured and legitimized result. What hides behind these criteria are assumptions of a performativity, held accountable by a system that regards a hierarchic epistemology as applicable to specific socio-economic tasks. This is where education is caught in a double bind, which Robbie McClintock characterizes as follows: "Insofar as it exists in the arts and sciences, the academic study of education is dispersed as a subsidiary interest in many different departments. Insofar as it exists in the schools of education, disinterested inquiry is subject to strong professional imperatives" (2005, p. 41). This is the logic of the practicist world, where what holds relevance is what is applied to the desired strictures of 'need': "If the performativity of the supposed social system is taken as the criterion of relevance (that is, when the perspective of systems theory is adopted), higher education becomes a subsystem of the social system, and the same performativity criterion is applied to each of these problems" (Lyotard 1989, p. 48).

Experience, Once Gained

The positivist distortion of practice and experience leaves us in a quandary. How could one reject experience and practice as categories of truth, when historically, and because of positivism, women and men were able to reclaim a materiality that rejected the theocracies that ruled intellectual history before the Enlightenment? How could we afford to reject materiality in a new century that is witnessing the gradual weakening of the secular state and the re-establishment of new theocracies? Historically, positivism was the battle cry of emergent social and liberal democracies, which in the name of progress and emancipation have effectively beaten the myth of god-given power and sepa-rated the state from religion. Yet in the name of the same historic progress, newer and subtler forms of oppression came into effect, creating new forms of alienation and accelerating the obfuscation of truth. It is also a historical fact that the scientific breakthrough of a politics aided with effective technologies and new empirical advances increasingly consolidates a corporate state that is ever more one-dimensional and less—all too less—emancipatory.

Given Greene's theoretical lineage, one cannot discount from this discus-sion Dewey's strong philosophical investment in experience and its central role in the development of philosophy of education. Dewey's pragmatism goes to counter the degeneration of liberty, more so when freedom has to be founded on the possibilities that arise from our own articulation of experi-ence, accommodated by a state that is designed to be secular, and therefore removed from ideology and religion. "Making more and more connections in their own experience, reflecting on their shared lives, taking heed of the con-sequences of the actions they performed [men and women] would become aware of more and more alternatives, more and more experiential possibilities; and this meant an increased likelihood of achieving freedom" (DOF, pp. 42–43). Here Greene traces a direct lineage between the recognition of experience and the outcomes of possible freedoms. Like Dewey she also puts in a caveat. The capacity of achieving such freedom has to be "continually nurtured, in-formed, and communally sustained." Greene's awareness of this pragmatist position is clear: "This recognition could not but feed into Dewey's articula-tions of a theory of experiential education and also into his descriptions of the social involvements and supports that eventually might lead to a 'great soci-ety'" (ibid.).

It stands to historical reason that the very notion of experience cannot be rejected, because from its philosophical inception it has represented an effort to find a suitable solution to the predicaments of the dualist stalemate be-tween mind and body, spirit and matter, theory and practice. This is a dualism that by and large is corroborated by the degeneration of positivism into practi-cism, where theory becomes stale and practice is parched out of any ethical, aesthetical or pedagogical value. Yet the question as to whether Dewey's theory of experience is robust enough to resist current and new challenges to phi-losophy, freedom and education remains. It goes without saying that to claim

Dewey as the ever-inspiring source of a self-renewing philosophy of education also implies continuous re-reading and re-formulation (Hansen 2006). But does Dewey's work portend a criticality that is forceful enough to shift the question of practice away from the dualisms it objects to? Does pragmatism, as inherited from Dewey, Pierce and James, and then renewed by contemporary thinkers such as Rorty and to some extent Cavell, offer the sharpness of the critical edge of existentialism, critical theory and deconstruction?

Although philosophical comparison is self-defeating—if not downright irrelevant—one cannot ignore the fact that the philosophy of education often remains stuck in pragmatic contexts that all too quickly take a shortcut into Dewey's work. It seems to many that his work remains the closest to the questions that continue to be core to the question of learning, and especially how learning is woven into our daily experiences and how, ultimately, education could affect our political being as members of an ever-expanding community. While there is a lot of mileage in any argument that supports the actuality of Dewey's work, even after so many years, it would appear that Dewey's philosophy is sometimes treated as a formula—which, in pragmatist terms, becomes nonsensical. Yet other progressive strands of educational philosophy, such as critical pedagogy, equally stand the risk of being as formulaic as their pragmatist relation, especially when it comes to holding onto the notion of practice as a form of praxis whose dialectic often remains positively construed. Even when there is no doubt that both pragmatist and critical philosophers of education are deeply dedicated to the agenda of equity, justice and effective change, the gradual encroachment of education by socio-economic strictures remains pretty much unchallenged, notwithstanding five decades of fierce resistance from pragmatists and critical theorists. Somehow the mounted logic of progress, as it has been diversely put within liberal and critical philosophies of education, starts looking like that logic whose flaws Nietzsche characterizes as follows:

> So far as the superstitions of the logicians are concerned, I will never tire of emphasizing over and over again a small brief fact which these superstitious types are unhappy to concede namely, that a thought comes when "it" wants to and not when "I" want it, so that it's a *falsification* of the fact to say that the subject "I" is the condition of the predicate "think." *It* thinks: but that this "it" is precisely that old, celebrated "I" is, to put it mildly, only an assumption, an assertion, in no way an "immediate certainty." After all, we've already done too much with this "it thinks": this "it" already contains an *interpretation* of the event and is not part of the process itself. (1973, §17)

So what are we missing when dealing with the paradox of a practical and experiential assumption of education? The suggestion in Nietzsche's dismantling of a logic—which not unlike that of progressive and liberal theories of education, seems to be trapped in its own rules—is that we seem to be missing the interpretative character of the *it*. The ensuing confusion between *interpretation* and the *process* that is often mistaken for the "it" of "I think it" amounts to putting the cart before the horse with the consequence that practice and theory are trapped in a tautology that heaps more fallacies on the assumption of empirical truth. Truth appears split between the *either-or* of theory and practice, when in effect theory and practice have become tautologies of *process*, forgetting that practice is never *processed* but is invariably *interpreted*.

In his discussion of what was then the new progressive alternative to a traditional education, Dewey is perturbed by the formulaic predicament of an *Either-Or*. His short yet bold *Experience and Education* opens with a stark scenario: "Mankind likes to think in terms of extreme opposites. It is given to formulating its beliefs in terms of *Either-Ors*, between which it recognizes no intermediate possibilities" (1997, p. 17). While fully supporting new and progressive pedagogical practices, Dewey was worried that what unified these new philosophies of education was a single strategy: the rejection of the old ways of doing education. This sounded alarm bells to his mind because a philosophy based on rejection could easily slip in the obfuscation of the real core of education: "Now we have the problem of discovering the connection which actually exists within experience between the achievements of the past and the issues of the present" (1997, p. 23).

Here one must clarify that the question of the past is not that of history, as understood to be the foundation of what we *are* in terms of what others *were*. Rather, Dewey's anxiety emerges over a body of experience that is mainly rejected on the pretext of traditional schooling: "We may reject knowledge of the past as the *end* of education and thereby only emphasize its importance as a *means*. When we do that we have a problem that is new in the story of education: How shall the young become acquainted with the past in such a way that the acquaintance is a potent agent in appreciation of the living present?" (1997, p. 23). The distinction between the knowledge of the past as an *end* and knowledge as a *means* has nothing to do with the mechanical strategy of means to an end. Often the problem with Dewey's philosophy is that in his dedication to accessible prose his work remains open to simplification. For Dewey the challenge was larger than the context of *just teaching* or *knowing the past*. The question has to do with how experience becomes a way of understanding the past, which is not simply objectified as a body of knowledge in a book or Canon, but which becomes pertinent to new forms of learning and therefore new forms of constructing the present.

The whole idea of experience is not a way of bringing things down to earth or making the familiar *teachable*. A new theory of experience, understood by Dewey as a way out of the *Either-Or* predicament, comes from the fact that experiential learning must be assumed from within its qualitative grounds because "everything depends upon the quality of the experience which is had" (1997, p. 27). This means that experience itself is taken out from its immediacy, and understood away from the quick fix of a practicist method whose measure is simply to fulfill one side of the *either-or* equation. In its Deweyan sense, experience is meant to provide a leap out of the quandary, and one could add that to date such quandaries still emerge from the quantified identification of experiential moments that are unitized and measured.

> I assume that amid all uncertainties there is one frame of reference: namely, the organic connection between education and personal experience; or that the new philosophy of education is committed to some kind of empirical and experimental philosophy. But experience and experiment are not self-explanatory ideas. Rather, their meaning is part of the problem to be explored. To know the meaning of empiricism we need to understand what experience is. (Dewey 1997, p. 25)

For Dewey experience emerges from two contexts: *continuum* and *interaction*. This is key to what one often forgets about Dewey: the Hegelian base from where his pragmatic view of history emerges in the forms of philosophical rectification that he, like other liberal philosophers, most notably Benedetto Croce, applies to both Hegel's dialectic of history and more so his aesthetics (Croce 2006; 1950). Dewey's philosophy "is a kind of naturalization of Hegel," says Rorty; "Hegel without the split between nature and spirit" (2006, p. 35). In this respect Dewey and Croce share what Granese calls the *pangaea* (*pangèa originaria*) of a common philosophical origin (Granese 2002, p. 69). Dewey assumes the experiential ground of continuum and interaction as the qualitative leap that keeps the realms of possibility open. Similarly, Croce front loads his philosophy with what he calls "absolute historicism" (*storicismo assoluto*), which not unlike a *concrete mind* frames human reality in continuous movement where the only absolute is constant change (Croce 1939a). We must also remember that Hegel's work evolves from idealism to a philosophy that ultimately yields to "a way of life," as Merleau-Ponty describes it. "What is certain in any case is that [Hegel's] *Phénoménologie de l'esprit* does not try to fit all history into a framework of pre-established logic but attempts to bring each doctrine and each era back to life and to let itself be guided by their internal logic with such impartiality that all concern with system seems forgotten" (1964, pp. 64, 65).

With all the concern with system forgotten, it is relatively easier to move with Dewey and engage with how experience works as a continuum of experiential qualities that negates the idea of a foundation, where the agency remains, by and large, that of *our* experiences. In other words, we discern the past and the present through what we qualitatively understand to be our experience. Yet a continuum does not come across simply by having experiences. As the experiential is interactive, an experience "is always what it is because of a transaction taking place between an individual and what, at the time, constitutes his environment, whether the latter consists of persons with whom he is talking about some topic or event, the subject talked about being also a part of the situation; or the toys with which he is playing; the book he is reading (...); or the materials of an experiment he is performing" (Dewey 1997, pp. 43–44). Dewey's characterization of this kind of relationship between past and present goes on to further quash assumptions of duality and the chasm that its split portends:

> The relation of the present and the future is not an *Either-Or* affair. The present affects the future anyway. The persons who should have some idea of the connection between the two are *those who have achieved maturity*. Accordingly, upon them devolves the responsibility for instituting the conditions for the kind of present experience which has a favorable effect upon the future. Education as growth or maturity should be an ever-present process. (Dewey 1997, p. 50, my emphasis)

Going with the assumption that *maturity* implies the capacity to take a critical leap beyond the mere immediacies of an unexamined experience, and therefore assumes a qualitative selection of a number of useful and not so useful experiences, one could argue that experience has to be seen from another angle, a trajectory that goes beyond *what happens now*.

"... summoned up imaginatively"

Though it is *felt* and *understood* individually, experience is also *shared*. Though I have my own experiences as someone, as an individual, I am also aware that my experience implies a plurality. Somehow because we *are* individuals we also participate in each other's experiences, because everyone's experience is the experience of an *other* someone. This is what lies at the base of the human species' ability to be moral. "Morality is possible," says Thomas Nagel, "only for beings capable of seeing themselves as one individual among others more or less similar in general respects—capable, in other words, of seeing themselves as others see them" (1997, p. 120). Only with others could one relate and interact with myriad qualitative experiences. And in valuing the quality of an experience we are able to forget and surpass a large *quantity* of immediate experiences that retain no consequence either for ourselves or for others. If this is, more or less, what we deem as experience beyond what the individual goes through in his private state, then experience must also be read within a wider concept of time as *durée*: "an ego which is *durée* cannot grasp another being except in the form of another *durée*," Merleau-Ponty argues. "By experiencing my own manner of using up time, I grasp it, says Bergson, as a 'choice among an infinity of possible *durées*'" (Merleau-Ponty 1963, p. 15).

The positivist limitation of accountability and measure cannot be unpacked unless a theory of experience like Dewey's is further supplemented with the notion of the embodied and lived subject. Only as such could one transcend a chronological account of experience to be able to enter it within possible forms of *anticipation*. Experience cannot, by itself, remain within the realms of practice, even when this is grounded in *quality*. In and of itself practice is just an iteration of a string of multiple experiences on which practice might critically dwell, but which it must also *defer*, if not *transcend*. A practicist limitation of experience becomes a mere accumulation of *retentions*. This accumulation is not unlike a banked quantity of knowledge, which simply makes us more "adaptable, manageable beings" (Freire 1996, p. 47). Quantifiable experiences, like banked knowledge, could never fully relate with the deeper dynamic being of a lived subject. For a lived subject to make something of experience—for a being to qualify experience—it must be ready to defy, by sometimes *residing within* the interstitial middles of the *Either-Ors* of immediacy. Somehow even the quantity-quality duality becomes irrelevant, and what remains is an order that could afford to gamble away its own myth of certainty.

It is this dialectical daring that is often missing in Deweyan philosophy. Even when Dewey famously aligned experience with the creative powers of the imagination, stating that "when old and familiar things are made new in experience, there is imagination" and "when the new is created, the far and strange become the most natural inevitable things in the world" (2005, p. 278), he lacks the verve of the dialectical reasoning by which Greene dares to infringe the polite affirmations of her pragmatist teacher: "I think in terms of expansion, of new connections in experience, of a sedimenting of texture or a layering of meanings, a thickening, if you like, a growing density of texture as persons allow their past experiences to feed into their present ones, as more and more is known" (1987, p. 19).

Just as Dewey dares his own Hegelian formation, Greene continuously pushes Dewey's work into ever-new contexts, as if she were testing how far she could go. What Greene undeniably brings to Dewey's work is the work of others, such as the human insights by which she carries Sartre, Camus and Woolf; the criticality by which she dialogues with the profundity of Arendt and Merleau-Ponty; and the insight that she gets from Bergson, Husserl and Schutz—to name but a notable few referents in the complex corollary that Greene's philosophy integrates into its own original métier.

Reading Dewey after Schutz, as it were, one could argue that for experience to defy the limitations of practicism—and its positivist immediacy—experience must be seen for how it becomes *protentive* (rather than *retentive*) of the lived body's events. Only as *protention*, as anticipation, could experience become critical and therefore able to refuse its being assimilated into an accumulation of the *known* certainties of familiar practices. This is what Schutz suggests in his discussion of Husserl's notion of experience:

> [O]ur actual experiences are not merely by retentions and recollections referred to our past experiences. Any experience refers likewise to the future. It carries along protentions of occurrences expected to follow immediately—they are so-called by Husserl as a counterpart to retentions—and anticipations of temporally more distant events with which the present experience is expected to be related. (1970, p. 137)

Schutz starts by explaining that Husserl was not interested in means of anticipation that are restricted to the measured projections of scientific and empirical investigation. Rather he "has convincingly proved that idealizations and formalizations are by no means restricted to the realm of scientific thinking, but pervade also our commonsense experiences" (Schutz 1970, p. 138). The way anticipation works is always conditioned on the possibility of future counter-evidence, and what is projected and idealized must be assumed as such, without the expectation of a systematization of what these projections might portend. "In other words, these idealizations imply the assumption that the basic structure of the world as I know it, and therewith the type and style of my experiencing it and of my acting within it, will remain unchanged—unchanged, that is, until further notice" (ibid.). This means that anticipations could come to nothing, and in this respect they remain indeterminate, which is where he poses a question over how such anticipations could move on, or whether they are simply meant to remain 'stuck' within a self-inflicted state of uncertainty.

While the prospect of uncertainty does not bode disaster to one's anticipation—unless one assumes that anticipation must be absolute (which defies the whole point of projection)—Schutz moves beyond Husserl and suggests that first our anticipations must be regarded as empty, and second, "not only the range but also the structuralization of our stock of knowledge at hand changes continually" (ibid.).

Here we have not ventured far from Dewey—which is where one must clarify that the scope of this discussion is neither to fail or oppose Dewey, nor to simply parrot what he said. Instead, it is important to understand how Greene's work operates at various levels and in different approaches with Dewey's work where on one hand she concurs with the basic terrain of his argument, and on the other, moves onto new grounds that she integrates and develops within her own philosophy. Thus while acknowledging Dewey's influence, Greene articulates the gap between the here and then. When she assumes Dewey's position, she then moves on. "There is always a gap, Dewey said, between the here and now of a present interaction and past experiences. 'Because of this gap, all perception involves a risk; it is a venture into the unknown'" (Greene 1987, p. 19). This sense of risk also pertains to the experiential contexts of the dialogue that one has with the *work*—whether it is a work of art, or literature, or philosophy or anything that holds the promise of anticipation. Citing *Art as Experience*, Greene states that what Dewey meant was "that present experience only becomes fully conscious when what is given is extended by meanings drawn from what is absent, *what can be summoned up imaginatively*" (ibid., my emphasis).

Greene plays to her philosophical and literary strengths when she takes experience into the aesthetic realm, but more so those of art. Here the gap articulates how works of art allow us to experience—while we anticipate—what we could take into the present from a presumed past. This experience never translates literally into a projection, but it is a semblance, a feeling whose gaps and structures keep changing, because they are, as Schutz suggests, empty and in constant flux. In this respect, one could say that the work of art acts as the ground on which one could hold what Schutz, after Husserl, characterizes as that which remains unchanged, "unchanged, that is, until further notice." As Greene reflects on her reading of *Moby Dick* and the process of assimilating one's reading with past experiences, she shows how this reading, this aesthetic experience, becomes an anticipation of new possible experiences, which are by and large also consciously held until further notice.

> As my present reading of Moby Dick is assimilated to past readings and past experiences, it somehow makes me *rewrite my own life story, makes me see what I have never seen, recognize what I have never noticed in the themes of my own life.* If it did not defamiliarize in that fashion, if my present reading only confirmed what I have always known, the resulting experience would have been routine and mechanical. My imagination would not have gone to work; I would not be wondering, questioning, re-experiencing even

now, reaching beyond where I am. Realizing how much the novel (even the paragraph I read) have made me see, I can only deeply agree that a work of art operates imaginatively by concentrating and enlarging immediate experience, by expressing the meanings imaginatively evoked. Pondering this, I think again about making works of art accessible in such a fashion to diverse young persons of different ages and with different biographies—and about the ventures into the unknown we can encourage as we provoke them to learn to learn. (1987, pp. 19–20, my emphasis)

As the experiential becomes an avenue for anticipating—and therefore *making possible*—my rewriting of my life story, or my seeing "what I have never seen" to "recognize what I have never noticed in the themes of my own life," experience takes a quality that categorically rejects any practicist assumption that corresponds to method or result. Thus, an "education for freedom must clearly focus on the range of human intelligences, the multiple languages and symbol systems available for ordering experience and making sense of the lived world" (DOF, p. 125). The way freedom and experience become categories of learning relies on the possibilities that could be explored only if what is possible is not predicated on a certainty that conditions freedom to start with. Based, as it is, on the unknown that makes possible new forms of knowledge, education could never be premised or legitimated by a correspondence theory of truth. If it were to rely on such theories, then learning precludes itself and becomes a self-affirmed myth. Correspondence theories deny the very anticipation of a counter-argument, and ultimately turn the possibility of learning into a series of platitudes. The empirical projections that often lie at the foundation of curricula or standards present the false claim that learning must be fulfilled as if by some predetermined vocation of cognitive growth or knowledge that is explained in programmed stages, where a generalized notion of *growth* practically nullifies the dynamics of *growing*, where growing is fulfilled by being meant as an accomplished growth, "that is to say, an Ungrowth, something which is no longer growing" (Dewey 1966).

This also recalls Adorno's remark: "If a life fulfilled its vocation directly, it would miss it" (1991, p. 81). As a 'fulfilled life' cannot be directly assumed by a vocation to be directly responded to—because such a thing is impossible, as no one can predict what a future-oriented vocation has in store—in the same entry in *Minima Moralia*, Adorno also reminds us that experience in itself is a fairly uneven ground, because "knowledge comes to us through a network of prejudices, opinions, innervations, self-corrections, presuppositions and exaggerations, in short through the dense, firmly-founded but by no means uniformly transparent medium of experience" (Adorno 1991, p. 80). This is where experience must travel on the undetermined horizon of aesthetics, because only here would it make sense to say with Greene: "I have spoken my piece on the arts, if not on love, and settled nothing" (1987, p. 22).

Art as "Futuring"

It is undeniable that Dewey's work stands for the rejection of fixity. As Croce puts it, "Dewey did not only struggle against the fixed truths of transcendental religions, but also those which laziness allows to become fixed and which tend to assume changing social conditions as immutable, [while] forgetting that the only rule is that of experience, that is, thought" (Croce 1939b, p. 252; Granese 2002, pp. 73–74). Throughout her work, Greene consistently recognizes this as the mainstay of Dewey's work, especially in the realms of aesthetic experience, which she chooses to think of "as a challenge to many kinds of linear, positive thinking, as well as to the taken-for-grantedness of much of what is taught," and later adding: "there is no question that this remains important, especially for those centrally concerned about breaking with the mechanical, the sporadic, the routine, and with challenging splits between ends and means" (LL, p. 171).

However, even with the dynamic character with which Dewey casts art as a form of experience, there remains an issue that has to do with the question of art that is distinct from aesthetic experience. Greene clearly recognizes this distinction. However, she does not dwell on the separation between aesthetic experience as it is found in the artist's and viewer's subjectivity *qua* expression, and the art form as the *object*, which is what Wollheim (1980) does in his critique of Croce's and Collingwood's aesthetics. (One must add that both Croce's *Estetica* and Collingwood's *The Principles of Art* are contemporary in both tenor and time to Dewey's *Art as Experience*.) Rather, Greene's attention is elsewhere. Her interest is specific to the function of the artist and the artwork. Citing Sartre, who argues that the artist "must break the already crystallized habits which make us see in the present tense those institutions and customs which are already out of date," where "to provide a true image of our time, he must consider it from the pinnacle of the future which it is creating, since it is tomorrow which will decide today's truth," Greene remarks that while aesthetic experience cannot be set aside, art must be recognized and engaged in terms of what she sees as its "problematic nature" (LL, p. 172).

Indeed, art implies a separate realm that allows certain things to happen without predetermining what these things *are* or *could be*. This kind of emphasis on art—and more specifically on what Etienne Gilson calls "the art that makes things" (*ars artefaciens*) as other than "the things which art makes" (*ars*

artefacta) (2000, p. 13)—is somewhat removed from the context of aesthetic experience. Dealing with art in terms of what, apart from making things, identifies a way of doing that radicalizes experiential anticipation into a distinctly
free *will* that seeks indeterminacy as a condition of the future, Greene opens
up a philosophical avenue that detracts from Dewey's interests.

> There are notable differences between this point of view and Dewey's, for all the fact
> that both Sartre and Dewey have treated the problem of fixity. For one thing, Sartre
> emphasizes the unique function of the artist and the work of art, a function that can-
> not be subsumed under whatever is understood to be the aesthetic experience. For
> another, in contrast to Dewey's emphasis on the present and the reconstruction of
> the past in the light of the present, Sartre's stress is on the reconstruction of the pre-
> sent in the light of future possibility. (LL, p. 172)

In this instance, Greene's dialectical approach takes on a trajectory projected toward something specific: what she calls *futuring*. As we have already
seen (in chapter four), Greene's core interest in existentialism revolves around
the idea of possibility. She regards existentialism as a philosophy that, while
recognizing the dread that the conditionality of situations produces, never
fixes its philosophical and pedagogical projection. The existentialist constantly
looks beyond, into a future that makes possible the surpassing of the present.
Dewey remains cautious when it comes to the future. He argues that "the ideal
of using the present simply to get ready for the future contradicts itself" because, according to him, "when this happens, the actual preparation for the
future is missed and distorted" (1997, p. 40). This caution is qualified by the
conditions for education, and to many extents Dewey's experiential concepts
remain pretty much closed within their own specificities—which, in this case,
seem to move between the contingencies of learning, education and schooling.
Dewey frequently makes reference to dispositions, although this is more to do
with adaptability (1966, p. 44) and does not dare the future in the same way
that Sartre or Greene assume futurity. It seems that Dewey is less interested in
what we now identify with critical consciousness, which in contemporary
pedagogical and political discourses we rightly and wrongly assume as a polity
of action that is not simply responsive of the time and place of learning, but
further seeks to alter present contexts. The political trajectory of a critical consciousness also recognizes *context* as mostly constructed through its own negation. This is totally alien to an affirmation of conditions that allow the
organism to adapt or simply ameliorate the situation, as Dewey suggests in his
concept of democracy and education.

Greene says that futuring relates "to the critical consciousness I would like
to stimulate" (LL, p. 173). Here the possibilities that arise would not simply

come from the experiential dispositions that gain ground as adaptable possibilities of the *new*. Because art and the artist give possibility to the contexts for critical consciousness, the conditions for change cannot simply happen by organic adaptation. Far from an adaptability that builds new grounds slowly, art portends an image that holds no fixed promise, because if it does, it would leave us in the midst of what we are, with the consequence of not being able to leap beyond the situations that more often than not obfuscate our positioning within the possible world of a future. Camus represents this in typical existential fashion in his *Betwixt and Between*, a collection of essays he wrote in 1937:

> One man contemplates and another digs his grave: how can we separate them? Men and their absurdity? But here is the smile of the heavens. The light swells and soon summer will be here. But here are the eyes and the voice of those whom I must love. I hold the world through all my gestures, to men through all my gratitude and pity. I do not want to choose between these two sides of the world, and I do not like a choice to be made. People don't like you to be lucid and ironic. They say: 'That shows that you are not good.' I cannot see that this follows. (...) Besides, how can I define the thread which leads from this all-consuming love of life to this secret despair? If I listen to the voice of irony, crouching underneath things, it slowly shows itself. Winking its small, clear eye: 'Live as if ...' In spite of much searching, that is all I know. (1967, p. 47)

The sense of an entrapment between he who contemplates and he who digs the grave appears to be the dilemma of the notion of leaping out of the condition that one seems to be *in* and *for*. If Camus appears confusing, it is because that is the condition of self-reflection. The choice of reflecting from within one's own experience traps one in the experience that one is supposed to *understand* and *stand out* of. As much as one argues for learning as beginning with being situated, the situatedness of learning constitutes the possibility and impossibility of one's ability to leap out. In his *Being and Nothingness* Sartre develops a whole philosophical elaboration of the possible *leap* through the concept of *ekstasis*. Rather than ecstasy, which implies some out-of-body experience that implies a great element of pleasure and sensual absolute, Sartre uses *ekstasis* in the context of the problematic of the nothingness that comes in, as that which allows us to disentangle ourselves from the situatedness that in the first place creates the need to learn about ourselves. Without detracting into a discussion of Sartre, we could say that the questions raised by the either-or with which Dewey struggles cannot be simply grounded on experience, even where this is understood in its interactive and as a continuum. To say that this is enough, in its elaboration, to solve the dilemma of experience is to forget that the whole question prompting this discussion is that of the possibility of freedom. This is why a positivistic separation of fact from

value redounds on the very assumption we make of freedom. "Values in actuality," says Sartre, "are demands which lay claim to a foundation. But this
foundation can in no way be *being*, for every value which would base its ideal
nature on its being would thereby cease even to be a value and would realize
the heteronomy of my will. Value derives its being from its exigency and not
its exigency from its being" (1956, p. 38).

If these needs are what give value being, then the experience and the
qualities that one derives, selects or assumes are themselves exigencies that
continue to spiral within the boundaries of needs feeding values. This is where
the whole notion of entrapment comes in, and where in the artistic realm one
finds that art starts to deconstruct these demands, these exigencies, by shifting
the parameters that we normally use in our construction of value. In other
words, art's exigencies and the ensuing values become radically different from
the day-to-day values that we assume in our situatedness. Why? The reason
goes back to the quandary of freedom, as it becomes bound by the experiential
exigencies reflected in our value systems.

> My freedom is anguished at being the foundation of values while itself without foun-
> dation. It is anguished in addition because values, due to the fact that they are essen-
> tially revealed to a freedom, can not disclose themselves without being at the same
> time "put into question," for the possibility of overturning the scale of values appears
> complimentarily as *my* possibility. It is anguish before values which is the recognition
> of the ideality of values. (Sartre 1956, p. 38)

This is even more problematic when in one's daily life one assumes values as
being forms of certainty. Throwing the whole value system into question as I
realize that they emerge from my own exigencies leaves me in a quandary. But
Sartre, Murdoch explains, "is concerned with the actual varying quality of our
awareness of things and people, rather than with the question of how, in spite
of these variations, we manage to communicate determinate meanings; he is
concerned with a study of the phenomena of awareness, and not with the de-
lineation of concepts" (1980, p. 42). As freedom turns labyrinthine in moments of reflection, consciousness is key, though Murdoch qualifies Sartre's
"picturing" of consciousness in what she sees as two contrasts. The first is between "the flickering, unstable, semi-transparent moment-to-moment 'being'
of the consciousness (...) and the solid, opaque inert 'in-themselves' of things
which simply are what they are" (p. 42). The second contrast "is that between
the flickery discontinuous instability of consciousness (...) and a condition of
perfect stability toward which it aspires" (p. 43).

This is why the question of freedom as it relates to experience cannot be
read from the reflection upon the qualitative choices that we make of experi-

ences and their applicability to other future ones. The notion of a future based on the selection is problematic, and it could only be surpassed by a form of leap, an *ekstasis*. To choose between the contrasting forms of consciousness, we find ourselves facing the way into possibility through the opaqueness of the nothingness that helps us avoid the certainty of the mundane exigencies.

In her reading of Sartre's *Being and Nothingness*, Greene prompts us to think of the possible leap as a way of breaking through the horizons of the ordinary:

> Sartre has written that people can never conceive the failures and lacks of their historical situation if they are immersed in it. They can only acknowledge the harshness of their situation, he said, "on the basis of what is not." And then: "It is on the day that we can conceive of a different state of affairs that a new light falls on our troubles and our suffering and that we *decide* that these are unbearable" (...). *I want to argue that encounters with the arts can lessen the immersion we see around us today, and that they may do so by enabling people to break through the horizons of the ordinary, of the taken-for-granted, to visions of the possible, of "what is not."* (LL, p. 173, my emphasis)

Only art can take us into "what is not." And this makes even more sense if the context that we are engaging with is that of learning. The reason for engaging with art as a special context for such possibility is because art is perhaps the only human activity that allows its inner contradictions to be evident, and not only that, but it makes of these contradictions, its essence. As the embodiment of making, art's purpose is to have no purpose, as Kant has established for the aesthetic (1974, §10). Its aim, purpose, is not to found itself on itself, as some misinterpret the notion of art's autonomy. Art is not there for art's sake; otherwise it would be unable to leap out of the limitations by which we seek to define works of art. Rather, we make art so that we *make* art, meaning that art is an act that is intrinsic to our need to take the leap out of the immediate needs. In a certain way, the most unhelpful thing to say about art and experience is to make them conterminous, and say that art is experience—which is why a distancing from Dewey becomes necessary if we are to understand how because of art we have to take the risk of going even beyond art itself. Art, says Adorno, "postulates itself as absolute, purpose-free, existing in itself, whereas after all the act of making, indeed the very glorification of the artefact, is itself inseparable from the rational purposefulness from which art seeks to break away" (1991, p. 226).

Failing to see the need to break away is the same as failing to see value as begetting being from our own demands. It is to fail to see that a qualitative grounding of experience has one major flaw—its *grounding*. It is to fail to understand why Emerson in his essay on experience makes the analogy of the painting that once seen must be taken leave of: "you shall never see it again. I have had good lessons from pictures, which I have since seen without emotion or remark" (1941, vol. 1, p. 245). Yet it is also because of the quandary of experience that we seek to anticipate the possible by risking all our certainties, including what we cherish most. This causes pain, and as Emerson tells us, this pain "is the plaint of tragedy which murmurs from it in regard to persons, to friendship and love" (ibid.). To leap off the ground is to leap into a strange world. To leave behind the friendships and loves of the familiar is to embark for a world that is always presumed to be foreign, somewhat *barbaric*—the barbarians being those who speak neither the language of Empire and the Law (Latin) nor that of Philosophy (Greek). Yet, as Cavafy asks, without the *barbarian* where would we be? "Those people would have been a solution, of sorts" (Cavafy 2007, p. 55).

CHAPTER SEVEN

Risking the Aesthetic

The motive or rather the premise of my new pictures is the same as that of almost all my other pictures: it is that I can communicate nothing, that there is nothing to communicate, that painting can never be communication, that neither hard work, obstinacy, lunacy nor any trick whatever is going to make the absent message emerge of its own accord from the painting process. I don't paint for the sake of painting.
— Gerard Richter, Letter to Benjamin H. Buchloh, May 23, 1977 (2005, p. 84)

My argument (...) has to do with wide-awakeness, not with the glowing abstractions— the True, the Beautiful, and the Good.
— Maxine Greene, *Landscapes of Learning* (LL, p. 162)

The wrong assumption that art's autonomy amounts to *art for art's sake* is often supplemented with another common fallacy: that art is an aesthetic experience. Whenever the arts are reduced to aesthetic experience, art becomes a conjecture of a life that is otherwise experienced in a truthful way. To say so would mean that unless one is an artist, everyone else's aesthetic experience would be limited to the things that art makes, which implies that feelings of pleasure, pain, dread and hope remain outside the aesthetic experience unless these are conjured by artists, musicians and performers. To limit art to an aesthetic experience and to say that aesthetic experience depends on the arts is to eliminate the necessary paradox that keeps art and aesthetics closely related yet clearly distinct.

From the artist's position, one makes art for other than art, even when only in art could one achieve this leap into this *other*. Richter does not paint for painting's sake. There is no such thing. Rather he wants to picture to himself what goes on, to gain a presence by reaffirming it. No tricks. No ruses. No secrets. "I want to picture to myself what is going on now. Painting can help in this, and different methods=subjects=themes are the different attempts I make in this direction" (2005, p. 84). When asked about his intentions as an artist, he replies: "To try out what can be done with painting: how I can paint today, and above all what. Or, to put it differently: the continual attempt *to picture to myself what is going on*" (2005, p. 92, my emphasis).

Looking at art from the spectator's position, Greene argues that

> Aesthetics, after all, involves an exploration of the questions arising when people become self-reflective about their engagements with art forms. They may wonder about the pleasure and pain certain engagements arouse, about their perceptions of beauty, horror, harmony, about the peculiar queries that rise up in them because of things read or seen. The burning questions, the significant questions probably arise after privileged moments of encounter with works of art. The content of such questions may well be derived from theory. (LL, p. 175)

To read theory in contradistinction to practice is to miss how Greene's position represents a *risk*—rather than just a *liberty*—taken with the notion of aesthetics. To separate art practice from the theory that ensues from within works of art, and the aesthetic experience that emerges from the audience's relationship with works of art, is to ignore what Richter says when he insists that art is neither hermetic nor solipsistic, but a *picturing of what goes on*. Greene's position is close. I see her risking the very notion of aesthetics as traditionally assumed within and outwith education challenging us to look and read again; to wake up, remain wide-awake and be provoked; to picture to ourselves what goes on. Here one must not forget the distinction between aesthetics and art, a distinction that must be taken into consideration when reading Greene's work. At the same time one, and at the risk of paradox, recognizes the close relationship between these two autonomous forms of human activity: "Works of art," she says, "are, visibly and palpably, human achievements, renderings of the ways in which aspects of reality are impinged upon human consciousness" (LL, p. 163).

While engagements with works of art create an environment for self-reflection, art and self-reflection must remain distinct. As people wonder about the pleasure and pain that their engagements with the arts arouse, these also reflect on the audience's perception of the experiences of pleasure and pain before their engagement with art. As one brings one's experience of pleasure and pain to the artwork, the encounter that happens will inform this experience as already learned, yet as it is enhanced, if or when further feelings of pleasure or pain are recollected. Though Greene does not call this experience a recollection, one could argue that an encounter with the arts is a form of *anamnesis* where we learn by remembering and critically reassessing our situatedness. How does this happen? Is there a way of learning our aesthetic experiences?

Are these encounters entirely reliant on previous experiences or knowledge? These are questions that will ensue in such a discussion. However, when discussing such questions one must also bear in mind the distinctions that are to be had. "Even more important," Greene clarifies, "in the aesthetic experience, the mundane world or the empirical world must be bracketed out or in some sense distanced, so that the reader, listener, or beholder can *enter the aesthetic space in which the work of art exists*" (LL, p. 164, my emphasis).

The encounter with artworks, then, is not the same as the encounter becoming an artwork, or the artwork becoming an encounter. The distinction between artwork, encounter and the person encountering the art is crucial both in terms of the qualitative instances this encounter implies and more so because this encounter is neither passive nor received, but *critical* and therefore *conscious*. "What distinguishes art from another (music from poetry, say, the dance from painting) is the mode of rendering, the medium used and the qualities explored. But all art forms must be encountered as achievements that can only be brought to significant life when human beings engage with them imaginatively" (LL, p. 163).

Agonized, If Only Beautiful

Greene's philosophical conversations about aesthetics get more and more distanced from both Dewey and Kant. This distance grows the more she continues to assert the necessary distinctions between art and aesthetic experience within the dialectical reasoning that recognizes the engagement between the two. While we inhabit the aesthetic space of art forms, we also realize that our situatedness requires that we refrain from aesthetizing the situation. Situatedness implies one's being critically conscious of being in a situation—which also implies a distancing from where one 'is'. Aesthetic experiences imply such forms of critical distance, because the imagination cannot happen when the object to be imagined is present. What art does is distance us from our situation by allowing us to take the leap from the ordinary into the extraordinary, thus affirming "the work of imagination—the cognitive capacity that summons up the 'as if', the possible, the *what is not and yet might be*" (Greene 1987, p. 14, my emphasis).

The aesthetic turn on possibility in Greene's work is neither invested in a necessary completeness nor in the idea that the aesthetic is meant to achieve such completeness for the sake of reason. On the other hand, Dewey's experiential trajectory poses the aesthetic as that which "cannot be sharply marked off from intellectual experience since the latter must bear an esthetic stamp to

be itself complete" (1997, p. 40). Though Dewey parts from idealist foundations, what he sees as an idea of completeness is not that distanced from the
'perfection' stressed in Kant's definition of the aesthetic. "Aesthetic perfection," as Kant states in his *Logic*, "consists in the agreement of cognition with
the subject and is based on the special sensibility of man. In aesthetic perfection (...) no objectively and universally valid laws can be applied, in accordance
with which this kind of perfection could be judged a priori in a manner universally valid for all thinking beings as such" (1988, p. 41). This is because, according to Kant, we need to establish a rational ground that is not marred by
personal tastes, but by sound judgment, judgment meaning the successful mediation between the particularly contingent and the necessarily universal:

> The beautiful is that which apart from concepts is represented as the object of univer-
> sal satisfaction. (...) For the fact of which everyone is conscious, that the satisfaction is
> for him quite disinterested, implies in his judgement a ground of satisfaction for all
> men (...) Consequently the judgement of taste, *accompanied with the consciousness of
> separation from all interest* must claim validity for all men without this universality de-
> pending on objects. (Kant 1974, §6, my emphasis)

Kant conceived aesthetic perfection as that "which contains the ground of
a subjective-general pleasure." This is what amounts to beauty: "This perfection is *beauty*: that which pleases the senses in *intuition* and for that very reason
can be the object of a general pleasure, because the laws of intuition are general laws of sensibility" (Kant 1988, p. 41). Dewey's stance on beauty is intrin-
sically critical of the latter: "Beauty is at the furthest remove from an analytic
term, and hence from a conception that can figure in theory as a means of explanation or classification. Unfortunately, it has been hardened into a peculiar
object; emotional rapture has been subjected to what philosophy calls hyposta-
tization, and the concept of beauty as an essence of intuition has resulted." In
this context, Dewey seems to prefer that beauty is articulated through experience: "In case the term is used in theory to designate the total esthetic quality
of an experience, it is surely better to deal with the experience itself and show
whence and how the quality proceeds. In that case, beauty is the response to
that which to reflection is the consummated movement of matter integrated
through its inner relations into a single qualitative whole" (1997, pp. 134–35).

Kant's and Dewey's contexts must be read as an affirmation of a discourse
that is distanced from an equivalence between aesthetics and the arts. However, their distinction is very different from Greene's. Their distinction brack-
ets the notion of beauty in an attempt to assume a grammar that would
ultimately allow us to bridge the various other provinces of human thought
and behavior. One must also be constantly reminded that aesthetics is a prov-

ince of philosophy, which, apart from appearing only two hundred and fifty years ago as a distinct discipline, has been prompted by far more expansive questions than the arts. It follows that a discussion of aesthetic education does not simply assume a terrain for the arts and literature in schools, but more a horizon that amounts to one goal: *freedom*. Schiller never hesitates to state as much in his *On the Aesthetic Education of Mankind*: "if man is ever to solve that problem of politics in practice he will have to approach it through the problem of the aesthetic, because it is only through Beauty that man makes his way to Freedom" (1967, §II, p. 9).

Like Kant, Schiller assumes freedom to be coterminous with a direct relationship, or mediation, between the true and the good through the powers of the beautiful—thereby meaning that aesthetic education implies the larger assumption of a whole. But rather than retain the assumption of a qualitative whole, albeit fluent and ever-changing, that seems to be an imperative to the arrangement which Dewey suggests for aesthetics, in Kant and in Schiller we find that this assumption for the aesthetic is assumed negatively—that is, as a desire to bridge the contingent and necessary worlds to achieve freedom. In this context, the aesthetic education of women and men takes on the task of breaking the cycle that comes about in what appears to be a mutually negating relationship between intellectual and moral education: "Intellectual education is to bring about moral education, and yet moral education is to be the condition of intellectual education?" (Schiller 1967, §IX, p. 55). Schiller does not see this as possible within the confines of the State. It was necessary that any form of political corruption will be tackled and gotten rid of, and somehow this would still pose a problem for future education. What he sees as a way out is the realm of aesthetics, as he sees it emerging from the arts, though here art must be read as that realm that retains its autonomy, and therefore becomes a safe territory for education.

> Art, like Science, is absolved from all positive constraint and from all conventions introduced by man; both rejoice in absolute immunity from human arbitrariness. The political legislator may put their territory out of bounds; he cannot rule within it. He can proscribe the lover of truth; Truth itself will prevail. He can humiliate the artist; but Art he cannot falsify. (ibid.)

This cannot be understood without going back to the notion of freedom—which remains at the center of any argument for aesthetic education. One must also recognize that the ideals of liberty that emerged from the Enlightenment remain a common ground between Schiller, Kant and Dewey. Yet this common lineage must also be re-examined in terms of a context where the very idea of freedom itself is reviewed and extended (if not changed) in terms of what it stands for. This is where an actual difference arises between the traditions of aesthetic education as inherited from Schiller and Dewey (in their diverse meanings) and what aesthetic education means to us when freedom cannot afford to be a hypostatized view of liberty that conflates ideals with truth. One could argue that Dewey begins to do this through his pragmatist reassessment of freedom. But as we have already seen in Greene's discussion of Dewey and Camus with regards to history (chapter three), and Dewey and Sartre with regards to art and freedom (chapter six), that new socio-economic and cultural realities require a further shift from the liberal assumption of freedom—especially when the freedom inherited from the great liberal revolutions of the past three centuries has resumed a hypostatized state where ideals may be enshrined in Constitutions and Laws, but whereas in reality many are experiencing freedom at best as a great ideal to aspire to and at worst as a form of propaganda that protects the power of the Establishment.

The fact that subsequent socialist revolutions have been disastrous with respect to the notion and practices of freedom neither justifies nor sustains what Rorty suggests that after the collapse of communism, "just ordinary liberal democracy is all the ideology anybody needs" (Rorty 2006, p. 60). Even though he goes on to qualify his statement by saying that liberal democracy works in times of economic prosperity but not in times of economic crisis, Rorty seems to invest the notion of freedom with prosperity—understood within the constructs of the same economic system sustained by liberal democracy. This seems to overlook the fact that such economic systems—which have now become global—remain sustained by inequity and exploitation, not merely in the classic terms of class domination, but more so within the one-dimensional reification of the human spirit into consumption, which is where freedom directly assaulted any notion of private radicalism, while severely impairing any sense of public solidarity or political resistance. Though one would recognize and agree with some of the basic tenors of Rorty's position (as one would do so with Dewey), especially where the notion of a predetermined foundation is concerned and its necessary critique and removal, with pragmatism there is an endemic problem of political practice, which Laclau sums up as follows:

> I think the merit of Rorty is to have reinscribed the problematic of American pragmatism within the wider field of the critique of the Enlightenment and the general discussion concerning the limits of modernity. It is certainly through this reinscription that a multitude of pragmatist themes can develop their full subversive and creative potential. Conversely, the limitation of Rorty's approach—as it has been developed so far—is that he has accepted at face value the politico-theoretical articulation of themes coming from liberalism, as if that articulation could not be, in turn, deconstructed.

For here the process should move in both directions: if the pragmatist reading of the Enlightenment can act as a fruitful corrosive of the latter, the tradition of Continental thought can react, in turn, by helping to shake some of the comfortable assumption of American liberalism. (Laclau, in Mouffe 1996, p. 64)

While human freedom is real and it remains central to men's and women's struggle to have a meaningful life, an aesthetic education that rests on a liberal notion of freedom that is trapped between a desired ideal and a lost reality would fail to recognize what contemporary art puts in stark evidence—which Adorno captures in one sentence: "The darkening of the world makes the irrationality of art rational: radically darkened art" (1999, p. 19). Rather than hopelessly attempt to bring together the true and the good via the beautiful, art refuses to hypostatize freedom as a bridge between ethics and metaphysics. It is also in this context that art cannot sustain a notion of freedom that is brought forward by Schiller and the heirs of the Enlightenment. This is not because one is averse to such notions of liberty, but because, as we have seen in the previous chapter, such a notion of liberty has become supplanted by its own liberal derivatives.

Focusing on the aesthetic-artistic dimension, one must begin with modern and contemporary art's critiques of the liberal logic. Discussing Kafka's power "of a negative feel for reality," Adorno remarks that "nothing is more damaging to theoretical knowledge of modern art than its reduction to what it has in common with older periods. What is specific to it slips through the methodological net of 'nothing new under the sun'; it is reduced to the undialectical, gapless continuum of tranquil development that it in fact explodes" (1999, p. 19). The question here is not to ideologize one form of art against the past in order to denounce art or the past, but to acknowledge that the historical ideologization of art reduces both art and history into a positive dynamic of harmonious growth that says nothing of history and far less about art. The fallacy of this notion of growth also comes in the form of a reification of art where a hypostatized notion of freedom is made to accommodate a system of values assumed on the exigencies of the few. Here art becomes one of those very exigencies that claim to have continuum and diversity. Consequently an aesthetic education that becomes part of this experiential concretization of freedom—which is what pragmatism aims for—falls into the entrapment of the ideologies that insist on a continuum that knows neither gap nor contradiction. It is not uncommon to find that often the very idea of progressive learning falls within this notion of freedom, which is why one must read art and philosophy from *beneath*, to find the radical roots that urge philosophers such as Greene to call for "discriminating awareness" and risk, rather than the fallacy of positive reinforcement (VBG, p. 24).

When Greene talks about "being fully present" in "our encounters" with works of art, she never argues for an indiscriminate enjoyment or use of the arts (VBG pp. 57ff). In her notion of aesthetic education one finds a constant insistence on the discrimination between art forms, an understanding that emerges from problematizing the relationship with meaning, and ultimately the need to take risks upon entering the aesthetic spaces that the arts inhabit. "We do not only want to make possible enhanced enjoyments of the arts; we want, in addition, to cultivate the disposition to choose to engage with diverse forms, to attend and explore and take risks" (VBG, p. 23).

Taken in the realms of learning, the risks are not playful exercises that remain positively tied to predisposed objectives. Risks represent an extraordinariness that emerges from our everydayness. This raises the interest "in what might happen when our students leave their classrooms, when they go beyond what they have been taught" (ibid.). Thus the learner exits the school and enters the world where the liberal's demarcation between the private and public is challenged because the risk is not a controlled explosion conducted in the safety of the classroom, but it is *political* and it pertains to the crude reality that a hypostatized freedom keeps renouncing. Once the demarcation between a circumvented notion of private learning and that of a dynamic engagement with the world is taken away, once the school and the art museum come out onto the streets and inhabit the squares, the diversity of perspectives, the gaps and contradictions of how we learn to be—whether aesthetically, rationally or politically—come closer to possibility. "The important thing," says Greene, "is for these perspectives to be sought consciously and critically and for meanings to be perceived from the vantage points of persons awake to their freedom. The arts are of focal significance in this regard, because perceptive encounters with works of art can bring human beings in touch with themselves" (LL, p. 165).

This business of being in touch with oneself is neither irenic nor sublime. As Sartre puts it, "poetry is the loser winning. And the genuine poet chooses to lose, even if he has to die, in order to win" (1965, p. 370). Far from bridging and rejoicing in the irenic assumptions of the true and the good, aesthetics are no less a loser winning than poetry is. Aesthetics pertains to an agonized world, even when it appears to be somewhat beautiful.

Art's *Other* Facts

Those who have sought to be educated by Greene and by her work might have some qualm with the assumption of aesthetics as pertaining to an agonized world and that such an aesthetic is indirectly attributed to Greene. Even when the recognition of dread and the condition of situatedness remain salient within Greene's existentialist philosophy, one could argue that, still, Greene's position on aesthetics remains charged with the idea of the possible and therefore with an underlying passion and optimism. Undoubtedly Greene's work, as especially accentuated in her works *Variations on a Blue Guitar* and *Releasing the Imagination*, would confirm the assumption that she stands for aesthetic education as she sees it grounded in a claim for meaning and freedom—the key to which is an imagination released from the clutches of standardized education and the philosophies of certainty. This remains the mainstay of her work. "Nothing can be predetermined or predicted in the artistic-aesthetic domain," Greene states, "But anything is possible. We only have to free ourselves, to choose" (VBG, p. 23).

Yet the question would invariably arise when, as done throughout this book, Greene's work is read from her existentialist and critical base, where, albeit indirectly, she pays close attention to the problematic, where, as she puts it in her commentary on Camus, "Decency is to keep thought alive in response to the awareness of the problematic, which is the desert, which is the absurd. Rebellion on behalf of decency is rebellion in the name of created others, exemplified by art" (EET, p. 94). This decency is existential and moral, but ultimately it sees itself as aesthetic-pedagogical. The action that Greene propounds has been, from its inception, an action that becomes intentionality, as an opening to a world that enables others to do so, where "the good teacher becomes an occasion for permitting a child to decide consciously on freedom and becoming" (EET, p. 72).

It is also in this openness that Greene seeks a dialectical framework for praxis. However, as she also remarks, "it is important to stress that *praxis*, while emancipatory in its purpose, is not a purely therapeutic exploration of consciousness" (LL, p. 99). In this way she assumes a critical position that surpasses its juxtaposition on the positivist assumptions of an uncritical world, and instead it seeks to be "a thinking about and an action on reality" (LL, p. 98). Though, as she reminds us, we tend to accommodate this notion into Deweyan forms of assurances on growth, Greene argues that praxis is different in that "praxis involves a transformation of that situation [shared by persons with common interests and common needs] to the end of overcoming oppressiveness and domination. There must be collective self-reflection; there must be an interpretation of present and emergent needs; there must be a type of realization" (LL, p. 100).

The dilemma for Greene is how would educators committed to "cultural transformation and far flung social change" confront not the outright poverty and struggle in developing countries where injustice is bare and in your face but one-dimensional society's "technical systems that deprive people of spontaneity and "erode their self-determination, their autonomy" (LL, p. 100). After Freire's suggestion of *intervention* in reality, Greene qualifies the idea of *awareness*, which "is only available to those capable of reflecting on their own situationality, their own historical existence in a problematic world" (LL, p. 102). More specifically she recognizes the centrality of hermeneutics, and thereby the interpretive roles that we take in our situational awareness, "the kind of critical reflection that can be carried on by persons who are situated in the concreteness of the world, by persons equipped for interrogation, for problematization, and for hermeneutic interpretation of the culture—of the present and the past" (LL, p. 108).

Reading this back into an aesthetic-pedagogical intentionality, the possible cannot simply happen without the criticality of a praxis that cannot disregard "the awareness of the problematic, which is the desert" (EET, p. 94). It is this awareness of the problematic that those reflecting on their own situationality have to somehow see through their blinded eyes and as in T.S. Eliot's *The Waste Land*, become a latter-day Tiresias who "perceived the scene, and foretold the rest" (Eliot 1999, III, pp. 31–32).

Eliot explains in his note to *The Waste Land* that "Tiresias, although a mere spectator and not indeed a 'character', is yet the most important personage of the poem, uniting all the rest (...) the two sexes meet in Tiresias. What Tiresias sees, in fact, is the substance of the poem" (1999, p. 42). In his *Metamorphoses* Ovid recounts how Tiresias becomes a woman after he disturbs two mating snakes by trying to kill them. This predicament hits him for seven years where he lives in transgendered form until he turns back into a man by daring the same snakes that happened to be copulating in the same place. In the meantime, Jupiter dared Juno on who achieves more sexual pleasure, the man or the woman. To settle the dispute they turned to Tiresias, who, having been both man and woman, had experienced both forms of pleasure. But Tiresias' response infuriates Juno, who in turn strikes him blind. Jove intervenes and consoling Tiresias, he gives him foresight, a gift that opened Tiresias' "inner eye, like a nightscope. See: The secrets of the future—they are yours" (Hughes 1997, p. 73).

Eliot's aesthetic image of the throbbing self that agonizes in the uncertainty that abject history brings to fore in the misery of war is certainly one of the most poignant in modern English literature. Tiresias's inner eye is the immanent vision of one who has been and who remains beholden by the imaginary world that begets truth in the woes of existence. Tiresias represents an alterity whose troubled life cost him his eyesight but gained him unlimited insight. Tiresias has been man and woman, self and other, and now he can see the past, present and future. This is why Eliot regards him as the personage who understands the essence of the poem by bringing it together. The imagery of *The Waste Land* is surely agonizing, albeit beautiful—which is where its inner dialectic makes it a work of genius. Here poetry offers no sense of reassurance. There is nothing therapeutic in it. Its decency comes from its rebellion. In Eliot we find a palpable example of rebellion on behalf of decency that remains "rebellion in the name of created others" that is "exemplified by art" (EET, p. 94).

Speaking of the power of incompleteness in the arts, Greene argues that "the disinterest that once was supposed to characterize the aesthetic attitude" (which, as we have seen earlier, comes from Kant's notion of disinterested taste) cannot help us "unconceal what is there for us, what is happening on the stage" (VBG, p. 156). On this occasion, she speaks of the engagement with flamenco, as it is layered with corporeal meaning, signified by a kinesthetic narrative that often requires a knowledge that we might feel as not having.

Though flamenco is a dance whose genre carries a specificity of its own, it cannot be engaged without the song and music, which Federico Garcia Lorca tells us originates in deep song (*cante jondo*) and the Gypsy siguiriya. Although Lorca considers flamenco as relatively paler than deep song, one is struck by how he describes the Gypsy siguiriya. It "begins with a terrible scream that divides the landscape into two ideal hemispheres," he explains. "It is the scream of dead generations, a poignant elegy for lost centuries, the pathetic evocation of love under other moons and other winds" (Lorca 1998, p. 4). Not unlike Eliot's poem, this song offers no solace, nor a cathartic closure. Rather, it is the "radically darkened art" that Adorno speaks of, where what appears as irrational is ultimately the very reason for art, and more so the reason for its autonomy, which, as in the case of Eliot and other avant-garde artists, becomes susceptible to elitist reinterpretation (Adorno 1999, p. 254).

But the notion of autonomy is not reserved to the avant-garde and has nothing to do with a willed cultural hierarchy. Rather art's autonomy must be read from within the 'stomach' of an intense confrontation with the threatened rejection of the immanent nature of aesthetic experience and, in turn, its dialectical resistance to art as form. In his great essay "Juego y teoría del duende" (Play and theory of the duende) Lorca internalizes flamenco within the *duende*—the *daimon* that characterizes the aesthetic verve and vision of present and future, as it struggles with the forms that we give it. Here Lorca chooses to characterize the duende by what may seem for some an unlikely figure—the Spanish mystic Teresa of Avila:

> Think of the case of Saint Teresa, that supremely "flamenco" woman who was so filled with duende. "Flamenco" not because she caught a bull and gave it three magnificent passes (which she did!) and not because she thought herself very lovely in the presence of Fray Juan de la Miseria, nor because she slapped the papal nuncio, but because she was one of the few creatures whose duende—not angel, for the angel never attacks—transfixed her with a dart and wanted to kill her for having stolen his deepest secret, the subtle bridge that unites the five senses with the raw wound, that living cloud, the stormy ocean of timeless Love. (1998, p. 58)

You could argue that Teresa's duende is, to use Greene's and Schutz's terminology, a heightened level of consciousness, a wide-awakeness that transforms and transcends the limitations of the situated condition, by recognizing in it the deepest secrets that, like a dart in the heart, become raw wounds felt in the dread of momentous historical events that only art could preserve as its *other* facts. About the aesthetic experience shared in the spaces of the flamenco dance, Greene tells her students: "We learned here to be participant and to participate against the consciousness and memory of our own lived lives, our own lived movements reflecting on our doing so, asking ourselves what we expect from what are called works of art and what happens when we make them ours, we cannot but be transformed" (VBG, p. 156).

Questioning Benignity

So the risk remains bold in that it continues to gamble away the relative safety of what has been traditionally accorded to aesthetics by Aristotle when he discerns the notion of catharsis in his theory of tragedy: where "a serious complete action, which has magnitude, in embellished speech, with each of its elements used separately in the various parts" is fulfilled "by means of pity and terror the catharsis of such emotions" (*Poetics* 1449b25, 1987, p. 7). In Greene we find that rather than a purgation, or catharsis of the emotions, we have a valorization of the same emotions taken into the realms, which though risky—because recognized and valued—are integral to the aesthetic. It could be argued that in Greene, more than catharsis or benign expurgation, risk becomes a foremost aesthetic category. It is where the imagination is 'let loose' and the idea of an "as-if"—or even an unanswered "what-if"—become catalysts of aesthetic autonomy.

Greene tells her students how "the inexhaustibility of works of art" opens the possibility where "each novel lent each one our lives" (VBG, p. 156). Unlike the tragedy, which takes us into the structured dilemma of the personages that are struck by the inevitable destiny of their deeds, here we are lent with our own lives. It is a life that becomes other than what we have, because it reflects but allows it to continuously reconstruct itself on a terrain that is speculative, and is therefore free. "We thought about writing our narratives as well and about the connection between our shaping our own life stories and these fictional shapings that made the 'as-if' lives somehow more intelligible than our own" (ibid.).

One cannot ascertain whether Greene would agree with Augusto Boal's critique of the theory of tragedy. Boal argues that although there are other aesthetic factors involved in Aristotle's formulation of tragedy, tragedy is an art form that has the political end of making the population of the city "*uniformly* content." "How to achieve this?" asks Boal. "Through the main forms of repression: politics, bureaucracy, habits, customs—and Greek tragedy" (2000, p. 25). As Boal gives an overview of tragedy within the setting of dramatic form and what he sees in its relationship with the political sphere, he is particularly critical of the notion of catharsis as the provocation by which tragedy achieves its ultimate aim: "And why is the repressive function the fundamental aspect of the Greek tragedy and of the Aristotelian system of tragedy? Simply because, according to Aristotle, the principal aim of tragedy is to provoke catharsis" (Boal 2000, p. 25).

Somehow the aesthetic merits of the tragedy have always been regarded through the idea of a structure that simulates a situation where an error that has been committed by a significant *someone*—the tragic personage—becomes the source of evil within the whole community. In effect the idea of the one person who takes upon all the sins of the community retains a presence in the Christian tradition. But unlike the Christ figure, in the case of the tragedy we have figures like Oedipus or Hamlet who unknowingly becomes the victim of destiny or the Gods, and whose role becomes both the cause and the solution of the cataclysms that affect the polis.

The whole concept of a separation of the one from the many, the figure from the chorus, has been central to commentators of tragedy who take from this a position of emancipation, where as Raymond Williams explains the separation from the chorus is "not an isolable metaphysical stance, rooted in individual experience, but a shared and indeed collective experience, at once and indistinguishably metaphysical and social, which is yet capable of great tension and subtlety" (1967, p. 18). Yet another interpretation could view this separation as implying, by default, a forced relationship between the assumed

objectivity of the polis and the subjective error of the anti-hero who has to expurgate himself to then become the hero, and thus return to the collective
whole. Somehow, this mechanism—which, for all intents and purposes, has a
pedagogical aim in terms of the audience that attends to it by becoming active
participants—also becomes a form of repression.

The discussion of tragedy that evolves from Hegel to Lukács positions the
cathartic experience in the same dynamic between the historical individual
and the community that embodies the necessity of the social. In his *Aesthetics*
Lukács argues that "every art[-form], every artistic effect evokes man's vital essence (...) as closely attached to a critique of life (...) Now, since (...) receptive
experience needs, in its immediacy, content as its character, it reveals this
complex (problem of catharsis) as the central content of that 'world' which the
work of art evidently reveals to its recipient" (1975, vol. I, p. 521). Williams
argues that rather than Marxist, Lukács's take is post-Hegelian: "This identification of the 'world-historical individual' with the 'tragic hero' is in fact doubt-
fully Marxist. It shifts attention from the objective conflict, which is present in
the whole action, to the single and heroic personality, whom it does not seem
necessary to regard as tragic if he in fact embodies 'the will of the world-spirit'
or of history" (1967, p. 35). This seems to recoup the Hegelian argument from
a specific Marxist tradition of aesthetics that, more often than not, took a
structuralist position. Given that Marx's aesthetic position has been rather
scant—some would say *lost* (Rose 1989) or *rigidified* (Marcuse 1977, p. 3)—
'Marxist aesthetics' has never been an identifiable system, but a broad church
of diverse and often opposed interpretations. In this respect, I have argued
elsewhere that "Lukács's notion of catharsis is intended as an objective process
where the individual's empathy responds to and takes place within a social
context. Lukács follows Hegel's definition of catharsis whose historic resolution of conflicts is, *per se*, tragic not epical" (Baldacchino 1996, p. 75). This
also implies that "plurality is a category of difference because the universality is
not an annulment but an emulation of the particulars. Catharsis and social
change follow this mediation to and from totality" (ibid., p. 77).

Marcuse takes a similar view of catharsis, though he stresses that it is an
ontological event. But contrary to Lukács's position on art, Marcuse insists on
"the critical, negating function of art" (1977, p. 7), which does not resolve itself into a return to the totality, as Lukács would see art's ultimate aim with
respect to men's and women's "teleological projects" (Lukács 1974, pp. 74ff).
In this respect, while catharsis is a form of psychological reconciliation, onto-
logically speaking it is not there to mend, but to perceive and help us recognize
the irreconcilable.

> The aesthetic form, by virtue of which a work stands against established reality, is, at the same time, a form of affirmation through the reconciling catharsis. This catharsis is an ontological rather than psychological event. It is grounded in the specific qualities of the form itself, its non-repressive order, its cognitive power, its image of suffering that has come to an end. But the "solution," the reconciliation which the catharsis offers, also perceives the irreconcilable. (Marcuse 1977, p. 59)

While Lukács's Hegelian engagement with catharsis as a category of social change and Marcuse's different though related reading that seeks to accentuate art's autonomy seem to assume an emancipatory notion of catharsis, a reading of Boal's position on catharsis might start from the same premises but would reach an altogether opposite conclusion when it comes to whether catharsis is a form of emancipation or oppression. Boal asks: "Catharsis is correction: what does it correct? Catharsis is purification: what does it purify?" (Boal 2000, p. 27). Boal is after the qualification of the pity and fear that catharsis is supposed to arouse in order to expurgate the source of malady that hits the polis, which, in terms of the audience's position, represents the moral imagination. In this context, he directs his attention to the exigencies of the political, which would ultimately deem something to be moral or immoral. To that effect, Boal goes on to qualify—or better seek a qualification *for*—the political context within which tragedy functions as an art form. While Lukács assumes that the context of tragedy is in itself a critical and thus an emancipatory form by dint of it being an art form that assumes a sociohistorical role, Boal seeks a qualification that makes tragedy and theater in general distinctly *political* and thereby *coercive*. Deeming art as an action that, with science, intervenes when nature fails, Boal concludes that

> [W]hen man fails in his actions—in his virtuous behaviour as he searches for happiness through the maximum virtue, which is obedience to the laws—the art of tragedy intervenes to correct that failure. How? Through purification, catharsis, through purgation of the extraneous, undesirable element which prevents the character from achieving his ends. This extraneous element is contrary to the law; it is a social fault, a political deficiency. (2000, p. 32)

Boal concludes his critique of catharsis with a caution: "We have to be better friends of reality: all of man's activities—including, of course, all the arts, especially theatre—are political. And theatre is the most perfect artistic form of coercion" (p. 39). Whether one takes Boal's position in its entirety or whether one assumes that a critical repositioning of the arts carries the risk of being a form of coercion, Boal's statement remains a cautionary tale when it comes to the whole argument of the aesthetic-pedagogic dynamic of the arts.

While the jury is still out as to whether Boal misrepresents Aristotle, especially when it comes to the pedagogical sphere (Winston 1998, pp. 61ff), the question that he raises touches upon the qualitative grounding of the aesthetic experiences that we often assume as being integral to education. Beyond the merits of Boal's Aristotelian exegesis, one cannot ignore the fact that the notion of the benign, or rather the positive assumptions made on categories such as learning, experience and more so the imagination, cannot be taken for granted. Greene talks about this aspect of aesthetic education extensively in her discussion of what she identifies as two issues about the imagination: one that triggers desperation and the other, bemused wonder. The first "has to do with the undeniable fact that imagination is not always benevolent." Greene recalls the Columbine killers "with their black lipstick and black raincoats, or the so-called skinheads drawn to the symbols of fascism" to whom one "cannot deny the fact that they too have been and are in search of some alternative reality" (VBG, p. 123). Citing Arendt, who states that the imagination cannot include Auschwitz or Belsen, Greene adds that conversely violent and horror films are appealing to some youth "offering them experiences they might consider much like aesthetic experiences." In view of this, she argues, "we should think more often about the kinds of spaces we can open for dialogue, for shared reflection" (VBG, p. 124). The other side of the imagination that strikes Greene with wonder is the realms of fantasy, which trigger in the young and old alike a "testimony for imaginative adventures." Greene cites Harry Potter and *Star Wars*. She wonders how or what these new vibrant forms of representation stand for in terms of education, in terms of how these new forms of fantasy and myth could affect issues of culture, race and gender.

> How do we answer, in any case, the accumulating questions about what ought to be categorized as art? Who has a right to impose, to publicize, to affirm that certain works change lives for the better, and others simply do not? How do we in aesthetic education deal with what is called 'hype'? What about works of other cultures, in other languages? How can we tell, here or abroad, what the relation is between adulthood and childhood—no longer empty, no longer innocent, no longer immune to pain and the dark? (VBG, p. 124)

It seems to me that the question of the benign rests on how far forms of art such as theater and film must be contextualized in terms of *willful reception* and *conscious act*. While the assumption of tragedy implies that the audience is approached by the art form, in its mechanisms that simulate a reality which often manipulates truth, the assumption of catharsis must be assumed as triggering a feeling that seems to have such potency that the participant becomes more passive rather than active. Yet this reception cannot be passive if *received willfully*. The question here is not so much focused on the cathartic mechanism, but more on the values—the *conscious acts*—that the assumed art form makes possible by addressing and in some cases *rectifying* a moral imaginary. This is where the notion of *choice*—a central argument in Greene's work—comes in full play. But does choice—that is, *personal* choice—necessarily guarantee a way out of the predicament of the imagination? Doesn't the skinhead have a choice when he assumes the role and rhetoric of hatred as his aesthetized forms of doing politics? Doesn't the risk of the aesthetic itself imply this possibility, when it assumes the role of a horizon where we are all encouraged to enter the unknown climes of aesthetic spaces?

Again the question falls back on the choice of freedom, and what this implies in the realm of the political. If the matter of choice is reduced to the measured facts that forget the alterity of art's *other* facts, then there is no way we could begin to deal with the questions of aesthetic education and choice. The Educationist's obsession with facts is a major obstacle when it comes to dealing with what is essentially a matter of how profound we must get when we are dealing with the notion of meaning without becoming a moralizing machine that oppresses everyone into the will of a majority. Greene recounts how in her experience she "was often accused of speaking in what was called 'soft' or even 'non-cognitive' language. I was often silenced by some saying, 'I don't know what you are talking about'. Often, too often, I repressed my dream—complying with those voices telling me to be sensible, to stay with the facts, to stop diverting myself with the arts" (VBG, p. 127).

Yet the matter of art and aesthetics is not about fact, but about the immanence that enables us to choose and recognize facts. Those who require facts from art and aesthetics are not going to get anything, because what aesthetics is all about is the recognition of an interiority that then gives definition to the factual world, which in itself remains meaningless. It is in this context of immanence that we could then start to assume what freedom means to the choices that we have to make. It is also because of this recognition that choices become a matter of responsibility and not exigencies that emerge from utility. What is necessary often comes in contingent forms. What we expect to be subliminal often appears to be a modest quotidian act. In this modesty one would eventually find that there is no hierarchy of need, but rather there is a horizon of values that we have to span and understand in order to be able to make decisions without becoming moralizers. It is this urge for meaning that Greene pits against the immediacy of meaninglessness.

This is where, as Nietzsche's Zarathustra tells us, from being the camel laden in the desert, the spirit becomes a lion that "wants to capture freedom and be lord in its own desert" where to the dragon of the Gods yelling 'Thou shalt!' the lion responds with 'I will'. Yet the metamorphosis is not complete unless the spirit turns from lion to child.

> But tell me, my brothers, what can the child do that even the lion cannot? Why must the preying lion still become a child?
> The child is innocence and forgetfulness, a new beginning, a sport, a self-propelling wheel, a first motion, a sacred Yes. (Nietzsche 1980, p. 55)

Pedagogical Imaginaries

[P]leasurableness does not mean the arts are to be used simply to "balance" what is thought of as the cognitively rigorous, the analytical, the rational and the serious. Nor should the arts be used as motivation. For one thing, participatory encounters with particular works may demand as much cognitive rigor and analysis as they do affective response. For another, *works of art cannot be counted upon to have beneficent, consoling, or illuminating effects*. Soul-chilling instances are multiple: we can recall *Oedipus Rex*, the Japanese film *Ran*, Toni Morrison's *Beloved*, the play *Marat/Sade*. Images of horror and distortion still emerge if we summon up memories of paintings by Zurbarán, Velázquez, Goya, Géricault, Picasso. From the instances of heartless violence in *The Iliad* to the murder of the little princes in *Richard III* to the transgressive energies of Blake's challenge to Locke and Newton (indeed to anything measurable and "moral") to modern novelist Kathy Acker's sleek obscenities, the arts *have not centered on depicting solely what is right and good*. Awakening imagination, they have brought our bodies into play, excited our feelings, opened what have been called the doors of perception. Yes, there have been lovely moments marked by blooming daffodils or children's laughter or the shimmer of water, and yes, there has been and will be a sense of wonder at moments of consummation, moments when the last chord finds a resolution. *But the role of the imagination is not to resolve, not to point the way, not to improve. It is to awaken, to disclose the ordinarily unseen, unheard, and unexpected.*

—Maxine Greene, *Releasing the Imagination* (RI, pp. 27–28, my emphases)

If there is an expectation that is central to our aesthetic and pedagogical experiences, this must boil down to the imagination. It is difficult to understand the arts and the notion of aesthetic experience without thinking about the role that the imagination plays in these *special* worlds. However, the imagination is also a bewildering human attribute, bewildering not because it scares people off, but because as with experience, the imagination is often misrepresented for a guaranteed, positive and agreeable human ability in which we have nothing to lose by investing it with a great deal of *hope* irrespective of what or whom it empowers.

Hope in its immediacy is not enough. Like experience and the imagination, hope needs to be mediated by occasions that we seek and fulfill in order to move from an impulse of hopeful existence to a meaningful context of a living that is possible to imagine and strive to realize. In *The Principle of Hope*,

Ernst Bloch argues that hope "requires people who throw themselves actively into what is becoming, to which they themselves belong. It will not tolerate a dog's life which feels itself only passively thrown into What Is, which is not seen through, even wretchedly recognized" (1986, p. 3). Like an immediate experience, an unmediated impulse of hope becomes self-defeating because even when the idea of a future fills us with the need to leap into the unknown, we remain prone to get dragged back into the certainties that trap the faculty of the imagination—and with it that of hope and possibility—into a self-affirming spiral, into a solipsism of false reassurances and outright ignorance. Greene is unequivocal about the role of the imagination: the imagination is not there to heal or resolve, but to awaken and to take us where we have never been, where we can somehow anticipate and therefore assume a fuller role in what others may have imagined, and where what has been imagined may not be necessarily to the benefit of the many, but is hegemonized by the capricious few, which is where we have to learn the imagination just as we learn how to make sense of experience and make it critically expedient for the benefit of the many. This is where the imagination is not just a matter of individual cognition but an activity of the mind that empowers us to engage with its larger context—that of the *imaginary*.

Our Imaginations ... Whose Imaginary?

In *The Human Condition*, Arendt compares the launching of Sputnik into space as the historical break where humans are no longer tied to Earth. Yet her notion of this unprecedented leap into new scientific and philosophical imaginaries where humanity could see beyond its own earthly condition is tempered by another scenario of *other* unprecedented possibilities. "This future man, whom the scientists tell us they will produce in no more than a hundred years, seems to be possessed by a rebellion against human existence as it has been given, a free gift from nowhere (secularly speaking), which he wishes to exchange, as it were, for something he has made himself," she says. "There is no reason to doubt our abilities to accomplish such an exchange, just as there is no reason to doubt our present ability to destroy all organic life on earth" (1998, pp. 2–3). Arendt adds that the answer to the questions that this ominous scenario raises cannot be scientific, but political, and it cannot be left to professional scientists or politicians to decide. A future that seems to be marked by a looming environmental catastrophe and an advanced way of life that remains regressive becomes a matter of the polity, where we must start to understand new situations that cannot be simply explained by empirical facts.

As earth-bound creatures, says Arendt, we are acting "as if we were dwellers of the universe" (ibid.).

Bearing in mind that this was written fifty years ago, one can discern the strength of Arendt's foresight when she states that we "will forever be unable to understand, that is, to think and speak about the things which nevertheless we are able to do" (ibid.) One could paraphrase this as a human inability to measure up to the consequences of the artificial intelligences that humans have created. As we have seen in previous chapters, Arendt takes this from the vantage point of what we are. This vantage point is not unlike Gerard Richter's view of the artist's intention where he paints to know what goes on. To know what goes on is to identify and take newer philosophical positions that have to measure up to these new situations. With respect to the fact that fifty years on the situation of a gap between what we do and what we understand remains (some would say it has become wider), the assumption of a political philosophy that seeks to assess and critically assume this gap within the sphere of the many remains essentially unchanged, both as a constant challenge and in terms of its tenor.

So could we argue that though we might discern on the horizon ever-new philosophical *needs* that are continuously prompted by new political and scientific imaginaries, these *needs* could only be discerned and tackled from the vantage points that we have—that is from within the limits of which we must always remain conscious—and thus *conscientized*? Do these philosophical needs include ever-changing aesthetic needs? And what do we mean when we assume that just as we have economic and political needs, we also have philosophical and aesthetic needs that we must address from our vantage points? Aren't these needs already part of the moral sphere that conditions such vantage points? How could our vantage points consist of what one *does* and what one *is*, without widening the gap between *what we do* and *what we could understand*? More so, how could we engage with such needs when in effect they do not come to us as a hierarchy, but as a horizon that keeps expanding because the communities that we belong to are equally expansive and plural?

One approach to the challenge of new situations that trigger ever-new imaginaries is to begin with "an awareness of our own awareness," which Greene insists should be cultivated. This implies a transactional procedure that can only come from the vantage point of what one does, where in a series of moments, "we grasp what is given, in which we thrust into the world." Greene qualifies this saying that "to be aware of such moments is to be sensitive to the ways in which we originate them; it is to be conscious of the fact that we are the motivators of what is happening, that we are subjects responsible to and for ourselves" (LL, pp. 199–200).

The inherent tension between the qualitative grounding of hope and imagination and the choices that we have to make must be read from the fact that by a 'vantage point' one does not mean an unquestioned situation, but to the contrary a situation that must be continuously and critically questioned. Why is the imagination necessary? What is its *praxial* nature? How does one take ownership and engage with its critical qualities? How does one discriminate between the adverse and the benign, when more often than not, the imagination is *received* as a benign assumption of the good and the beautiful?

It could be argued that whereas we individually engage with the imagination as a faculty of consciousness by which we anticipate experience in view of other experiences, we have to cross the juncture between the imagination per se and the imaginary as a wider representation of a plurality of imaginations. In English the word *imaginary* (as a noun, not as an adjective) often loses some of its meaning implied in the romance rendition of *l'imaginaire* in French, *l'immaginario* in Italian or *el imaginario* in Spanish. While *the imaginary* broadly implies either something that exists only within the imagination, or the horizon of the imagination as a collective human activity, the *imaginary* also involves the noetic—the intellectual-cognitive—aggregate that comes from the *images* that we present and anticipate in our teleological projections and aesthetic anticipations. In his book *L'Imaginaire* Sartre describes the image "neither as illustration or support for thought" nor as something different from thought (1948, p. 137).

> An imaginative consciousness includes a knowledge, intentions, and can include words and judgments. And by this we do not mean that a judgment can be made *on* the image, but that, in the very structure of the image judgments can enter in a special form, namely, in the imaginative form. (ibid.)

Sartre gives a mundane example where one is confronted with a staircase that one does not particularly know. However upon discerning the image of the object, one realizes that now the staircase has a carpet laid on it. In this way one adjusts his original 'judgment' of the situation and the object before him by "conferring on the object of [one's] image the quality 'recovery of a cover'" (ibid.). Sartre argues that this decision gives rise to a particular sort of judgment he calls "imaginative assertion" (p. 138).

> What we ordinarily designate as *thinking* is a consciousness which affirms this or that quality of its object but without realizing the qualities on the object. The *image*, on the contrary, is a consciousness that aims to produce its object: it is therefore constituted by a certain way of judging and feeling of which we do not become conscious as such

but which we apprehend on the intentional object as this or that of its qualities. In a word: the function of the image is *symbolic*. (p. 138)

While this does not begin to comprehensively explain Sartre's theory of the imagination, one can appreciate how the relationship between consciousness, thought and image remains underpinned by a qualitative grounding that is not dissimilar to what Greene constantly alludes when she refers to experience and the imagination.

Sartre opens *L'Imaginaire* with the qualifier that what the book aims to describe is "the great function of consciousness to create a world of unrealities, or 'imagination' and its noetic correlative, the imaginary" (1948, p. 1). The notion of consciousness is, in Sartre's term, explained within concrete structures such as the consciousness of the image. To that effect the imaginary is grounded in a consciousness that is qualified by other than a passive notion of 'being conscious'. The imagination emerges as the consciousness of the image, postulated as "a consciousness that aims to produce its object" (p. 138). This neither happens by chance nor is it caused by a series of eventualities. "The imaginative attitude," says Sartre, "represents a special function of mental life. If such an image appears, in place of simple words, of verbal thoughts or pure thoughts, it is never the result of a chance association: *it is always an inclusive and* sui-generis *attitude which has a meaning and a use*" (p. 174, my emphasis).

Greene underlines the imaginative attitude with the concreteness of the image that we encounter and try to make sense of. The image is not just a spatial situation like a staircase, or a painting that we might be able to understand by virtue of its abstract nature. The *image* understood in the context which Sartre gives us could well be a political situation, a situation of inequality that emerges from the absence—or rejection—of someone else's imaginative attitude. "Is it not imagination," asks Greene, "that allows us to encounter the other as disclosed through the image of that other's face? And is this face not only that of the hurricane survivor or the Somalian child or the homeless woman sitting on the corner but also of the silent or the fidgety or the hopeless child in the classroom, be that child girl or boy?" (RI, p. 37).

The political image, then, becomes other than a spatial situation like a staircase that seems right but needs to be corrected once we realize that it has a carpet laid on it. As we are confronted by the image of the *polis* and its *agôn* of learning, we might just realize that based on the assumptions that we usually take before we are confronted by the political image of learning we have to lay further meanings *qua* images, or, to use Sartre's phrase, we have to confer the quality that is identified with a *recovery of a further meaning*. As the child that appears out of place becomes part of the image that I expect from the *agôn* of learning, I realize that the child's disinterest in what is going on in class is a recovery of *my* pedagogical imaginary, and not the child's. Here the pedagogical imaginary of exclusion, which the standards-based system of schooling assumes as a 'failing student', is turned on itself. The political quality of the child's exclusion widens and teaches *me* as *the teacher* that something is amiss in the education of this child. Something is amiss because the child's own imaginative attitude is switched on a world that he or she is seeing differently from what I was expecting him to see as a school pupil. The child may see the poverty, or the abuse, which actually cause his apparent 'loss of interest' in learning. Yet as a teacher I must be able to see, or at least imagine, what the child sees. But I fail, because my pedagogical imaginary does not match the child's expectations. This might also be the case of gender, race or culture, or any other situation that causes imaginaries different from the one that the school or the teachers expect. This also amounts to a direct challenge to teachers in that they have to open their own imaginaries to myriad other imaginaries with which their students present themselves to the world. This is the context within which I read Greene's comment: "Imagination is as important in the lives of teachers as it is in the lives of their students, in part because teachers incapable of thinking imaginatively or of releasing students to encounter works of literature and other forms of art are probably also unable to communicate to the young what the use of imagination signifies" (RI, p. 36).

The question remains: *whose* imaginary is justifiable enough to enable teachers, artists, philosophers, politicians, mentors, carers, parents and the like to release their or their mentees' imagination? If the imaginary that prevails in schools assumes that only those who 'succeed' are worth reinforcing and enhancing, then the imagination becomes a means of exclusion. If on the other hand the notion of the imagination is read, as Sartre suggests, as pertaining to the image in the sense of an "imaginative consciousness," then it would imply that the imagination is qualitatively assumed and therefore potentially resistant to the prevalent imaginaries that more often than not remain at the root of the manufactured consent that the School presents.

As the matter moves from the psychology of the imagination to its correlative imaginaries, it becomes more a matter of the polity and how it is confronted by the value of subjectivity. "Subjectivity strove to break out of its inwardness into the material and intellectual culture," Marcuse remarks in *The Aesthetic Dimension*. "And today, in the totalitarian period, it has become a political value as a counterforce against aggressive and exploitative socialization" (1977, p. 5).

Presenced Truth

Greene's work tends to keep a distance from psychological analyses of the imagination. Her argument is closer to Marcuse's and to what Sartre has to say about art, but not so much to Sartre's psychology of the imagination or Marcuse's psychoanalytical references to *eros* and *thánatos*. What remains important to her notion of a released imagination takes on the qualitative grounding that turns on to consciousness as the location of criticality, as read from an aesthetic-pedagogical context. Here criticality is a pedagogic *turn* that cannot be isolated within specific individuals, though at the same time it is a "liberating subjectivity" that, Marcuse tells us, "constitutes itself in the inner history of individuals—their own history, which is not identical with their social existence" (1977, p. 5). This relationship between the self as subject, and the social sphere as the dialectical terrain of the imagination, lies at the core of how Greene's notion of the social imagination operates. Greene does not front-load the social as the only signifier of subjectivity and the imagination. Just as the imagination is never subsumed in the social, she is careful to keep the imagination away from those solipsistic realms that open subjectivity and imagination to one-dimensional imaginaries. This balancing act is achieved through her extensive reference to the community. Community is achievable, Greene argues, and we cannot afford to see the fortunate alienated "from those who remain tragically in need." Then she adds: "Again, it may be the recovery of the imagination that lessens the social paralysis we see around us and restore the sense that something can be done in the name of what is decent and humane" (RI, p. 35).

Communities, therefore, must be assumed intersubjectively. Like freedom, community "has to be achieved by persons offered the space in which to discover what they recognize together and appreciate in common; they have to find ways to make intersubjective sense" (RI, p. 39). In this respect the role of the individual as a lived subject cannot be relegated to a socialized reduction of individuality. The social tenor of community lies in the intersubjective possibilities that are achieved by an interaction between awakened imaginations. Marcuse argues that "the rejection of the individual as a 'bourgeois' concept recalls and presages fascist undertakings" (1977, p. 38). Read from the very need to shift away from the deterministic positivism that dominated the Left's ideological traditions, Marcuse remains unequivocally critical of any concept that is pitted against the individual: "Solidarity and community do not mean absorption of the individual. They rather originate in autonomous individual decision; they unite freely associated individuals, not masses" (1977, p. 39).

Likewise Greene remarks: "Community is not a question of which social contracts are the most reasonable for individuals to enter. It is a question of what might contribute to the pursuit of shared goods: what ways of being together, of attaining mutuality, of reaching toward some common world" (RI, p. 39).

The fact that communities are ever-expanding and becoming a larger presence within the realization of present and future possibilities in the arts, education and across many sectors also means that the "imaginative awareness that enables those involved to imagine alternative possibilities" (RI, p. 38) is always in a state of becoming, a state that cannot be lost because otherwise the community as a coming together of plural subjects disappears into a mass. As communities expand, the definitions of civil society, the law and ensuing ethical-moral constructs also take on new meanings, and have a direct effect on what we as individuals do in the realms of learning, the arts and everyday life. By 'law' I do not simply mean the law of the land—although this cannot be discounted—but the general assumptions that civil society has in terms of its expectations of the rules by which we engage with each other. Although the law does not involve aspects of life such as manners and the way we live our normal lives—except for norms of public behavior—as members of civil society we are continuously aware of the ever-changing lifestyles that directly affect us. There is a lot to be said about this in pedagogical terms, where the education of women and men is often lacking in the unseen, tacit forms of civic behavior, and where, instead, priority is given to the consumption of syllabi and standard examinations. It is also in these tacit norms and expectations—often concretized in the arts as possibilities to try out the unconventional and the unacceptable—that the idea of a social imagination gains center stage. To understand the social aspect of the imagination is to take on, aesthetically and ethically, those *yet-to-be-accepted* assumptions that we only harbor in the intimacy of our own individual self in the form of experiential anticipations or teleological projects.

As I read Greene through her literary and philosophical interlocutors—like Camus, Morrison, Arendt and Woolf—the notion of a social imagination clearly emerges as an anticipation that appears to be factually impossible. These anticipations constitute an investment in hope where the times are dark. They amount to a need to find a home where the teacher, like the artist and philosopher, will always be a stranger. They are the anticipations of the emarginated that challenge the status quo. This is where the matter of thinking, imagining and anticipating is not just a narrative or a life's story. The anticipation happens beyond the experiential limitations of the here and now. Reflection is not an exercise of thinking what happened to me, but it is concerned with what I want to be doing in the future. The limitation of stories is evidently something that remains always on Virginia Woolf's mind—the mind of that great author whose life is interlaced with her act of writing by which she is "doing what is far more necessary than anything else" but which she also regards as the artist's "most obscure elements in life that has never been much discussed. It is something left out in almost all biographies and autobiographies" (Woolf 1985, p. 73). This is why to Woolf stories of life are not enough.

> Up to this point in telling the story of Orlando's life, documents, both private and historical, have made it possible to fulfil the first duty of a biographer, which is to plod, without looking to right or left, in the indelible footprints of truth; unenticed by flowers; regardless of shade; on and on methodically till we fall plump into the grave and write *finis* on the tombstone above our heads. (Woolf 1994b, p. 51)

Dogged stories, whose assumptions are a linear recounting of *what happened*, fail to anticipate the truth of one's life, especially when this someone is a figure of constant futuring, like Woolf's Orlando. "One's life is not confined to one's body and what one says and does," says Woolf, "one is living all the time in relation to certain background rods or conceptions. Mine is that there is a pattern hid behind the cotton wool. And this conception affects me every day" (1985, p. 73). Greene argues that without the imagination Woolf would have succumbed to the "blows" that challenged her in trying to make sense and meaning of life (RI, p. 27). It follows that episodes of futurity have to emerge from this wrestling with the hermetic blows of the present. When Woolf comes to write about a crucial episode in Orlando's life, she invites the readers to act as interpreters, to assume a hermeneutic stance—almost to play a game of reasoning and sleuthing: "it is dark, mysterious, and undocumented; so that there is no explaining it. Volumes might be written in interpretation of it; whole religious systems founded upon the signification of it. Our simple duty is to state the facts as far as they are known, and so let the reader make of them what he may" (Woolf 1994b, p. 51).

In the intimacy of the darkest self, then, the possible futuring of our anticipated projects could happen on the condition of what the self may not even know what it means to live a life beyond mere fact and daily happenings. Yet to take hold of meaning and to interpret what this tacit assumption of a lived body means is also to gain from deep subjectivity a way of understanding and anticipating a reality that is recognized by all as being broadly a matter of interpretation. As we exchange our interpretations, we also engage in a future that is bound to happen in the expanded communities that are open to the articulations of further interpretative grounds.

Does this mean that communities are just a matter of imaginative futuring? Does it mean that communities emerge simply from interpretations of dark selves? Definitely not. The community is an act of *presencing*, which one should read as an actualization of the ever-expanding imagination that occurs as we engage with the realities of our being situated. To be present means to be yourself. One's reality cannot happen if the dark unknowable depth of subjectivity remains entangled in itself. Presencing happens when in the first place we are present to ourselves, as this then becomes a presencing to others:

> We are, therefore, now left entirely alone in the room with the sleeping Orlando and the trumpeters. The trumpeters, ranging themselves side by side in order, blow one terrific blast:—
>
> 'THE TRUTH!'
> at which Orlando woke.
>
> He stretched himself. He rose. He stood upright in complete nakedness before us, and while the trumpets pealed Truth! Truth! Truth! we have no choice left but confess—he was a woman. (Woolf 1994b, pp. 105-6)

The imagination loses most of its potential and meaning unless individuals come together as autonomous subjects in solidarity. The solidarity of the trumpet's "Truth!" is the image-symbol of one's presence to oneself, just as he or she is present to a physical situation that is hardly *known*. But indeed the knowledge is there, because the self is lived, and like Orlando there comes a moment when one realizes that there is a wide-awake reality beyond somnolent existence. This is where as lived bodies we realize what we know about ourselves. This is also the moment of real learning, the consummation of the Delphic commandment: *gnothí seauthón, know thyself!* That the imagination is a leap into the future does not mean a permanent state of flux. Rather, the imagination is the presencing act of an intersubjective intentionality, where the subject presents him- or herself by his or her own *presence with others*. This also gives us the ability to *present* ourselves continuously to new situations and images, because when we are present we cannot be present alone, but our presence must be signified and recognized by those who are present to us.

When in her *Existential Encounters for Teachers* Greene cites the work of Martin Buber, she highlights his argument that "the individual is a fact of existence in so far as he steps into a living relation with others" (EET, p. 140). Buber also argues that neither the individual nor the aggregate (community) could be considered separately and in themselves, as that would amount to "a mighty abstraction." Reading Buber back into the classroom situation, Greene shows how "an emphasis upon the discoveries which take place through and by means of dialogue and shared endeavor" would avoid isolation so that "the existing person be conceived *as prior to his group*" (EET, pp. 141, my emphasis). The existing person can only come *prior* in terms of being *before* his group when this happens within an intersubjective assumption of *a* group; which is why Buber's position is not contrary to Marcuse's notion of the autonomous individual, but reinforces it by what Buber qualifies as the fundamental fact of human existence as being man with man, or better put, *human with human.*

"Only a *subject* ... can choose"

A pedagogical imaginary cannot happen without the consciousness that emerges from the lived body, as in the moment of Orlando's Truth: "he was a woman." Orlando knows she is a woman not because she appears naked in the presence of truth, but because she re-presents herself as the "female subject" as the truth of *her* self. Luce Irigaray argues: "(re-) discovering herself, for a woman, could only signify the possibility of sacrificing no one of her pleasures to another, of identifying herself with none of them in particular, of never being simply one. A sort of expanding universe to which no limits could be fixed and which would not be incoherence nonetheless" (1985 p. 30).

Presencing is the moment of truth, as it does not act as within a neutral relationship. Presencing is gendered, classed, sexed, cultural and even racial. It could be as evil as it turns to be benign, and it is sharply attendant to the relational state of the community, mainly through the orders of 'meaning' that we assume in coming to terms with our presencing through the implements of word and image, that imply the power of speaking and representing. Is there anything between the two? Can we discern a situation that lies in other than the relational grounds of language? Does presencing imply more than the *imaging* by which we realize the potential to signify meaning in figure? Greene argues that "all of us know that interstices can be found in the structures; communities can be created; desires can be released" (RI, p. 56). But here Greene takes these interstices into what communities could achieve. In other words, how far would communities reach beyond the limitations of images and languages. These communities are not socialized forms of togetherness, as in forced and artificial assumptions made in schooled communities, but in real-existent situated human beings who find themselves needing to enter the interstices of the given conventions of languages and symbols, because to make a community is not to limit oneself to the polities of word and image.

It is here that a third *place* or even a third *genre—and gender—*is 'evidenced' by how other meanings come into play. If we can call this a space, place or indeed a gap, it is definitely an interstitial one. It has left behind the assumptions of language and image, where the imagination has to operate with the unusual and the unfamiliar, and where we as subjects seek to move beyond the duality of image and word. This space has been identified with what Plato calls the *khôra* that is a 'space' between a reality that is intelligible—attributed to the word as logos—and the other reality that is sensible—discerned through forms of representations, the realm of the mythos (Plato [1989] *Timaeus* 52b1-3). Derrida argues that "a discourse on the *khôra*, as it presents itself [to us], does not proceed from the natural or legitimate *logos*, but rather from a hybrid, bastardized form of reasoning (*logismô nothô*)" (1993, p. 17). This is a third space that is corrupted in the parameters of the word and the image, because it looks formless, and it seems impossible to identify; in other words, it needs more than the symbolic imaging that we attribute to the imagination.

Julia Kristeva (1984) sees the *khôra* as pertaining to the place before the beginning, to the sensibility that happened before we acquire language, even before we are born. One could say, perhaps beyond Kristeva's intended interpretation, that the idea of this gap, this undefined *khôra*, remains a potent memorial assumption that we seem to have forgotten or indeed suppressed. Yet one wonders how this genre, this reality that is neither intelligible nor sensible, could remain "beyond categories, above all those categorial oppositions, which in the first place have allowed it to be approached and to be uttered" (Derrida 1993, p. 17). For the sake of our discussion one wonders how this gap—in its semiotic, political or indeed pedagogical implications—actualizes itself in the unknown possibilities to which we leap by means of our imagination. Elsewhere I have argued that just like the discourse of the *khôra*, pedagogy surpasses its immediate teleological possibilities by remaining *paradoxical*: "pedagogy is the discourse of dispute and not simply the haven of *paedeia*. While the latter sustains the betterment of the child, the former implies a ground that is not dissimilar to the *khôra*—a ground that carries the dilemmas of that 'something other' than word or image" (Baldacchino 2007, p. 16). If we read this back into the imagination, we can see how the idea of a place, a *something other* that is neither word nor image, brings about an interpretation of the world from another dimension, which would have to begin with the recognition from one's being *present* in *this* world.

Presencing is political because one is present to a polity as an individual who assumes—and is in turn *assumed*—according to the plurality of the otherness that remains integral to the self. This also clears any doubt as to whether situatedness is some sort of passive assumption of being. To *be there* means to assume one's self with whatever one *is*, at the risk of being rejected, and with the mindset of presenting one's imagination to prevalent imaginaries. Thus the female subject also takes on the larger picture and is not an assertion of 'equality' understood as an equivalence of identities, or even identical imaginaries. "Gender difference is not, as customarily believed, limited to biology," states Irigaray (2000, *np*). "Neither is it, as often believed to be, constructed of social stereotypes. It is primarily a difference of relational identity. Verified (...) by an analysis of language."

The relational essence of language as it names and defines myriad communities is an ever-shifting ground on which we speak and talk, shout and whisper, denounce and announce, swear and pray, utter truths and falsehoods. On these linguistic and symbolic grounds new arrangements of meaning provide us with new locations for our own presencing to each other. Reading *Orlando* after Irigaray's *This Sex Which Is Not One* helps us understand what the qualitative grounding of the imagination means, as it presents and at the same time becomes a presence for the truth of the subject, where "she" represents other than herself by means of "her," and distinguished from "his," *lived* self.

> "She" is indefinitely other in herself. This is doubtless why she is said to be whimsical, incomprehensible, agitated, capricious (...) not to mention her language, in which "she" sets off in all directions leaving "him" unable to discern the coherence of any meaning.

> Hers are contradictory words, somewhat mad from the standpoint of reason, inaudible for whoever listens to them with ready-made grids, with a fully elaborated code in hand. For in what she says, too, at least when she dares, woman is constantly touching herself. She steps ever so slightly aside from herself with a murmur, an exclamation, a whisper, a sentence left unfinished. (Irigaray 1985, p. 28)

In this relational situatedness, tempered by the leap into a possibility that has always been suppressed and "sutured" (Irigaray 1985, p. 26), "her" imagination ultimately predicates the core moment of learning to be "she." This is what we learn from the moment of being authentic to one's self, authentic, that is, against all odds, against all forms of invisibility, against imposed indentitarian imaginaries. The female subject is just one of many subjects. In identifying the female subject, Irigaray opens the notion of difference as a realm of the subject, where the subject becomes plural. This is potent because the female subject is the most plural of subjects—in terms of emotions, location of desire and the possibilities that a gendered discourse presents. This also means that the male subject needs to be revalued and reassessed in the presence of other subjects. As this notion is widened, the notion of a politics of difference becomes crucial to a notion of distribution. However, this is not a straight-laced narrative of plural subjects, but a recognition—if not a warning—that the plurality of subjects is an epiphany marked by the irreconcilable, where, as in the female subject, woman "enters into a ceaseless exchange of herself with the other without any possibility of identifying either," where we come to under-stand that this must radically question "all prevailing economies" (Irigaray 1985, p. 31). If there is a moral to Woolf's Orlando, it is that the subject is an economy of being that must be *redistributed*.

Just as the much-heralded ideal of the redistribution of wealth has always been kept within the realms of utopia by the liberal-democratic establishment, because it was either denounced as communistic or as simply impossible, the redistribution of subjects and their diverse imaginaries has always been, and remains, a leap into the unknown. However, the human struggle for the right to imagine and to be present to the undefined possibilities of the *khôra* re-mains at the core of women's and men's struggle against oppression. If there is anything inevitable, it is that the inevitable remains marked by uncertainty. In this respect, women and men have exercised their right to leap into the un-known, even when the harshest of autocratic regimes did their best to contain human knowledge within the 'safety' of dogma. The leap into the unknown is a leap into knowledge as a gnoseological possibility rather than an epistemo-logical rubric.

Galileo Galilei, whose scientific discovery represented the prohibited truth of the cosmos, is a great example. In *The Philosophical Imaginary*, Michèle Le Doeuff gives a possible explanation as to how a revolution in our knowledge of reality could happen: "Galileo's case might lead us to say (...) that a revolu-tionary scientific idea may, precisely because of its unfamiliarity, be born among metaphors and confusion and attain its 'fine abstract pointing' only afterwards, by integration into a scientific system not yet constituted at the time of its initial appearance" (2002, p. 38). Likewise, discussing Kant's notion of the *noumenon*, which as a *thing-in-itself* remains an elusive and incomprehen-sible concept to present human intelligence, Gramsci assumes a materialist reading, where *noumena* are concepts that *will* be understood once the condi-tions of knowledge will afford women and men with their comprehension. Rather than denounce the *noumenon* as an idealist trifle, Gramsci the political philosopher considers *noumena* in their future possibilities where "one could make a historical forecast that simply consists of a thought projected in what is to come as a process of development like that which has been hitherto verified in the past" (1975a, p. 48). Gramsci redistributes the possibility of what remains out of the bounds of human comprehension, implying that one could already imagine that such concepts are possible, albeit in the future.

In both Gramsci's and Le Doeuff's examples we find that even where knowledge approaches the prospect of the objective world—whether this is a concept that cannot be seen as other than a *noumenon*, as in Kant, or whether it is a discovery that has no existing scientific consensus to be floated on, as in Galileo—the presentation of the objective world invariably comes from the conscious power of subjectivity by which we could imagine and ultimately present the truth to ourselves and others.

Just as the teacher presents herself in her uninformed encounter with her pupils, and just as individuals present themselves to the communitarian *agón*, so we must *image*—as a verb—our realities by insisting on our right to be plural subjects. It is because we approach this as plural that we could gain a way out of the morass of sameness. In *imaging* the present, we are enabled to project possibility into the near future where we aim to transform mere existence into meaningful realities. Yet this can only happen because we as plural subjects also insist on the right to choose to imagine. The imagination is neither objectified nor could it even be identified within an identitarian and unified object. As women and men become female and male subjects who recognize that even gender is not a univocal assumption but one of many further subjects, we realize that we can choose. Greene tells us that "only a *subject*, after all, can choose—can decide to break from anchorage and insert himself or herself into the world with a particular kind of identity and responsibility, a particular mode of valuing what lies around and of straining toward what ought to be" (RI, pp. 70–71).

This amounts to a fundamental choice that is as much political, as it is aesthetic, ethical and indeed pedagogical: it is the choice of difference. Yet this difference is also a challenge and the choice still looks insurmountable even as we stand on the shoulders of giants such as Mahatma Gandhi, Dr. Martin Luther King, Teresa of Calcutta, Nelson Mandela and many others who gave their lives to the struggle for the human right to be equal by dint of being different. Yet there is no other way but to insist on such a struggle. "Since the days of de Tocqueville," says Greene, "Americans have wondered how to deal with the conflicts between individualism and the drive to conform."

> They have wondered how to reconcile the impassioned voices of cultures not yet part of the whole with the requirements of conformity, how not to lose the integrity of those voices in the process, how not to allow the drive to conformity to determine what happens at the end. The community many of us hope for now is not to be identified with conformity. As it is shown in Whitman's way of saying, it is a community attentive to difference, open to the idea of plurality. That which is life-affirming in di-

versity must be discovered and rediscovered, as what is held in common becomes always more many-faceted, open and inclusive, and drawn to untapped possibility. (RI, p. 167)

As we reappraise the differences that we have gradually recognized and learned to see as part of the wider horizon of subjectivities, we also continue to learn that humanity is far from being delivered from the evil of forced conformity. Thus as we continue to claim that we have reached a modicum of emancipation, we soon realize that there are still women being defaced, mutilated and killed by their spouses and brothers because they dare to want a different life; that there are still gay men being hanged in public; that ethnic genocides are not a thing of the past; and that the social divide between rich and poor has become even wider. This is why Greene also argues that "it is not enough to emancipate individuals or to disclose their lived worlds for their enlightenment and our own" (RI, p. 59). For Greene the radical choices remain in the ambiguous, and in the in-between:

> Lived worlds themselves must be open to reflection and transformation. The culture and its traditions compose part of the context—so do the languages of the present and the noxious clouds, hoarded books, and socioeconomic phenomena of the world. I hope we can ponder the opening of wider and wider spaces of dialogue, in which diverse students and teachers, empowered to speak in their own voices, reflect together as they try to bring into being an in-between. (RI, p. 59)

To educate in order to learn is not enough, just as to emancipate is only a way of revealing what needs to be further taken apart. This is why the inevitable uncertainties of our need to leap beyond the immediate also require that we claim back our right to assume the in-between—that is, the ambiguities by which we empower ourselves to challenge injustices, even, or especially so, when such injustices emanate from an establishment that often assumes the right to be called *educational*.

Education Beyond Education

Thought waits to be woken one day by the memory of what has been missed, and to be transformed into teaching.

—Theodor W. Adorno, *Minima Moralia* (1991, p. 81)

The matter was thus clear. This was not a method for instructing the people; it was a benefit to be announced to the poor: they could do everything any man could. It sufficed only to *announce* it. (...) And he indicated the way of that "universal teaching"—*to learn something and to relate to it all the rest by this principle: all men have equal intelligence.*

—Jacques Rancière, *The Ignorant Schoolmaster* (1991, p. 18)

We are interested in education here, not in schooling.

—Maxine Greene, *Variations on a Blue Guitar* (VBG, p. 7)

By now it should be clear that this book's reading of Greene's work lays particular emphasis on the inherent dialectic with which possible freedoms are sustained. What is valued more is an investment in the *as-if* and the *what-is-not-but-yet-might-be*, and less so in *what-is* or *what-should-become*. This reading might jar with the expected educational affirmations of positive values, expedient beauty and good prospects. Rather than the naturalist *flow* of learner-centeredness or even a militant call for emancipation, my reading of education in dialogue with Greene's work opts for the need to problematize learning at all levels without resolving to the usual comforts with which conservative, liberal and even progressive philosophers of education seem to approach the issue. Rather than self-affirmation and credo in the necessity of education, readers are urged to doubt and become critical. While this book unfailingly endorses Greene's work as an effective philosophy that brings the discussion of learning and education right into the contexts of current conditions, this same reading could invariably raise questions such as Does this reading portend the impossibility of a full representation of learning and ensuing notions such as social emancipation, personal freedom and knowledge? What prompts such a position that seems to put education in contradistinction with the school? Does this imply a degree of *unease* or even some *hostility* to education?

Questions such as these are not uncommon when it comes to taking a view that seems to look at education from the 'outside'. Similar questions have been raised against Greene's own work. As we have seen her recall, Greene has often been "accused of speaking in what was called 'soft' or even 'non-cognitive' language." In her own words, she has been silenced by the accusation that her comments are not understood while she has been urged to "be sensible, to stay with the facts" and stop being diverted by the arts (VBG, p. 127). The accusation of 'not being understood' is often leveled at arguments that seek to problematize education in the way Greene presents the question of learning.

Sometimes one gets the impression that education is stuck in the mantra of equal opportunity and learner-centeredness, with the result that these noble causes become sidetracked either because they become too obvious or because equality and learner-centeredness begin to look like tired slogans. While indeed learning is about equality and the agency of the learner in an environment that is conducive to learning, the question of learning cannot begin and end with schooling. One cannot deny that schools per se remain fundamental to education. One could never dream of arguing against school provision, especially in countries where children still do not have any education provision at all. However, schooling is one aspect of a much larger context of learning, and to concentrate just on schooling would first and foremost disarm teachers and educators from the real power and potential that they have beyond the School and more so beyond the systematized assumptions of learning in the established nomenclature of 'education'. Greene's work drives home the argument that learning cannot be taken *as is*.

Learning and schooling could neither be relative nor absolute. This sounds obvious to say, but more often than not education is prone to inherent forms of relativism where learning is reduced to measured contexts that seek to assume learning from statistical numbers drawing quick conclusions from what are hailed to be 'scientific facts'. Another form of relativism happens when under the pretext of diversity, a curricularized education forgoes any notion of what Jacques Rancière (1991) calls the "equality of intelligence." To forgo this fundamental notion of equality is to have an education provision that remains relative to a hierarchy of learner responses that are typified according to assumed epistemological Canons. This form of relativist 'differentiation' is often mistaken for pedagogical differentiation where learners are addressed according to their needs. However, the question as to what sort of *needs* learners are expected to have is never clearly addressed because schools must operate within specific parameters. Relativist inequality is at the heart of meritocracy, which as discussed earlier emerges from the mistaken assumptions of freedom as an individualized concern.

Underlying the relativist approach is a state of affairs where schooling becomes an absolute, and where whole societies become schooled in totalized assumptions of knowledge. Thus Schooling comes to stand for two opposite meanings: as a space for learning, and (one hopes) liberation, and as an institution of oppression—what Althusser (1971) calls an "ideological state apparatus." Unlike overt institutions of repression, *ideological state apparata* uphold their image of distinct and specialized institutions, and are not in themselves oppressive. However, an ideological state apparatus like the school inherently represents the Establishment in both its ideological assumptions and its socializing force.

Greene's work makes us all too aware of the relativist and absolutist dangers that remain inherent in education. While it values education and schools, it also makes distinctions where necessary. It tends to pay more attention to education because schooling is not necessarily coterminous with it, especially when such institutions become instruments of hegemony. Greene also treads carefully when it comes to relativist assumptions of learning, because she knows that if learning becomes trivialized by sophistic argument, then we lose track of learning in its central concern. This is why Greene's philosophical strategies for education and learning emerge from two fundamental premises: endorsing the *incomplete* and becoming a *stranger*.

"Exercising imagination, the individual (...) is liable to come awake as seldom before, to call out, 'I see, I hear, I feel, I *know*'." However, Greene quickly qualifies this, adding: "This happens, however, mainly when there has been a sense of incompleteness, of something not yet attained" (VBG, pp. 154-55). Incompleteness warrants a perspective that cannot be determined by certainty or familiarity. The idea of incompleteness cannot be misunderstood for something broken. Rather, it is a situation that retains potentiality for future possibility. The context of the incomplete, as evidenced in the arts, is a potent form of retaining possibility from being exhausted by the semblance of completeness. Complete lives are one-dimensional affairs. Incompleteness sustains the notion of autonomy, an autonomy that is not just a formal complexity, as assumed by art, but intimately tied to the individual autonomy by which we all make choices within society.

Marcuse likens the world of art to another *reality principle* of estrangement, where "only as estrangement does art fulfill a cognitive function: it communicates truths not communicable in any other language: *it contradicts*" (1977, p. 10). Incompleteness gives the vantage point of those truths that are often incommunicable. Education is not just there to teach the teachable. To go beyond what seems impossible or indeed unteachable one must also take a step *outside* the familiar and become a *stranger*:

> To take a stranger's vantage point on everyday reality is to look inquiringly and wonderingly on the world in which one lives. It is like returning home from a long stay in some other place. The homecomer notices details and patterns in his environment he never saw before. He finds that he has to think about local rituals and customs to make sense of them once more. For a time he feels quite separate from the person who is wholly at home in his ingroup and takes the familiar world for granted. (TAS, pp. 267-68)

Janet Miller recalls how after she first heard Greene arguing for the teacher as stranger she realized how these perspectives never informed her undergraduate teacher preparation or her own high school teaching. "There I was pressured to present predetermined, sequential, skills-oriented, and measurable versions of 'English' to my students—hardly ways to encourage looking 'inquiringly and wonderingly on the world'" (Miller 1998, p. 146). In Greene's work, Miller "at last found theoretical, philosophical, and political imperatives for what had been considered among some of my colleagues as 'subversive' attitudes and perspectives about teaching." As she read Greene she was no longer guilty or apprehensive about knowing that perspectives remain contingent and that there is no such thing as a complete picture (ibid.).

In an altogether different vein, Greene's willful repositioning of herself as a 'stranger' is—albeit indirectly—appreciated also from the critical pedagogical position of Peter McLaren, who, although taking the stance of a critical friend with respect to what he sees as Greene's "left-liberal" position, states that what he greatly appreciates in Greene's work is "the nuanced manner in which she embraces epistemological heterogeneity":

> I admire the finesse of argumentation she brings to urgent ethical issues, the wide range of interpretive frameworks she draws upon, and the sensitive strategies she employs when examining the myriad dimensions of social life: brushing them against existing properties and conventions without succumbing to a wispy, ethical relativism. (McLaren & Torres 1998, pp. 193-94)

Here McLaren is not admiring Greene's style, but he hones on the interpretative strategies she takes. These strategies are forms of action. I would also qualify them as political strategies and in view of the reality of what McLaren attributes to a left-liberal context, I would argue that the same strategies turn out to be *radical* in their portent and effectiveness. This may sound as a disagreement with McLaren's 'liberal-left' description of Greene's work of which he remains a great admirer. Far from disagreeing, I would offer a different take on Greene's strategies, basing my observations on McLaren's own friendly critique. In my own reading, I invite readers to consider Greene's positioning within the pragmatic peculiarities of the educational sphere and how it begins with what appears to be a familiar terrain of Deweyan pragmatism only to qualify her position with the radical assumptions found in Existentialism and more so in Arendt's critique of oppression. Greene adopts a radical stand, especially when she has to operate within the parameters of the 'liberal-left'. This sounds like a contradiction, but Greene's political philosophy does not *follow* an agenda: she *makes* the agenda. In this context her politics are founded on the situatedness of learning that is evidently classed, gendered and attentive to all the social forms of oppression that the toiled history of liberal democracy has brought up—more so when it comes to the thorny issues of racism and sexism. Apart from declaring herself as a Humanist card-holder in her various contributions to *The Humanist* (1964; 1965), Greene does not identify herself with any specific political creed or ideology. Thus she refuses to assume the politics of *karamasovism* (see chapter five, this volume) because it would be "relatively easy to take the path of vengeance or rejection, especially when most rational people seem to support one's notion of what is right and wrong" (Greene 1964, p. 34).

As McLaren rightly argues, Greene's work is robustly anti-relativistic—and this even when we know that it renders ineffective any notion of objective foundation. As I have argued in chapters four and five, Greene's radical stance comes from her attention to the very roots of oppression, which she identifies in the existential encounters we discover while we cling to the very core of our claims for autonomy. Such autonomy makes no sense unless it is underlined by the dynamic of choice, which is not simply couched in a liberal assumption of the individual, but where the autonomous self becomes plural and recognizes the need to radicalize the very foundations of democracy. This is also why Greene is fiercely critical of meritocracy, against which she pits a strategy for expanding communities. Again McLaren's comments are spot on when he states that Greene's "is not a strident or militant standpoint in the sense that it excludes a ludic or playful poetics of knowing grounded in a praxis of telling. It is, rather, a tough-skinned probing of contemporary issues" (McLaren & Torres 1998, p. 200).

While so many comments and essays on Greene's work speak for themselves, citing Miller and McLaren and Torres just goes to confirm that Greene radically repositions everything when it comes to how we engage with education. In the ever-growing field of Maxine Greene Studies, Greene becomes ever more the unlikely champion of a field of human concern in which she exhorts us all to take to the margins and seek new places. I say 'unlikely' because against all odds Greene comes from the side, if not the periphery, of Education and takes on an institution and a discipline that have altogether been and broadly remain dominated by the power of 'fact' and 'corresponding truths'. Greene comes into the 'fold' of schools of education only to tell educators that there are *many other places* and that to find hope for other than the *status quo* the first place to look for is the dread of existence, its absurdity and the radical possibilities by which women and men could potentially assume (and resume) their situations by means of the power of the imagination.

By way of concluding this dialogue with Greene's work, I would like to venture within these often-perceived-as-*unlikely* places. Here I also want to follow her example and claim further spaces and other voices beyond what often remains so stiflingly certain in the realms of philosophy and education.

The claim for a willful departure from the familiar requires that one understands what a place for learning is all about. Maybe the best way to do so is to assume this in reverse, and realize that such places do not hold any specificity, because once one specifies a place then it becomes fixed in a world that accepts neither anomaly nor paradox. In effect the world with which we all claim to be *familiar* remains most *un*familiar. Whenever the worlds of norm and normality are presented as valid by dint of their 'familiar nature', we know that this is a self-imposed assumption. We impose such worlds on each other because we are always anxious that otherwise we run the risk of having no truth, or beauty or goodness—or so they tell us. But as Greene states, we should be concerned with wide-awakeness "not with the glowing abstractions— the True, the Beautiful, and the Good" (LL, p. 162).

Here I want to revisit three *other* 'places' that have emerged in this book's discussion of Greene's work. These are the *polis*, the *agôn* and the *khôra*. One assumes that it is now abundantly clear that this discussion goes beyond the original context and usage of these Greek terms. We now speak of the *polis* as a community within which we assume a political space that is mostly dominated by language and the imaginaries that emerge from our argument and conversation. One would find that we assume a *polis* by how we *image* and *imagine* the world. As to where and how the *polis* is engaged in conversation and imaging, we inhabit many spaces that in their diversity are all considered as forming an *agôn* of learning. Thus the *agôn* denotes the space that is defined by the places where argument, dispute as well as leading and learning give form to future possibilities. But before we get comfortable with the *polis* and the *agôn*, we also find ourselves confronted by another place: the *khôra*. The *khôra* is not only intangible, but also illegible and hard to represent. We are still not sure whether such a place exists, and if so, whether it *is* a place. Does the *khôra* stand for the interstices within which we could figure out another definition of our physical existence? Is it a psychological awareness that we attribute to the fetal origins of the self? Or is the *khôra* an equivocal sense of existence by which we could ultimately recognize everything else—almost by way of elimination?

As I see the *polis*, *agôn* and *khôra* broadly corresponding to the *political*, the *polemical* and the *indefinable* as interrelated places, I also remain intent on trying to explain what it means to argue for an education that must be posed *beyond* itself. This business of a *beyond* cannot be simply understood as a historical or ideological surpassing of the current state of education. Likewise the beyond does not denote a dismissal of one definition of education for another. To me, an education beyond education is an invitation to estrangement, which, in line with Greene's position to refuse to delineate overarching conclusions or even recommendations about education, continues to defy any idea of closure or grounding. To borrow Greene's words: "we are unwilling to end this book by spelling out overarching purposes or slapping still another proclamation on the schoolroom wall" (TAS, p. 272). So rather than proclaim another recipe for an education beyond the education that we have got, I suggest that we must revisit what has been assumed; that we continue to re-read what has been already read; and more important that we closely critique and problematize what has been and continues to be proclaimed in the name of education.

To do so, we must revisit learning as a multiplicity of occasions for the political, polemical and the indefinable. As we cast an eye on education, and more specifically on the intent of engaging learning beyond the limits that the very idea of a place would yield, we also start to rethink the whole vision of what it means to have an education that moves beyond itself. To do so, education must estrange its own ontological plurality—that is, its diverse modes of being—from the basic tenets of those standardized epistemological consequences, which constitute the knowledge base that systems of education claim to have. This is why any space that could effectively problematize human learning could never gain specificity or be assumed as a *ground*. There is no special case for human learning except for its ability to identify those inherent polemical possibilities within a polity that far from being bound by a fixed notion of civil society remains indefinable by dint of the constant expansive communities that continuously change and redefine the polis.

To take a position that Greene may not see in these same terms, I regard this direction as one of groundlessness. Groundlessness implies a refusal to adopt necessary grounds of understanding. Groundlessness emerges from the reality and value of what Agnes Heller recognizes as "historical contingency." For Heller "there is no wager for or against this contingency, since there is no ignorance about it" (Heller 1993, p. 16). Elsewhere I have argued that even when the contingency leaves us in an unresolved quandary, because we are often unprepared to cope with a state of affairs that continuously shifts and changes, there "is no excuse for the restoration of a ground for certainty in art or education. The ill-fated histories of 'progressive' and 'traditional' forms of teaching and learning (…) teach us that the notion of a model in education, whether 'open' or 'closed', remains equally interested and tied to the narratives by which the School has been de-historicised" (Baldacchino 2005, p. 3). The state of groundlessness allows us to read history as it is in its inherent contingencies and not as we want to reconstruct it in terms of absolutes.

I happen to think that the contingency by which we moderns have realized that there are limits to what we wish to have *completed* is to many extents a good turn. As we realize that this is all we have, we also realize that it is up to us to continue to move on and imagine the possibilities that we could achieve beyond the limits. If all was complete and if we had a universalized knowledge that stopped the contingent and the accidental, life would be far more cruel and unfair than it already is. And this has been proven in history when men imposed absolute systems on each other, and when the singular subject refused to see the plurality of other subjects and the point of communities that expand.

Greene argues that because "no one can predict precisely the common world of possibility we will grow to inhabit" and because we can never justify "one kind of community over another" we still retain the potential to affirm values like justice and equality and freedom and commitment to human rights. "Only if more and more persons incarnate such principles, choosing to live by them and engage in dialogue in accord with them, are we likely to bring about a democratic pluralism and not fly apart in violence and disorder" (VBG, p. 166). Without having to postulate or scaffold newly fixed forms of non-fixedness, we have to realize an opening that critiques foundational philosophies, and accept that our ultimate historical responsibility—of which we remain contingent—is in our hands. Even without fixed grounds, the values of freedom, justice and equality have to remain. We do not need certainty to be just. We do not need positivist measure to have knowledge. We do not assume facts to make art. More so we have to learn as unfinished subjects. Objective grounds do not construct an ethical self. Rather it is the ethical self that provides the possibility of values—with or without objective assumptions.

Greene argues that "unable to provide an objective ground for such hopes and claims, all we can do is speak with others as eloquently and passionately as we can about justice and caring and love and trust" (VBG, p. 166). The one condition for these possibilities beyond an objective ground is that we assume plurality as the quality of these values. One must insist that a *quality* is radically different from a fixed *ground*. A quality inheres in the value and it gives the value all the possibility it needs. It is also within the prospects of qualities that such learning enters the political, polemical and the indefinable. If values of justice, equality and freedom appear within an awareness of the plural subject, then learning must relate to a political sphere that is equally open and in continuous expansion. Because the political implies the polemical and the indefinable, learning must be staked on this dialectical dynamic, where rather than pose an objective world or assume a system of values that we assume as instantly *human*, we assume this world in its essentially groundless *condition* as undefined and thus incomplete.

Here we could argue that the power of incompleteness takes on a pedagogical turn, not to mend the incomplete, fix middles or universalize knowledge, as many Educationalists seem to think, but to understand that education is itself the place for the polemical and the indefinable. To polemicize is to test the assumptions of the power of argument itself. Likewise to assume the indefinable is to claim meaning as a necessity that continues to reach beyond its fixed nature. Without such states, which more often than not appear averse and sometimes *inhuman*, learning disappears—resulting in the pedagogical possibilities being foreclosed by surrogate forms of definition.

Somehow, when we speak of learning we often get nervous and either state the obvious or seek to rationally settle what reason already obstructs. "As if reason had no doubt," states Lyotard, "that its vocation is to draw on the indeterminate to give it form, and that it cannot fail to succeed in this. Yet it is only at the price of this doubt that reason reasons" (1991, p. 4). The temptation to systematize what must not be closed is part of the *humanity* by which we assume that the unresolved could be accommodated as a new system. Yet this is not what is meant when one reaches for an education that lies *beyond*. Beyond education there are no mended grounds by dint of the groundless—as if an indefinable moment were to be mummified in a state of non-being and then presented as a new assumption for learning. That would amount to a new familiarity where the stranger finds his or her way back into a community while forgetting why he or she went back in the first place. To return to the fold as a stranger and to sustain the possibilities of the indefinable is to take the polemical character of the *agôn* back into the pedagogical. This also means that the return implies new interpretations that sustain learning as an engaging conversation without ever imposing an objective ground.

'Education beyond education' delimits the notion of education and takes it back into the realms of learning. It identifies the challenges that Greene's work poses in terms of the ethical imperatives by which education cannot sustain itself as a foreclosed structure and could not presume itself to be certain. This is how I would sum up the thrust of this book. Like any conclusion here I only offer a promise and like Adorno I 'hope' that the memories we have missed return to teaching, provided that what we are taught goes back to our memories to retrieve further learning without ever assuming a certain pose. What is certain about this need of incompleteness is that even as we read other people's memories and learn from what they have to teach, these would neither presume nor preclude what they have to offer. This is how Greene regards her own work. As she tells me, no one has the last word. And with this in mind I want to say how right she is especially when we realize that education is only one of the many steps toward a truthful, real and *just* world.

Bibliography

Works by Maxine Greene

Main works

When referring to Greene's books the following abbreviations have been used:

DOF: Greene, M. (1988). *The Dialectic of Freedom*. New York: Teachers College Press.

EET: Greene, M. (1967). *Existential Encounters for Teachers*. New York: Random House.

LL: Greene, M. (1978). *Landscapes of Learning*. New York: Teachers College Press.

PSPV: Greene, M. (1965/2007). *The Public School and the Private Vision*. New York: New Press.

RI: Greene, M. (2000). *Releasing the Imagination. Essays on Education, The Arts and Social Change*. San Francisco CA: Jossey-Bass.

TAS: Greene, M. (1973). *Teacher as Stranger. Educational Philosophy for the Modern Age*. Belmont CA: Wadsworth Publishing.

VBG: Greene, M. (2001). *Variations on a Blue Guitar. The Lincoln Center Institute Lectures on Aesthetic Education*. New York: Teachers College Press.

Other works

All referred by date. ND indicates *No Date* available.

Greene, M. (NDa). "Between Past and Future: The Becoming of Teachers College." Convocation address to Teachers College Columbia University. Typewritten MS. Teachers College Library Archive. Electronic access, http://pocketknowledge.tc.columbia.edu

Greene, M. (NDb). "Existentialism and Education," *Education Synopsis*. pp. 6–9. Electronic access, http://pocketknowledge.tc.columbia.edu

Greene, M. (NDc). "Wide-awakeness in Dark Times." *Educational Perspectives*. pp. 6–13. Electronic access, http://pocketknowledge.tc.columbia.edu

Greene, M. (1959). "Philosophy of Education and the Liberal Arts: A Proposal." *Educational Theory*. Vol. IX, No. 1, pp. 50–55.

Greene, M. (1964). "The Word into Action." *The Humanist*. No. 2, pp. 34–35.

Greene, M. (1965). "Man Without God in American Fiction." *The Humanist.* May/June 1955, pp. 125–28.

Greene, M. (1966). "The Humanities and Social Work Education." *Education for Social Work.* Spring issue, pp. 21–31.

Greene, M. (1967). "Teaching the Literature of Protest." *The English Record.* October 1967, pp. 2–9.

Greene, M. (1968a). "The Whale's Whiteness: On Meaning and Meaninglessness." *The Journal of Aesthetic Education.* Vol. 2, No. 1, January issue, pp. 51–72.

Greene, M. (1968b). "Literature and Human Understanding." *The Journal of Aesthetic Education.* Vol. 2, No. 4, October issue, pp. 11–21.

Greene, M. (1973). "The Matter of Justice." *Teachers College Record.* Vol. 75, No. 2, December issue, pp. 181–91.

Greene, M. (1975). "Education, Freedom and Possibility." Inaugural lecture as William F. Russell Professor in the Foundations of Education. October 23. New York: Teachers College Columbia University.

Greene, M. (1979). "Language, Literature, and the Release of Meaning." *College English.* Vol. 41, No. 2, October issue, pp. 123–35.

Greene, M. (1987). "Creating, Experiencing, Sense-Making: Art Worlds in Schools." *The Journal of Aesthetic Education.* Vol. 21, No. 4, Winter issue, pp. 11–23.

Greene, M. (1990). "The Passion of the Possible: Choice, Multiplicity and Commitment." *Journal of Moral Education.* Vol. 19, No. 2, pp. 67–76.

Greene, M. (1991). "Aesthetic Literacy in General Education." *18th Yearbook of the National Society for the Study of Education.* Chicago: University of Chicago Press.

Greene, M. (1992). "The Passions of Pluralism: Multiculturalism and the Expanding Community." *Journal of Negro Education.* Vol. 61, No. 3, pp. 250–261.

Greene, M. (1994a). "Epistemology and Educational Research: The Influence of Recent Approaches to Knowledge." *Review of Research in Education.* Vol. 20. pp. 423–464.

Greene, M. (1994b). "Postmodernism and the Crisis of Representation." *English Education.* Vol. 26. pp. 206–219.

Greene, M. (1998). "An Autobiographical Remembrance." *The Passionate Mind of Maxine Greene: 'I Am ... Not Yet'.* Ed. William F. Pinar. London: Falmer.

General Bibliography

Adorno, T.W. (1990). *Negative Dialectics.* Trans. E.B. Ashton. London: Routledge.

Adorno, T.W. (1991). *Minima Moralia.* London: Verso.

Adorno, T.W. (1999). *Aesthetic Theory.* Trans. R. Hullot-Kentor. Ed. G. Adorno, R. Tiedemann. London: Athlone.

Adorno, T.W. (2000). *Problems of Moral Philosophy.* Cambridge: Polity Press.

Adorno, T.W., et al. (1976). *The Positivist Dispute in German Sociology.* London: Heinemann.

Adorno, T.W., Horkheimer, M. (1979). *Dialectic of Enlightenment.* Trans. J. Cumming. London: Verso.

Allende, I. (2003). *My Invented Country. A Memoir.* Trans. M. S. Peden. London: Flamingo.

Althusser, L. (1971). *Lenin and Philosophy and Other Essays.* New York: Monthly Review Press.

Arendt, H. (1978). *The Life of the Mind: Thinking* (vol. 1) *Willing* (vol. 2). Two volumes in one edition. New York: Harcourt.

Arendt, H. (1998). *The Human Condition.* Chicago: University of Chicago Press.

Aristotle. (1987). *Poetics.* Trans. R. Janko. Indianapolis: Hackett.

Ayers, W. (1998). "Doing Philosophy: Maxine Greene and the Pedagogy of Possibility." *A Light in Dark Times: Maxine Greene and the Unfinished Conversation.* Ed. W. Ayers, J.L. Miller. New York: Teachers College Press.

Ayers, W., Miller, J.L. (Eds.). (1998). *A Light in Dark Times: Maxine Greene and the Unfinished Conversation.* New York: Teachers College Press.

Baldacchino, J. (1996). *Post-Marxist Marxism: Questioning the Answer.* Aldershot: Ashgate.

Baldacchino, J. (2005). "Hope in Groundlessness: Art's Denial as Pedagogy." *Journal of Maltese Educational Research.* Vol. 3, No. 1, pp. 1–13.

Baldacchino, J. (2007). "The Pedagogy of Culture. Cultural Theory within the Politics of a 'Third Space'." *Interactive Discourse.* Vol. 1, No. 1, pp. 3–20.

Barnes, H.E. (1956). "Translator's Introduction." J.P. Sartre. *Being and Nothingness. An Essay on Phenomenological Ontology.* Trans. H.E. Barnes. New York: Philosophical Library.

Beckett, S. (1979). *Waiting for Godot. A Tragicomedy in Two Acts.* London: Faber and Faber.

Bergson, H. (1983). *Creative Evolution.* Trans. A. Mitchell. Lanham MD: University Press of America.

Bloch, E. (1986). *The Principle of Hope.* Trans. N. Plaice, S. Plaice, P. Knight. Cambridge MA: MIT Press.

Boal, A. (2000). *Theatre of the Oppressed.* London: Pluto Press.

Camus, A. (1967). *Lyrical and Critical.* Trans & Ed. P. Tody. London: Hamish Hamilton.

Camus, A. (1986). *The Outsider.* Trans. J. Laredo. Harmondsworth: Penguin.

Camus, A. (2000). *The Myth of Sisyphus.* Trans. Justin O' Brien. London: Penguin.

Carroll, L. (1996). *Through the Looking-Glass and What Alice Saw.* London: Macmillan.

Cavafy, C.P. (2007). *The Canon. The Original One Hundred and Fifty-Four Poems.* Original Greek with English translation. Trans. Stratis Haviaras. Ed. Dana Bonstrom. Cambridge MA: Harvard University Press.

Christie, A. (1984). *The Mysterious Affair at Styles.* New York: Berkley.

Clark, T.J. (1999). *Farewell to an Idea. Episodes from a History of Modernism.* New Haven CT: Yale University Press.

Croce, B. (1939a). "Il concetto della filosofia come storicismo assoluto." *Il Carattere della Filosofia Moderna.* ["The concept of philosophy as absolute historicism". The Character of Modern Philosophy] Reprinted in Benedetto Croce (1955). *Filosofia Poesia Storia. Pagine tratte da tutte le opere a cura dell'autore.* [Philosophy Poetry History. Pages edited by the author and selected from his work] Milano: Riccardo Riciardini.

Croce, B. (1939b). *Conversazioni Critiche.* [Critical Conversations] Bari: Laterza.

Croce, B. (1950). *Estetica come scienza dell'espressione e linguistica generale.* [Aesthetics as a science of Expression and General Linguistics] Bari: Laterza.

Croce, B. (2006). *Saggio sullo Hegel, seguito da altri scritti di storia della filosofia*. [An Essay on Hegel, followed by other writings on the history of philosophy]. Napoli: Bibliopolis.

Derrida, J. (1993). *Khôra*. Paris: Éditions Galilée.

Dewey, J. (1966). *Democracy and Education: An Introduction to the Philosophy of Education*. New York: Free Press.

Dewey, J. (1989). *Freedom and Culture*. New York: Prometheus.

Dewey, J. (1997). *Experience and Education*. New York: Touchstone.

Dewey, J. (2005). *Art as Experience*. New York: Penguin /Perigee.

Eliot, T.S. (1999). *The Waste Land and Other Poems*. London: Faber and Faber.

Elytis, O. (1998). *Journal of an Unseen April*. Original Greek with English translation. Trans. D. Connolly. Athens: Ypsilon Books.

Emerson, R.W. (1941). *The Works of Ralph Waldo Emerson*. Four Volumes in One. New York: Tudor Publishing Company.

Foucault, M. (1991). *The Order of Things. An Archaeology of the Human Sciences*. London: Routledge.

Freire, P. (1996). *Pedagogy of the Oppressed*. London: Penguin.

Gilson, E. (2000). *The Arts of the Beautiful*. Champaign IL: Dalkey Archive Press.

Gramsci, A. (1975a). *Il Materialismo Storico*. [Historical Materialism] Torino: Editori Riuniti.

Gramsci, A. (1975b). *Gli Intellettuali*. [The Intellectuals] Torino: Editori Riuniti.

Granese, A. (2002). "Pragmatismo deweyano e filosofia dello spirito crociana." [Deweyan Pragmatism and Croce's Philosophy of Spirit] *Croce e Dewey: Cinquanta Anni Dopo*. Ed. P. Colonnello, G. Spadafora. Napoli: Bibliopolis.

Hansen, D.T. (Ed.). (2006). *John Dewey and Our Educational Prospect, A Critical Engagement with Dewey's Democracy and Education*. Albany NY: State University of New York Press.

Heller, A. (1993). *A Philosophy of History. In Fragments*. Oxford: Blackwell.

Horkheimer, M. (2003). *The Eclipse of Reason*. New York: Continuum.

Hughes, T. (1997). *Tales from Ovid. Twenty-four Passages from the Metamorphoses*. London: Faber and Faber.

Illich, I. (1999). *DeSchooling Society*. London: Marion Boyars Publishers.

Inglis, F. (1982). *Radical Earnestness: English Social Theory, 1880-1980*. Oxford & Cambridge MA: Martin Robertson with Basil Blackwell.

Irigaray, L. (1985). *This Sex Which Is Not One*. Ithaca NY: Cornell University Press.

Irigaray, L. (2000). "Io donna non sarò più te uomo" [I woman, would never be again you, man]. Interviewed by Bruno Gravagnuolo. *L'Unità*. April 13.

Joyce, J. (1992a). *Ulysses*. London: Minerva.

Joyce, J. (1992b). *Finnegans Wake*. London: Minerva.

Kant, I. (1974). *Critique of Judgement*. Trans. J.H. Bernard. New York: Hafner Press, Collier-Macmillan Publishers

Kant, I. (1988). *Logic*. Trans. R.S. Hartman, W. Schwarts. New York: Dover.

Kristeva, J. (1984). *Revolution in Poetic Language*. Trans. M. Waller. New York: Columbia University Press.

Kundera, M. (1999). *The Unbearable Lightness of Being.* Trans. M. H. Heim. New York: Harper-Perennial.

Laclau, E. (1993). "Politics and the Limits of Modernity." *Postmodernism A Reader.* Ed. Thomas Docherty. London: Harvester Wheatsheaf.

Laclau, E. (2005). *On Populist Reason.* London: Verso.

Le Doeuff, M. (2002). *The Philosophical Imaginary.* New York: Continuum.

Lorca, F.G. (1998). *In Search of Duende.* Trans. C. Maurer. New York: New Directions.

Lukács, G. (1971). *Prolegomeni a un' Estetica Marxista, Sulla categoria della particolarità.* [Prolegomena for a Marxist Aesthetic. On the Category of Particularity] Rome: Editori Riuniti.

Lukács, G. (1974). *Conversations with Lukács.* Trans. D. Fernbach. Ed. T. Pinkus. London: Merlin Press.

Lukács, G. (1975). *Estetica.* [Aesthetics] Italian Trans. A. Solmi. Ed. F. Fehér. Turin: Piccola Biblioteca Einaudi.

Lyotard, J.F. (1989). *The Postmodern Condition: A Report on Knowledge.* Trans. G. Bennington, B. Massumi. Manchester: Manchester University Press.

Lyotard, J.F. (1991). *The Inhuman. Reflections on Time.* Trans. G. Bennington, R. Bowlby. Stanford CA: Stanford University Press.

Marcuse, H. (1977). *The Aesthetic Dimension.* Boston: Beacon Press.

Marcuse, H. (1986). *One Dimensional Man.* London: Ark Paperbacks.

Marx, K. (1977a). *Economic and Philosophic Manuscripts of 1844.* Moscow: Progress Publishers.

Marx, K. (1977b). "The Bourgeoisie and the Counter-Revolution." Marx, K., Engels, F. *Selected Works.* Vol. 1. Moscow: Progress Publishers.

Marx, K., Engels, F. (1988). *The Communist Manifesto.* New York: Prometheus.

McClintock, R. (2005). *Homeless in the House of Intellect: Formative Justice and Education as an Academic Study.* New York: Laboratory for Liberal Learning, Columbia University.

McKibbin, R. (2008). "An Element of Unfairness." *London Review of Books.* Vol. 30, No. 13, pp. 7–10.

McLaren, P., Torres, C.A. (1998). "Voicing from the Margins: The Politics and Passion of Pluralism in the Work of Maxine Greene." *A Light in Dark Times: Maxine Greene and the Unfinished Conversation.* Ed. W. Ayers, J.L. Miller. New York: Teachers College Press.

Merleau-Ponty, M. (1963). *In Praise of Philosophy.* Trans. J. Wild, J.M. Edie. Evanston IL: Northwestern University Press.

Merleau-Ponty, M. (1964). *Sense and Non-Sense.* Trans. H.L. Dreyfus, P. Allen Dreyfus. Evanston IL: Northwestern University Press.

Merleau-Ponty, M. (1989). *Phenomenology of Perception.* Trans. C. Smith. London: Routledge.

Mészáros, I. (1996). *Beyond Capital: Towards a Theory of Transition.* London: Merlin Press.

Miller, J.L. (1998). "Autobiography and the Necessary Incompleteness of Teachers' Stories." *A Light in Dark Times: Maxine Greene and the Unfinished Conversation.* Ed. W. Ayers, J.L. Miller. New York: Teachers College Press.

Morrison, T. (1980). *Sula.* London: Picador.

Mouffe, C. (Ed.) (1996). *Deconstruction and Pragmatism: Simon Critchley, Jacques Derrida, Ernesto Laclau, Richard Rorty.* New York: Taylor & Francis.

Mouffe, C. (2005). *On the Political.* London & New York: Routledge.

Murdoch, I. (1980). *Sartre: Romantic Realist*. New York: Harper & Row/Barnes & Noble.

Nagel, T. (1997). *The Last Word*. Oxford: Oxford University Press.

Nietzsche, F. (1973). *Beyond Good and Evil*. Trans. R.J. Hollingdale. London: Penguin.

Nietzsche, F. (1980). *Thus Spoke Zarathustra. A Book for Everyone and No One*. Trans. R.J. Hollingdale. London: Penguin.

Nietzsche, F. (1995). "Schopenhauer as Educator." Trans. R.T. Gray. *Unfashionable Observations*. Stanford CA: Stanford University Press.

Peters, R.S. (1967). *Ethics and Education*. Chicago: Scott, Foresman & Co.

Pinar, W.F. (Ed.). (1998). *The Passionate Mind of Maxine Greene: 'I Am ... Not Yet'*. London: Falmer.

Plato. (1989). *Timaeus*. Trans. B. Jowett. *The Collected Dialogues of Plato*. Ed. E. Hamilton, H. Cairns. Princeton NJ: Bollingen Series LXXI, Princeton University Press.

Poole, R. (1972). *Towards Deep Subjectivity*. New York: Harper & Row.

Poole, R. (1993). *Kierkegaard. The Indirect Communication*. Charlottesville VA: University Press of Virginia.

Poole, R. ([1978] 1995). *The Unknown Virginia Woolf*. Cambridge & New York: Cambridge University Press.

Rancière, J. (1991). *The Ignorant Schoolmaster. Five Lessons in Intellectual Emancipation*. Stanford CA: Stanford University Press.

Rancière, J. (2006). *The Politics of Aesthetics. The Distribution of the Sensible*. New York: Continuum.

Richter, G. (2005). *The Daily Practice of Painting. Writings 1962-1993*. Trans. D. Britt. Ed. H.U. Obrist. London: Thames & Hudson.

Rorty, R. (2006). Take Care of Freedom and Truth Will Take Care of Itself. Interviews with Richard Rorty. Ed. E. Mendieta. Stanford CA: Stanford University Press.

Rose, G. (1992). *The Broken Middle. Out of Our Ancient Society*. Oxford: Blackwell.

Rose, G. (1997). *Mourning Becomes the Law. Philosophy and Representation*. New York: Cambridge University Press.

Rose, M.A. (1989). *Marx's Lost Aesthetic. Karl Marx and the Visual Arts*. New York: Cambridge University Press.

Sartre, J.P. (1948). *The Psychology of Imagination*. New York: Philosophical Library.

Sartre, J.P. (1956). *Being and Nothingness. An Essay on Phenomenological Ontology*. Trans. H.E. Barnes. New York: Philosophical Library.

Sartre, J.P. (1965). *The Philosophy of Jean Paul Sartre*. Ed. R. Denoon Cumming. New York: Modern Library/Random House.

Sartre, J.P. (1982). *Nausea*. Trans. R. Baldick. Harmondsworth: Penguin.

Schiller, F. (1967). *On the Aesthetic Education of Man in a Series of Letters*. Trans. E.M. Wilkinson, L.A. Willoughby. Oxford: Clarendon Press.

Schutz, A. (1970). *On Phenomenology and Social Relations*. Chicago: University of Chicago Press.

Searle, J. (1999). *Mind, Language and Society*. London: Weinfeld and Nicolson.

Skinner, Q. (1998). *Liberty Before Liberalism*. Cambridge & New York: Cambridge University Press.

Solzhenitsyn, A. (1973). *One Day in the Life of Ivan Denisovich*. Trans. R. Parker. London: Penguin.

Thatcher, M. (1987). "Aids, Education and the Year 2000!," interview with Douglas Keay. *Women's Own Magazine*, October 31, pp. 8–10. *Margaret Thatcher Foundation* http://www.margaretthatcher.org/speeches/displaydocument.asp?docid=106689, accessed July 29, 2008.

Valéry, P. (1963). "Narcisse Parle" [Narcissus Speaks]. *The Penguin Book of French Verse. The Twentieth Century*. Harmondsworth: Penguin.

Williams, R. (1967). *Modern Tragedy*. Stanford CA: Stanford University Press.

Wimsatt, W.K., Beardsley, M.C. (1954). "The Intentional Fallacy." *The Verbal Icon: Studies in the Meaning of Poetry*. Lexington: University of Kentucky Press.

Winston, J. (1998). *Drama, Narrative and Moral Education: Exploring Traditional Tales in the Primary Years*. London: Falmer.

Wittgenstein, L. (1979). *Wittgenstein's Lectures Cambridge 1932-1935*. Ed. A. Ambrose. Oxford: Basil Blackwell.

Wollheim, R. (1980). *Art and Its Object. With Six Supplementary Essays*. Cambridge: Cambridge University Press.

Wollstonecraft, M. (1987). *A Vindication of the Rights of Woman*. Ed. C.H. Poston. New York: W.W. Norton.

Woolf, V. (1985). *Moments of Being*. Ed. J. Schulkind. New York: Harvest/Harcourt Brace Jovanovich.

Woolf, V. (1994a). *Mrs. Dalloway*. London: Flamingo, HarperCollins.

Woolf, V. (1994b). *Orlando*. London: Flamingo, HarperCollins.

Woolf, V. (1995). *To the Lighthouse*. London: Flamingo, HarperCollins.

Index

• I •

• J •

• K •

TEACHING
❧CONTEMPORARY❧
SCHOLARS

Joe L. Kincheloe & Shirley R. Steinberg
General Editors

This innovative series addresses the pedagogies and thoughts of influential contemporary scholars in diverse fields. Focusing on scholars who have challenged the "normal science," the dominant frameworks of particular disciplines, *Teaching Contemporary Scholars* highlights the work of those who have profoundly influenced the direction of academic work. In a era of great change, this series focuses on the bold thinkers who provide not only insight into the nature of the change but where we should be going in light of the new conditions. Not a festschrift, not a re-interpretation of past work, these books allow the reader a deeper, yet accessible conceptual framework in which to negotiate and expand the work of important thinkers.

For additional information about this series or for the submission of manuscripts, please contact:

Joe L. Kincheloe & Shirley R. Steinberg
c/o Peter Lang Publishing, Inc.
29 Broadway, 18th floor
New York, New York 10006

To order other books in this series, please contact our Customer Service Department:

(800) 770-LANG (within the U.S.)
(212) 647-7706 (outside the U.S.)
(212) 647-7707 FAX

Or browse online by series:

WWW.PETERLANG.COM